# Garbage Wars

**Urban and Industrial Environments**
series editor: Robert Gottlieb, Henry R. Luce Professor of Urban and
Environmental Policy, Occidental College

Maureen Smith, *The U.S. Paper Industry and Sustainable Production: An
Argument for Restructuring*

Keith Pezzoli, *Human Settlements and Planning for Ecological
Sustainability: The Case of Mexico City*

Sarah Hammond Creighton, *Greening the Ivory Tower: Improving the
Environmental Track Record of Universities, Colleges, and Other
Institutions*

Jan Mazurek, *Making Microchips: Policy, Globalization, and Economic
Restructuring in the Semiconductor Industry*

William A. Shutkin, *The Land That Could Be: Environmentalism and
Democracy in the Twenty-First Century*

Richard Hofrichter, ed., *Reclaiming the Environmental Debate: The
Politics of Health in a Toxic Culture*

Robert Gottlieb, *Environmentalism Unbound: Exploring New Pathways
for Change*

Kenneth Geiser, *Materials Matter: Toward a Sustainable Materials Policy*

Matthew Gandy, *Concrete and Clay: Reworking Nature in New York
City*

Thomas D. Beamish, *Silent Spill: The Organization of an Industrial Crisis*

David Naguib Pellow, *Garbage Wars: The Struggle for Environmental
Justice in Chicago*

# Garbage Wars

The Struggle for Environmental Justice in Chicago

David Naguib Pellow

The MIT Press
Cambridge, Massachusetts
London, England

First MIT Press paperback edition, 2004

Set in Sabon by The MIT Press.
Printed and bound in the United States of America.

Library of Congress Cataloging-in-Publication Data

Pellow, David N., 1969–
Garbage wars : the struggle for environmental justice in Chicago / David Naguib Pellow.
p. cm. — (Urban and industrial environments)
Includes bibliographical references and index.
ISBN 978-0-262-16212-8 (hc. : alk. paper)—978-0-262-66187-4 (pb. : alk. paper)
1. Environmental justice—Illinois—Chicago. 2. Refuse and refuse disposal—
Social aspects—Illinois—Chicago. I. Title. II. Series.
GE235.I3 P45    2002
363.7'02'0977311—dc21

2001060360

10 9 8 7 6 5

# Contents

Preface    vii

1  Waste, Politics, and Environmental Injustice    1

2  A Social History of Waste, Race, and Labor, Part I: Movements, Technology, and Politics, 1880s–1930s    21

3  A Social History of Waste, Race, and Labor, Part II: Waste Management and Waste Conflicts, 1940s–2000    41

4  The Movement for Environmental Justice in Chicago and the United States    67

5  Working for the Movement: Recycling Labor at the Resource Center    101

6  The Next Evolutionary Stage: Recycling Waste or Recycling History?    131

7  Toward Environmental Justice    161

Appendix: The Principles of Environmental Justice    171
Notes    175
References    207
Index    229

# Preface

This book is a study of conflicts over solid waste and pollution in urban areas, particularly in communities of color and in neighborhoods and workplaces where immigrants and low-income populations live and labor. Using ethnographic and historical methods, I uncover a fascinating cycle involving social movements, government, and industry. This "movement-policy cycle" reveals the power of social movements to influence politics and to shape waste-management practices in urban areas.

Much of the research on the social impacts of pollution and toxic substances concludes that low-income persons and people of color bear a disproportionate burden of environmental hazards—often termed environmental racism or environmental inequality. However, we have yet to see a coherent conceptual framework that might explain the emergence of environmental inequalities. I propose a framework that views environmental inequality as a process involving various stakeholders engaged in struggles for a range of resources within the political economy—struggles that result in the uneven distribution of the benefits and costs of those resources. The environmental justice framework emphasizes the importance of process and history, the roles of multiple stakeholders, the effects of social stratification by race and class, and the ability of those with the least access to resources to shape the struggle for environmental justice.

I frame the "garbage wars" as struggles against environmental racism, rather than simply battles over natural resource management and community resources. Although the latter characterization is accurate, if we do not view the garbage wars as environmental justice conflicts we miss a major portion of what activists and workers in communities of color think about the concentration of Chicago's trash in their neighborhoods. I also focus a much more critical eye on environmental and environmental justice organizations, rendering the distinctions between heroes and villains less clear. Although large companies, various levels of government, and affluent white communities certainly are to blame for perpetrating acts of environmental racism, I demonstrate that people of color and even environmental justice advocates are often implicated in these tragedies. My case studies raise disturbing questions about what constitutes environmental racism and how we might achieve environmental justice, a cause to which I am deeply committed.

I am indebted to numerous persons who guided and supported me during the ten years since I began this project. Lisa Sun-Hee Park is my collaborator, life partner, best friend, best critic, and the true source of all my intellectual ideas. Allan Schnaiberg, my dissertation advisor, mentor, and friend, teaches his students to think critically and independently, to write and publish, and to always pursue humanistic goals in the academy in the face of pressures to do otherwise. My good colleague, collaborator, mentor, and friend Adam Weinberg gives far more than he receives. Kenneth Gould has inspired me with his success at living the life of a true activist-scholar. Aldon Morris, Albert Hunter, and Charles Payne advised me diligently during my master's thesis and dissertation thesis trials. Dorceta Taylor provided me with a role model for a struggling young African American scholar. Evelyn Hu-DeHart is without question the best boss a professor could ever have. I also thank J. Timmons Roberts, Dennis Mileti, Michael Ames, Ed Barber, and Patricia Limerick.

James Schwab, Ofelia Miramontes, and Harold Henderson provided intellectual support and positive feedback on my work. My wonderful editors, Clay Morgan and Robert Gottlieb, deserve accolades for believing in this book and for making it happen. And I thank Patricia Jackson, Orrin Williams (a brilliant man and great friend), the late Carretta McCarter, Cheryl Johnson, Hazel Johnson, Sara Parran, Bob Ginsburg, Charles Lee, Robert Bullard, Stefan Noe, Jim Burris, Ken Dunn, Bill Eyring, Kevin Greene, Ann Irving, Joanna Hoelscher, Keith Harley, Jeff Tangel, and Marian Byrnes for their activism and their passion for environmental justice.

This project sustained me during my time at three universities, which means that I placed burdens on generous colleagues all across the United States. I am forever grateful to my incredible research assistants and colleagues Mary Beth Slusar, Jon Dennis, Alyssa Schuren, Dana Sevakis, and Sabrina Hodges. They provided thousands of hours of labor transcribing interviews, researching archives, and analyzing data. Financial support for this project came from the Ford Foundation Minority Fellowships Program, the Robert Wood Johnson Foundation Scholars in Health Policy Research Program (University of California at Berkeley); Northwestern University's Graduate Fellowship Program, Department of Sociology, John D. and Catherine T. MacArthur Foundation Summer Fellowship Program, and Institute for Policy Research Graduate Fellowship Program; and the University of Colorado's Undergraduate Research Opportunity Program, Implementation of Multicultural Perspectives and Approaches in Research and Teaching program, Department of Ethnic Studies, and Department of Sociology.

I also wish to extend warm thanks to all the librarians and staffers at Northwestern University; to Chicago's Harold Washington Library; to the Chicago Historical Society; to Maryann Bamberger of the University of Illinois at Chicago Library's Special Collections; to the Illinois Regional Archives Depository; and to Deborah Hollis and Peggy Jobe, stellar, incomparable librarians and scholars at the University of Colorado.

As an activist in the movement for environmental justice, I hope that this book will inspire its readers to engage in the critical thinking and constructive action necessary to achieve environmental justice for all people and for the biosphere upon which we depend.

# Garbage Wars

# 1

# Waste, Politics, and Environmental Injustice

From a sociological perspective, it is never sufficient to point to the environment as having been protected. The question must always be asked, for whom and from whom?[1]

Solid waste is a fact of life. Waste production is an unavoidable function of all living organisms. Similarly, cities and civilizations—as aggregates of human existence—produce waste as a matter of course, and they have struggled with the myriad problems associated with garbage disposal and pollution for thousands of years.[2] With the rising world population, the closure of landfills, and high per capita waste generation (particularly in the global North), garbage disposal practices are becoming more and more problematic. These practices frequently divide public opinion, and they have led to major political conflicts between groups concerned with natural resource conservation and those focused on social justice. But, as a representative of a waste hauling company in Chicago once told me, "the garbage has to go somewhere."[3]

Although all human beings contribute to the waste stream, we rarely share the burden of managing garbage and pollution equally. Moreover, in most parts of the world, those social groups that consume the most natural resources (environmental "goods") and create most of the waste and pollution are the least likely to have to live or work near the facilities that manage those environmental "bads."

Consider the case of Pat James, who told me that her boss "has [a] philosophy about recycling, but . . . has no philosophy about humans."[4] James is an African American woman employed in a waste recycling facility on the South Side of Chicago. Chicago has more landfills per square mile than any other city in the United States. While the city was officially practicing recycling in order to "clean up the environment," the people who actually did the work got more than they bargained for. Workers were routinely exposed to numerous health and safety threats in these plants, such as unregulated toxic substances with which they came into physical contact while sorting recyclables. In addition, workers confronted psychological intimidation and harassment by management while being overworked at low wages. Finally, the recycling facilities were placed in low-income neighborhoods and/or communities of color around Chicago, exacerbating already high levels of noise and pollution in these areas.

In many ways, this is perhaps the worst type of environmental inequality because of the cruel irony that recycling should be about cleaning up the environment when, in fact, this particular program dumped more garbage on African Americans and Latinos at work and in their communities. Environmental racism is the unequal exposure to pollution, toxics, and other hazards that the poor and people of color confront every day.[5] This includes solid waste facilities (garbage dumps, transfer stations, sewage treatment plants, incinerators), other polluting industries (chemical plants, steel plants), highways, dangerous jobs, and a range of "locally unwanted land uses" (LULUs).[6] So when Pat James pointed out that recycling facilities (ostensibly built to prevent waste from entering landfills and incinerators in already overburdened neighborhoods) were creating hazards for both workers and communities, she concluded that the irony was overwhelming. Despite its promises, recycling was just one more example of environmental inequality, stemming from a long line of waste management practices as old as the local city dump and as old as human civilization. Pat's story was the inspiration for this book.

## Why Study Garbage Wars?

This is a historical and ethnographic study of conflicts over solid waste and pollution in urban areas, particularly in communities and workplaces where people of color, immigrants, and low-income populations live and labor. Specifically, I explore the ways in which our garbage is imposed upon vulnerable populations and how it impacts those of us who are forced to live on or near it and those of us whose job it is to dispose of it. I investigate the historical origins of environmental inequalities in Chicago's communities of color and in workplaces where municipal and industrial solid wastes are collected, processed, and eventually dumped. Within communities, these struggles typically emerge in the form of social movements and neighborhood politics over how to repel or attract waste. In the workplace, these conflicts reveal the nature of the dirtiest of "dirty work" and its related occupational hazards that immigrants, African Americans, Latinos, and Asian Americans confront in Chicago.

I begin with the early days of the horse and cart and move on to the compactor trucks and dumpsters and the official and unofficial (i.e. illegal) city dumps, incinerators, reduction plants, sanitary landfills, and materials recovery facilities of the US waste management and recycling industry. Through this sampling of both crude and "high-tech" waste management practices, I follow the trash, the pollution, the hazards, and the human beings who face these by-products of our civilization every time they take a breath in their homes and communities, and every day they go to work. Although we in United States produce more waste and pollution than any other nation, we want it out of sight and out of mind. Hence we engage in constant battles to keep it out of our communities and in others: "garbage wars."

Scholars have typically argued that environmental injustices occur when the poor or people of color are dumped on or exposed to hazards because they are less powerful than corporations and the state. The following is one such perpetrator-victim scenario:

Typically, a corporate producer or waste facility or military production site would locate itself unannounced in a poor, non-white neighborhood. Once the facility was set up, the emissions or waste often had detrimental health impacts on the residents of the area. Groups of residents got together to discuss their immediate health concerns or worked to detect the source of a particular health threat. They demanded more information on the facility causing the damage, or sought the right to know what was causing their immediate health problems.[7]

I argue that environmental racism unfolds in ways that are more complex, more disturbing, and more unsettling than most written accounts of environmental justice (EJ) struggles reveal. Not only are industry and government often guilty of perpetrating these acts of injustice, but many times our own community leaders, our own neighbors, and even environmentalists are deeply implicated in creating these problems.

I propose an EJ framework in order to understand how and why environmental racism destroys communities. This framework emphasizes the importance of history, the role of the many people and organizations involved, the impacts of social inequality, and the power of the disenfranchised and dispossessed to shape the outcomes of these tragic battles.

This is the first in-depth study of the waste industry's history of environmental conflicts in a major city. Only by engaging in careful historical analysis can we hope to answer the question driving this book: what are the origins of environmental inequality and environmental racism with regard to policies on the management of solid waste? By highlighting conflicts over waste dumping, incineration, landfilling, and recycling, I provide a broad historical and contemporary view of this industry through the life cycle of waste and the people it touches in many ways. I do so with a particular focus on the city of Chicago while also locating these trends and conflicts in a broader geographic context.

Chicago is an appropriate setting for several reasons. First, it is one of the first great industrial cities in the United States, and therefore it is one of the most polluted. Previously known as the "slaughterhouse to the world," Chicago was the undisputed capital of the meat packing industry during the nineteenth and twentieth centuries. That industry was the leading source of water and land pollution during that era, making the "Windy City" one of the filthiest places in the world.[8] Chicago is also the site of many world-class battles between labor and capital and between various racial and ethnic groups. From the massacres of workers by police during the Haymarket Square riots (1886) and the Republic Steel strike (1937) to the racial violence during the great Pullman strike (1894) and the Race Riot of 1919, Chicago's air, water, and soil have been stained with the blood of workers and people of color murdered by mobs of women, men, and children fighting for jobs, schools, neighborhoods, and beaches free of "undesirable" ethnic or racial groups.[9]

For the rest of the twentieth century, Chicago was also the site of many defining struggles in the neighborhood, anti-toxics, and environmental justice movements. For example, the community organizer Saul Alinsky made his mark on Chicago with a range of innovative movement tactics. His Industrial Areas Foundation and its aggressive, take-no-prisoners style of neighborhood organizing achieved many victories for working-class ethnic neighborhoods. However, Chicago's history as a "city of neighborhoods" has also been its Achilles' heel, in that neighborhoods often fight over resources and differ dramatically in their perspectives on many environmental, social, and economic issues. In chapter 4, I will use the case of the Village of Robbins to drive this point home. Robbins, a historic African American town in desperate economic straits, was the focus of an incinerator battle that pitted African Americans against African Americans and raised difficult questions about what exactly environmental racism is or is not. The modern environmental justice movement got its start in Chicago long before the Robbins battle. The year 1982 is the date many activists and scholars view as the beginning of this nationwide mobilization (because of a major protest in North Carolina over a hazardous waste landfill—see chapter 4). During that same year, on Chicago's far Southeast side, a new organization was founded: People for Community Recovery. PCR was focused on fighting the scourge of waste and polluting industries inundating the African American community in this industrial landscape. The organization's founder, Hazel Johnson, was soon thereafter referred to as the "black mother of the environmental movement" and became a major figure in the environmental justice cause. PCR and several other organizations later found themselves in a controversy over one of the largest garbage incinerators and waste recycling programs ever devised. These conflicts revealed that EJ groups sometimes make mistakes that produce future environmental inequalities. Most of the EJ battles in Chicago revolved around solid waste landfills, incinerators, and recyclers. In the chapters that follow, I will chronicle these important events in order to understand why they happened and what their implications for the movement and environmental policy are.

Why focus on the solid waste industry? The waste industry is vitally important because it was, and remains, the major driver of the environmental justice movement and the academic and policy debates surrounding environmental racism. All across the United States (and indeed the global South), communities have risen up against the waste industry's efforts to locate facilities in their back yards. And the uncontested holder of the distinction as the most vilified waste hauler in U.S. history is Waste Management, Inc. (WMX), headquartered in Oakbrook, Illinois, a Chicago suburb. WMX has always called Chicago home and is also the largest waste hauler in the world. Indeed, the waste industry itself was first organized around business associations based in Chicago, so this city must be at the front and center of any history of garbage and environmental justice conflicts in the United States. I will explore the historical and more contemporary battles this corporation has been involved with in chapter 6.

More important, however, I focus on solid waste because garbage, rubbish, trash, refuse, detritus, or waste—whatever term you might prefer—has always been a part of life in human settlements. As long as we exist on this planet we will produce waste. The vital questions are "How much or how little can we produce?" and "What do we do with it?" Thus far the answer to the first question appears to be: a wide range, from very little (as in the case of nomadic peoples and indigenous populations) to an infinitely large volume (as in the case of the average US consumer). The answer to the second question is: Since large human settlements came into existence, we have generally been either very careless with our wastes by dumping them into the streets, the air, water, and our back yards, or downright unfair by deliberately placing them in close proximity to those least powerful segments of society. Thus, I propose that we ask more piercing questions that seek to understand how this process originates and how we can restructure our social, political, and economic systems in ways that produce environmental justice rather than environmental injustice.

In addition to answering the big question (What are the roots of environmental racism?), I will ask: How have class and racial politics influenced the development of the waste industry throughout the history of Chicago and that of the United States? What are the roles of social movements and workers in defining, resisting, and shaping solid waste practices in the United States? What is the future of this industry, and what are the prospects for building sustainable and environmentally just communities where people of color and other marginal populations live, work, and play?[10]

Much of the research on the social impacts of pollution and toxic substances concludes that low-income persons and people of color bear a disproportionate burden of environmental hazards. However, we have yet to see a conceptual framework put forward that would explain the emergence of environmental racism and environmental inequality. This book offers such a framework, and it builds upon earlier studies by analyzing the processes by which environmental injustices are created.

How is environmental racism produced? To answer this question, I propose a framework that emphasizes

• the importance of the *history* of environmental racism and the processes by which it unfolds,
• the role of *multiple stakeholders* in these conflicts,
• the effects of *social stratification* by race and class,

and

• the ability of the least powerful segments of society to *shape the struggle for environmental justice*.

In each of the cases detailed in this book, I find that workers and residents with minimal political power are the most vulnerable to environmental inequality. However, departing from conventional accounts of environmental racism, this study also concludes that class and political privilege often place certain people of color—or organizations in communities of color—in a position to benefit from (and perhaps perpetrate acts of) environmental racism. When EJ struggles take this direction, the very claim that environmental racism is at work comes into question. These dynamics add an ingredient long absent from much of the literature: the way that class and political power often divide communities and racial groups, creating intra-racial, intra-community, and class tensions. These internal community dynamics are important, but they often serve to divert attention from the larger political economic structures wherein affluent whites still remain in the cleanest, most secure living and working environments. Readers familiar with world history will immediately note that environmental racism in the United States bears a strong resemblance to the age-old practice of "divide and conquer" observed in the interaction between Western nations and their colonies.[11] Even so, I argue that, ultimately, the fates of all communities—whether "clean" or contaminated—are deeply linked.

## Research on Environmental Racism

Many scholars, activists, and policy makers who use the terms *environmental justice* and *environmental racism* do so with little attention to how to define these concepts, often using them interchangeably. My first task in this section will be to define these concepts so as to develop a shared understanding of the basic terminology used so casually in verbal and written discourse.

The sociologist Bunyan Bryant defines environmental racism as follows:

It is an extension of racism. It refers to those institutional rules, regulations, and policies of government or corporate decisions that deliberately target certain communities for least desirable land uses, resulting in the disproportionate exposure of toxic and hazardous waste on communities based upon prescribed biological characteristics. Environmental racism is the unequal protection against toxic and hazardous waste exposure and the systematic exclusion of people of color from decisions affecting their communities.[12]

Environmental racism is a form of *environmental inequality* (which occurs when a particular social group—not necessarily a racial or ethnic group—is burdened with environmental hazards). From a social movement perspective, environmental racism and inequality are what activists are fighting against. But what are they fighting *for*? That brings us to environmental justice. Again, Bryant's clarity is helpful here:

Environmental justice . . . refers to those cultural norms and values, rules, regulations, behaviors, policies, and decisions to support sustainable communities where people can interact with confidence that the environment is safe, nurturing, and productive. Environmental justice is served when people can realize their highest potential. . . . EJ is supported by decent paying safe jobs; quality schools and recreation; decent housing and adequate health care; democratic decision-making and personal empowerment; and communities free of violence, drugs, and poverty. These are communities where both cultural and biological diversity are respected and highly revered and where distributive justice prevails.[13]

Whereas *environmental racism* denotes the disproportionate impact of environmental hazards on communities of color, *environmental justice* is focused on improving the overall quality of life for those same populations. Environmental racism is based upon problem identification, environmental justice is based upon problem solving.[14] Thus, environmental justice seeks both "justice as fairness" and justice as "mutual respect . . . owed to human beings as moral persons."[15]

Over the last three decades a growing number of scholars, activists, and policy makers have begun to pay attention to the distributive impacts of environmental pollution across dimensions of class and race.[16] The predominant finding to emerge from this research is the environmental racism thesis—the argument that, through the location (intentionally or otherwise) of environmental hazards, the poor and people of color "bear the brunt of the nation's pollution problem."[17] (See table 1.1.) Although there are hundreds of reports that support this conclusion, the major studies in this vein include the following:

• A 1983 congressionally authorized General Accounting Office study that revealed that three out of four off-site commercial hazardous waste landfills in the southeast United States were located within predominately African American communities, even though African Americans made up just one-fifth of the region's population. The report concluded that it was unlikely that this uneven distribution of waste in African American communities was the result of race-neutral decision making.[18]

• *Toxic Wastes and Race in the United States,* a study issued in 1987 by the United Church of Christ Commission for Racial Justice. This was the first national study to correlate waste facilities and demographic characteristics and found that race was the most significant factor in determining where waste facilities are located in the United States. Among other findings, the study revealed that 60 percent of African Americans and Latinos live in communities with one or more uncontrolled toxic waste sites, and that 50 percent of Asian Pacific Islander Americans and Native Americans live in such communities.[19]

• A 1990 Greenpeace report on the siting of incinerators concluded that communities with *existing* incinerators had people of color populations 89

**Table 1.1**
Indicators of environmental inequality and/or racism.

| |
|---|
| Widespread unequal protection and enforcement against hazardous facility siting in poor neighborhoods and communities of color |
| Disproportionate impact of occupational hazards on the poor and workers of color |
| The abrogation of treaties with native populations, particularly with regard to mining, waste dumping, and military weapons testing |
| Unsafe and segregated housing |
| Discriminatory transportation systems and zoning laws |
| The exclusion of the poor and people of color from environmental decision making |
| The neglect of human health and social justice issues by the established environmental movement |

percent higher than the national average, and communities with *proposed* incinerators had people of color populations 60 percent higher than the national average.[20]

• "Unequal Protection: The Racial Divide in Environmental Law," a 1992 study published in the *National Law Journal*, uncovered significant disparities in the way the US Environmental Protection Agency enforces the law: "There is a racial divide in the way the US government cleans up toxic waste sites and punishes polluters. White communities see faster action, better results and stiffer penalties than communities where blacks, Hispanics, and other minorities live. This unequal protection often occurs whether the community is wealthy or poor."[21] This study therefore provided some indicators of the *causes* of environmental racism: government inaction and officially sanctioned discrimination at the hands of corporations. This report also underscored that *racism* impacts people of color at all socioeconomic levels.[22]

• A 1992 edition of the *EPA Journal* and a 1992 EPA report titled Environmental Equity: Reducing Risk for All Communities highlighted the agency's efforts to acknowledge and remedy the problem of unfair and unequal environmental policy making.[23]

• In 1999, the Institute of Medicine published a report titled Toward Environmental Justice: Research, Education and Health Policy Needs. This report concluded that government, public health officials, and the medical and scientific communities need to place a higher value on the problems and concerns of non-white communities with regard to environmental health issues.[24]

This body of evidence that environmental racism impacts millions of US residents provided a level of scientific legitimacy to the EJ movement. "Unequal protection" became a common protest theme. The unequal protection against locally unwanted land uses includes exposure to lead smelters, coke ovens in steel mills, sewage treatment plants, municipal, chemical, and medical waste incinerators, municipal and hazardous waste landfills, waste transfer stations, and chemical plants. And that's just for starters.[25]

And although a few scholars argue that race is less salient than class in the siting of hazardous facilities, or that market dynamics explain away any allegations of environmental racism, the overwhelming majority of EJ studies by social scientists, legal scholars, government agencies, and non-profit organizations corroborate the environmental racism thesis.[26] Thus, the majority of this research remains focused on the distribution of hazardous facilities in vulnerable communities and on local responses to these policies. The latter category of studies generally centers on the importance of organized community-based resistance to facility siting—the environmental justice movement. There are several other areas of EJ concern that researchers have begun to explore, including the workplace, housing, and transportation.[27] In the next section, and throughout the book, I will address the workplace and occupational health dimensions of environmental justice.

## The Workplace

The majority of environmental justice research utilizes communities as the primary unit of analysis. But since factories and firms create pollution, it is surprising that we have few studies that focus on the workplace, or what Karl Marx called "the point of production." There is, however, an extensive literature on hazardous work that has largely been unconnected to EJ studies. Numerous links might be made between these literatures.

The growing body of environmental justice research demonstrates that, in addition to being subjected to disproportionately high environmental impacts in their communities, people of color, the poor, and immigrants tend to confront similar hazards at work as well.[28] This body of the EJ literature was partly born out of long-standing concerns over the plight of farm workers exposed to pesticides. Reports estimated that 1,000 farm workers die each year from pesticide poisoning and that more than 300,000 become ill.[29] Moreover, 90 percent of this population consists of people of color and immigrants. The United Farm Workers and their charismatic leader Cesar Chavez articulated these concerns in the 1970s.

Much of the research on workplace hazards and social stratification—while not focused on EJ issues per se—lends support to the environmental racism thesis through the use of existing large data sets.[30] For example, using the Panel Study of Income Dynamics, the Current Population Survey, the Survey of Economic Opportunity, the Quality of Employment Survey, and the National Longitudinal Survey, Robinson demonstrates that African Americans face greater health threats in the workplace than the average white worker of the same socioeconomic status.[31] African Americans are

37 percent more likely to succumb to an injury or illness on the job than their white counterparts. In California, African American and Latino men are, respectively, 40 percent and 80 percent more likely to suffer injury or illness on the job than their white counterparts. For African American women and Latinas, the figures are 40 percent and 60 percent, respectively. African Americans make up 20 percent of the steel industry's work force but occupy 90 percent of the positions in the coke ovens, where exposure to the carcinogen benzene is known to produce high rates of leukemia. In Silicon Valley's high-tech sector, 70 percent of the production workers are Asian and Latino immigrants and 60 percent are women. While making the microchips, printed wire and circuit boards, and other components of the computers that millions of Americans depend upon, these workers are exposed to more than 700 different chemicals. Studies estimate that illnesses in this industry are three times that of any other basic industry.[32] People of color, immigrants, and politically marginal ethnic groups currently and historically occupy the lowest-status, highest-risk, lowest-paying jobs in this society. In every way, the workplace is an environmental justice issue.

Other research, while recognizing racial inequality, proposes a more class-oriented thesis of occupational health and safety, arguing that the practice of maintaining poor working conditions must be understood within a broader theory of capitalist exploitation of the working class.[33] For example, Vincente Navarro develops a class theory of health and stress under advanced capitalism and argues that the capitalist class engages in the "absolute expropriation of health from workers."[34] Thus, any discussion of environmental injustice in the workplace must integrate the social components of risk—namely, who pays the price, who benefits, and how.

Some of the most exciting EJ research aims to redefine what is meant by the word 'environment', moving beyond a nature-centered ecology toward a human-centered ecology that includes the social and "built" environments. That is, while traditional conceptions of the environment and environmental problems dealt mostly with natural resource conservation, the EJ discourse re-frames environmental issues as public health and quality of life concerns.[35] As one author put it, environmental justice research should be concerned with where the poor and people of color "live, work, and play."[36]

Much of the literature focuses on proving or contesting the existence of environmentally unequal siting *outcomes* without a thorough understanding of how these outcomes are produced.[37] The *causes* of environmental injustice referenced in the scholarly literature include institutional racism in housing, discriminatory zoning and planning practices, the lack of community access to environmental policy making, the absence of many people of color as elected officials, the historically rooted tendency for corporations and governments to "follow the path of least resistance" in facility siting, "market dynamics," and the exclusion of low-income individuals and people of color from the dominant environmental movement.[38] In the social science literature, the most exciting research on the causes of environmental inequality to date consists of historical analyses of single cases. Studies by Hurley, by Hersch, by Pulido et al., and by Szasz and Meuser stand out as models.[39] Each demonstrates how racism, classism, and our changing knowledge of environmental hazards interact to burden different populations with risk over time. Most important, these studies reveal that stakeholders are constantly jockeying for quality living and working environments and that concerns over social stratification and environmental quality are always on the minds of urban planners, corporations, workers, and residents. Other scholars have conducted longitudinal studies using statistical analyses to demonstrate how hazards and people have shifted over time.[40] However, we have yet to see a conceptual framework put forward that would explain the emergence of environmental racism.

In this book I build on the literature by analyzing the processes by which environmental inequalities are created, reproduced, and sometimes challenged. That is, I make a conscious effort to move away from quantitative analyses of large data sets to a different set of methods—historical and ethnographic analyses of EJ conflicts. Using historical data, I not only uncover where the people and hazards are located; I also provide a social and political context for environmental policy and environmental struggles. Historical methods offer a way to uncover the origins of environmental inequality and reveal "how we got into this mess," or, in a traditional scientific sense, they lead us to clues about "cause and effect." Through ethnographic investigation, researchers might be able to observe how managers at firms and regulatory agencies think about and make decisions regarding toxic exposure to residential and worker populations. Ethnographers might also be able to analyze how workers and residents themselves experience, negotiate, and challenge these exposures.[41]

These methods inform my conceptual framework and provide tools for understanding environmental inequality as a social process involving and impacting many actors, institutions, and organizations. These actors, or stakeholders, often include social movement organizations, private sector firms, the state, residents, and workers. Each group's interests are complex and often involve cross-cutting allegiances. Thus, it is often difficult to distinguish between heroes and villains. The environmental justice framework allows us to move beyond a view of environmental racism where hazards are unilaterally and uniformly imposed upon victims, who then react, toward a scenario wherein many actors are viewed in their full complexity and would-be victims become active agents in resisting and shaping environmental inequalities before, during, and after they emerge. Within this framework, we also move beyond a view wherein outcomes simply consist of the presence or the absence of hazards to one wherein we can account for variations in patterns of environmental inequalities—that is, how environmental inequalities emerge and change over time and place. This component of the framework underscores the importance of history and process. For example, in the case studies I present, different stakeholders get access to varying amounts of resources depending on the circumstances. Environmental inequalities may be more or less pronounced across cases because residents, workers, or environmentalists have less or more power vis-à-vis government, and corporations. In its present state of development, the environmental justice literature does not provide an adequate account of why these variations occur.

Thus, the framework I am using makes it possible to unpack the process by which environmental inequalities emerge. Without an adequate understanding of how environmental inequalities are produced, diluted explanations for why and how people suffer from them handicap policy makers (and perhaps activists) who might seek to remedy these social problems.

How does environmental racism occur? When different stakeholders struggle for access to valuable resources within the political economy, the benefits and costs of those resources become distributed unevenly. That is, those stakeholders who are unable to effectively mobilize resources are the most likely to suffer from environmental inequality. Conversely, those stakeholders with the greatest access to valuable resources are able to deprive other stakeholders from that same access. This perspective captures the dynamic nature of environmental inequality. Valuable resources can include clean living, recreational, and working environments. They can also include power, wealth, and status. Thus, inability to gain access to these resources often means living and working under dangerous conditions, with very *little* power, wealth, or status. Conversely, those stakeholders with greater ability to access these resources live and work under safer, healthier conditions with *more* power, wealth, and status. In communities where environmental inequality is evident, immigrants, people of color, low-income populations, and politically marginal groups tend to bear the brunt of the pollution, the toxins, and the risk. Environmental racism has a negative impact on people's physical and psychological well-being and on the health of entire communities.

The framework I am using (see table 1.2) has four major points: the importance of process and history, the role of multiple stakeholder relationships, the impact of social stratification such as institutional racism and

**Table 1.2**
A new environmental justice framework.

The historical origins of environmental racism are crucial to understanding these conflicts and promoting solutions. The socio-political processes by which hazards are created and distributed must be the focus.

Environmental inequality involves and impacts many actors and institutions ("stakeholders") with often contradictory and cross-cutting allegiances (the state, workers, environmentalists, residents, private capital, neighborhood organizations). These stakeholders are engaged in struggles for access to valuable resources (clean and safe working and living environments, natural resources, power, profit). Environmental inequalities are rarely characterized by simple "perpetrator-victim" interactions. Rather, they involve stakeholders with varying degrees of access to resources such as political power.

Institutional racism and other forms of inequality play a decisive role in environmental justice struggles. Specifically, those populations of workers and residents with the least access to political resources are generally low-income and/or people of color and are therefore more likely to suffer environmental injustices.

Despite the yoke of racism and classism (among other forms of inequality), marginal groups can sometimes create or exploit openings in the political process to mitigate or change the nature of environmental racism they confront. That is, through resistance they can shape environmental inequalities. Thus environmental inequalities continuously evolve and vary over time and context, rather than simply consisting of a pattern of unequal outcomes.

classism, and the ability of those groups with the least access to resources to resist toxics and other hazards.[42] It should be evident from these four points that environmental inequalities are not always simply imposed unilaterally by one class or race of people on another. Rather, like all forms of stratification, environmental inequalities are relationships that are formed and often change through negotiation and conflict among multiple stakeholders. Environmental racism is about oppression. But it is also about opposition to that oppression.[43] This is why I include worker and community resistance as a part of the process whereby environmental inequalities emerge, rather than simply as a reaction to them.

Undergirding this framework are several political economic theories, the main one being Allan Schnaiberg's "treadmill of production."[44] On that treadmill, corporations and individuals invest and reinvest capital to seek maximum economic returns. This behavior places strains on the ecosystem and on social systems because economic growth is fueled by the continuous withdrawal of natural resources for industrial feedstocks. Industrial production and private consumption create effluents, waste, and other forms of ecological disorganization. Capital intensification of production becomes the most profitable path in most industries, resulting in increased worker displacement and underemployment. These ecological and social strains place pressure on the state, communities, workers, and corporations to address these ills—often, ironically, through future pro-growth policies.

This model of environmental conflict is useful for understanding how environmental injustices are reproduced. It is also helpful for explaining why achieving environmental justice is a Herculean task in view of the enormous institutional pressures by corporations, shareholders, the state, consumers, and workers to sustain economic growth, profits, and race and class privileges for affluent and white populations and for middle-class people of color. The history of environmental racism in general and of solid waste conflicts in particular demonstrates that these institutional pressures are not simply a "rich versus poor" or "whites versus people of color" dynamic. The drama is much more complex, as different stakeholders often choose one set of goals that displaces another, or persons in the same racial or ethnic community make choices that put them at odds with others. In the case of recycling (see chapters 5 and 6), community-based environmental organizations supported recycling's economic benefits while ignoring its environmental and social costs. It also meant that many African Americans indirectly supported the continued subjugation of other African Americans in this system (in the form of increased occupational hazards and importing more garbage into the community). These intra-ethnic and intra-movement divisions are played out in several of the cases presented in chapters 4–6. These complex cross-pressures within stakeholder communities, combined with the systemic biases of the market place, tend to go unnoticed by many observers.

## Introduction to Cases and Methodology

Data for this study were gathered between 1992 and 2000 as part of a companion project examining the social and economic dimensions of recycling in Chicago's communities of color.[45] I conducted a systematic content analysis of the leading recycling and waste management trade journals. From several archives I also collected numerous newspaper articles and government documents on garbage and other waste conflicts, labor struggles, and racial strife in Chicago and around the United States from the late 1800s to the present. The story presented in this book is also based on accounts from thousands of memos, reports, internal documents, and studies from various grassroots and advocacy organizations. For the chapters on recycling and occupational health, I employed both participant observation and interviews. I conducted semi-structured interviews with managers of recycling facilities, workers, environmentalists, and government officials directly involved in solid waste policy making in Chicago. I was allowed access to the shop floors of several recycling facilities for a close examination of work practices and factory design, and I interviewed workers both on and off site. I also rode in collection trucks on pickup routes and worked on a volunteer basis in one firm. Many workers insisted on anonymity, so most names printed herein are pseudonyms. Also, all workers are African American, Latino, or Asian, unless otherwise noted. The majority of the managers were white, middle-class men. This general racial division of labor is representative of the entire recycling industry.

A growing movement of scholars is arguing that a new methodology is needed in the academy to respond to the various crises and needs of communities. This methodology is "advocacy research," the practice and theory of making the scholarly enterprise more application oriented, more sustainable, and more relevant to communities.[46] Advocacy researchers argue that scholars ought to give something back to communities from which they have taken so much for so long. Moreover, these scholars argue that the entire tradition of peer review ought to be revamped to include laypersons as peers who should have as much say as (and perhaps more at stake than) any scholar with regard to the validity of a particular research endeavor.[47] Scholars practicing advocacy research, therefore, view themselves, their students, their research informants, and the public as stakeholders in the knowledge production process. Although I do not presume to practice pure advocacy research, this book was produced in the spirit of this tradition. I therefore view myself not only as a scholar, but as an activist-scholar.[48]

The plan of the remainder of this book is straightforward. In chapters 2 and 3 I explore the early history of the garbage wars in Chicago and the United States, paying special attention to the role of labor, race, and social conflicts. Chapter 4 is an in-depth presentation and analysis of the US environmental justice movement with a particular focus on Chicago. Here I present two defining moments where the movement took unexpected turns, challenging race, class, and movement loyalties. The battles over the Robbins Incinerator and the Operation Silver Shovel scandal exposed ugly divisions within African American communities that produced environmental injustices without the usual cast of suspects to blame. I also locate these conflicts in the national context in which they emerged. Chapters 5 and 6 are case studies of attempts to create working models of environmental justice and sustainability. I focus on two recycling businesses: a nonprofit community-based center that emerged from the environmental movement of the 1960s and a facility run by the largest private waste hauler in the world. These chapters invite the reader in for a closer look at how different organizational forms produce, exacerbate, reduce, and prevent hazardous working conditions and pollution in communities of color. In these two chapters I demonstrate that workers respond to environmental injustices through a variety of strategies. Workers locate their oppressive circumstances in a broader understanding of social and racial inequality. These findings support other studies' conclusions that racially biased social structures within and outside industry keep a disproportionate number of people of color in occupational "sacrifice zones."[49] Chapters 5 and 6 reveal the origins of recycling in social movements. The recycling center in chapter 5 *is* a social movement organization; the recycling program in chapter 6 was devised as a direct result of a movement campaign to shut down a municipal waste incinerator. As in chapter 4, these two cases reveal both intra-ethnic and intra-movement cleavages that complicate our conventional understanding of environmental racism. So between chapters 2 and 6 I present the evolution of the solid waste industry in its many forms (dumps, incinerators, sanitary landfills, recycling) and link environmental racism in communities with environmental racism in the workplace. Chapter 7 is an effort to bring the major themes of Chicago's garbage wars together in a coherent environmental justice framework.

Waste management and waste disposal are basic requirements for cities to exist and function properly. How we decide to handle our waste in the twenty-first century will invariably be linked to neighborhood and global political economic realities. Perhaps the questions I explore in this book will open the door to more sensible, sustainable, and just solutions for urban areas in the future. The environmental justice movement is concerned with the inequalities that lead to disproportionate environmental impacts on the poor and on people of color. It is my hope that this book will provide a better understanding of the structural roots of this problem and point to opportunities to achieve true environmental justice.

City dump, Back of the Yards area, c. 1902. Courtesy of Chicago Historical Society (negative ICHi-22713).

"Leaving the Dump," Back of the Yards area, 1905. From Mary McDowell Settlement House collection. Courtesy of Chicago Historical Society (negative ICHi-23826).

Trimming counter in slaughterhouse, date unknown. Courtesy of Chicago
Historical Society (negative [none]-00498).

Alley between Congress Street and Harrison Street, 1910. Courtesy of Chicago Historical Society (negative ICHi-21030).

New City Pier Dumps at Grand Avenue and the Lake, 1914. Photo credit: Chicago Daily News. Courtesy of Chicago Historical Society (negative DN-0063685).

Garbage dump, Western Avenue and Grace Street. Photo credit: Chicago Daily News. Courtesy of Chicago Historical Society (negative DN-0061236).

Commonwealth Edison plant at Pulaski and Chicago River, February 1953. Photo credit: Florian Plonka. Courtesy of Chicago Historical Society (negative [none]-00495).

Ken Dunn at Hyde Park Recycling Center. Courtesy of Chicago Historical Society (negative ICHi-34684).

# 2

# A Social History of Waste, Race, and Labor, Part I: Movements, Technology, and Politics, 1880s–1930s

The degree of civilization attained in a community is indicated by the efficacy with which domestic and other wastes are disposed of in that community.[1]

On November 19, 1913, Mary McDowell addressed the City Club of Chicago. McDowell, an activist associated with Jane Addams's Hull House (center of the Reform Movement), was widely known as "the Garbage Lady."[2] She and other reformers were leading a battle against the city's unhealthful and exploitative practice of concentrating garbage dumps in immigrant neighborhoods. McDowell and her colleagues were, without question, early environmental justice activists, not only fighting against environmental injustices directed at European immigrant populations in her ward but also speaking out against violence and discrimination directed at African Americans.[3] The City Club requested that she address its members about "Chicago's Garbage Problem."[4] Her remarks that day in 1913 are illuminating with regard to EJ struggles of nearly a century ago and today:

... let me say that here in Chicago the people in the "back yard" of the city are awake. We can never go back to the old outrageous conditions. The old attitude of mind was represented by a lawyer before the Finance Committee in the City Hall when he said: "*Gentlemen, in every great city there must be a part of that city segregated for unpleasant things, and, of course, you know that people in that part of town are generally not sensitive.*" Now, Chicago dare not have that attitude. We must take a new attitude of mind toward these other districts because the people are thinking in those districts and the standard is growing higher every day. ... We must make it so that it will not be tolerable to the citizens even on the edge of town.[5]

The italicized portion of this quotation is, without a doubt, a disturbing revelation, a "smoking gun" of environmental injustice.[6] That powerful leaders and institutions behave in ways that create environmental injustices is hardly a question. However, many EJ activists (and scholars) experience a nagging question as to whether or not those stakeholders actually *intended* to do so. This quote is evidence of a conscious, even nonchalant, ideological framework that supports the production of environmental injustices as an inherent necessity of urban life and politics.

Environmental racism is not just about dumping toxics on people of color, immigrants, and the poor. Environmental racism is the result of continuous struggles among many groups for access to valuable resources—ecological, material, social, political, psychological, and symbolic. Those groups least able to access these resources must contend with environmental injustices. McDowell makes this clear in her statement above. Groups involved in Chicago's early garbage wars included the Hull House, the city of Chicago, private waste haulers and dumpers, and the immigrant ethnic groups constituting the wards and neighborhoods where dumping was occurring. These stakeholders were in conflict over *the* seminal environmental justice issue: the distribution of solid waste in neighborhoods populated by less powerful socioeconomic or ethnic groups. McDowell's very presence at the City Club of Chicago indicates that the protests that emerged over this crisis had caught the attention of the media, policy makers, and influential institutions. She also notes that the system was in transformation precisely because of local neighborhood consciousness of environmental injustices, thus creating a "standard [that] is growing higher every day." McDowell was carrying on a tradition begun by Jane Addams as early as 1895, when Addams was appointed garbage inspector of the 19th Ward, a section of the city where Russian Jews and Italian immigrants lived amidst massive city dumps. In short, McDowell's statement nicely illustrates the framework for understanding environmental racism that I proposed in chapter 1. She demonstrated that the *history* and the *process* of waste management and dumping were changing; that multiple stakeholders were involved in this drama, not just dumpers and community residents; that long-standing traditions of institutional racism and classism were at work in these practices; and that ordinary people—residents targeted by these practices—were challenging these environmental injustices.

In order to fully understand how contemporary waste management and disposal policies have produced environmental racism in communities and workplaces, one must examine the history of this industry. By presenting this history, I will paint a picture of the process that led to the unequal outcomes we observe today in the waste management industry with respect to communities and workers being exposed to hazards. This process centers on the interactions among several stakeholders—industry, the state, labor, communities, and the environmental movement—involved in Chicago's garbage wars and in other social conflicts.

### The Politics of Pollution and Waste: Inequality and Resistance

The difficulties associated with the management of solid waste have been with us since human beings first settled in cities. First and foremost, these problems included the foul stench, unsightly blight, and the public health impacts of garbage disposal. Equally noteworthy is that environmental inequalities have been evident since the first cities were founded several thousand years ago. For example, in great ancient cities like Cairo, Rome, and Athens, those groups who were poor or politically powerless generally bore the brunt of solid waste problems. That is, as in contemporary cities, the presence of affluence was marked by the absence of effluents. The "non-elites" and "despised minorities" not only were saddled with the duty of cleaning up the refuse of ancient cities, they also tended to live in the quarters where this waste was eventually placed.[7] These were early stakeholders who were unable to exert sufficient political muscle to secure clean living and working environments, and thus suffered environmental inequalities. Research by social historians indicates that these trends continued through the Middle Ages in Europe and into the nineteenth and twentieth centuries[8]: "Before the turn of the [twentieth] century . . . many city officials were forced to confront the cost of expedience. For example, many cities, especially those not situated along waterways [where waste could be conveniently deposited], dumped refuse on vacant lots or near the 'least desirable' neighborhoods."[9]

The "solid waste crisis," while certainly a media buzzword during the 1980s, was in many ways an even more urgent urban problem during the 1880s, particularly in industrial centers like Chicago and New York: "Household garbage and debris were for years thrown out into the street, where pigs or other animals ate anything edible and scavengers and scrap merchants also took their share. Anything unwanted simply remained where it was dropped. The streets of European and American cities until as recently as the nineteenth century were filthy beyond the most fertile imagination."[10]

Air and water pollution too were considered menaces around 1900. Environmental inequalities—in the form of the uneven application of city services—were also hallmarks of this era, when "garbage collection remained uncertain, with rotting mounds of garbage and ash a common site in immigrant neighborhoods."[11] In classic Social Darwinian form, many intellectuals and political leaders of the time defined sanitation problems and occupational hazards as the result of careless health behaviors.[12] In the United States this was the dawn of the Progressive Era, an era that saw the emergence of the Sanitarian movement. The Sanitarians—not unlike the mainstream contemporary environmental movement—included engineers, chemists, physicians, businessmen, women's movement reformers, and socialist and labor leaders. Much of the Sanitarian movement was concerned with the fate of the modern city. Engineers and chemists typically understood the problems in narrow scientific and planning terms. Scientists and physicians were encouraged by the emergence of bacteriology as a significant breakthrough in understanding disease around the turn of the century. Reform-minded businessmen viewed the pollution crisis as a deterrent to attracting more industry to cities. Leaders from the women's movement, socialist groups, and labor unions placed pollution in a larger context of the oppression of women and the working classes. As in today's political economy, the Progressive Era featured a distinct array of stakeholders who engaged in both symbolic and political struggles over how to define this problem and how to access the resources to challenge or maintain the status quo.[13]

The enormous volume of pollutants produced by industrialization around 1900 was at once evidence of great fortune for the affluent and of the reality that millions of workers and residents were living an environmental nightmare.[14] Fortunately, communities were not always passive about the problems associated with pollution. Many activists saw fit to seek protective legislation in this regard. For example, in 1881, America's first pollution control law went into effect in Chicago. The Chicago Smoke Control Ordinance explicitly recognized the link between industrial effluents and public health. A decade later, the first professional association concerned with "smoke control" was formed. There was a great deal of community resistance to waste and polluting facility siting in Chicago during the late nineteenth and early twentieth centuries. There was also a lot of complicity by government officials in allowing these noxious industries to thrive. For example, in 1881, one citizen wrote to the *Chicago Tribune* regarding a particularly offensive meat packing house:

Petitions by the dozen have been drawn up and signed concerning it, successive Health Officers have been begged to interfere, Grand juries have been informed of the facts, and the civil courts have been invoked for relief: but the ramshackle old packing-house, so greasy with long occupation that itself is an offense to any pair of nostrils that comes within three blocks of it, still stands defiant of the laws and regardless of the public health, a nuisance and a destroyer of business in the neighborhood where it is situated.[15]

This letter goes on to tell the story of several workers at a nearby lumber yard who "went home sick" as a result of inhaling odors from the packing house. The Health Department inspectors, summoned by telephone, promised to "have the matter looked into" but never arrived. The writer notes that a *Tribune* reporter actually showed up and made a report of the matter, while no one from the city even bothered. He concludes: "The municipal march towards sanitary improvement is a slow and dignified measured trend, which no stress of unsanitary circumstances can hasten."[16]

The year 1881 in Chicago was a very active time for residents raising grievances about smoke, pollution, and solid waste emitted from the steel mill stacks and packing houses into the air, land, and water. In fact, residents continued to protest locally unwanted land uses during the 1880s and the 1890s with regularity. The media were major players in framing these debates and motivating both the public and city officials to action.[17] And because of this type of protest and public embarrassment, the City Health Department stepped up its vigilance against waste dumpers and unmitigated pollution. Thus the local activists and the media appear to have had a temporary positive impact on influencing the city's inspection practices (and therefore, an indirect impact on those packing houses' business practices).[18]

During the early 1880s, the *Chicago Tribune* appointed a task force of Health Commissioners who conducted regular investigations of businesses and tenements and reported them in the paper. They routinely and harshly criticized the city's Health Department over its lack of vigilance, with headlines like "District Health Inspector Very Negligent in His Duties" or "Disgraceful Neglect and Criminal Indifference."[19] In one report they address seminal issues that are still heavy on the minds of environmental justice scholars and activists today:

> The *Tribune* Health Commissioners sallied forth on another tour yesterday afternoon and were again abundantly successful in their search for bad sewerage and the foul evils arising therefrom. The first place visited was Tilden street, . . . most commonly known to residents of the Eighth Ward as "Devil's Lane," a name which came to it from the non-angelic nature of its inhabitants. . . . The tenants of these houses are poor people, and, if there can be an excuse for dirt, their poverty provides it. If the impression prevails that the poorer residents of the city are not alive to the value and importance of sanitary measures, especially the leading one of good sewerage, it is a mistaken one. Of course in the poorer parts of the city the defects in this line are more frequent than in the richer, but the sufferers from it submit because they feel that what cannot be cured must be endured, and if many of them become reckless and at last utterly disregard all sanitary decencies it is from despair of receiving that assistance in the direction of cleanliness which their landlords and the city authorities decline to give them.[20]

One of the major issues here is to what degree there are real differences in environmental concern between affluent and poor populations. Common wisdom in lay and academic circles has it that people of color and the poor have a "hierarchy of needs" wherein they must prioritize subsistence concerns (food, shelter) over more abstract environmental concerns.[21] Recent research has challenged these theories and argues that people of color and the poor do indeed possess deep environmental values, the real problem is that academics and environmentalists often fail to recognize this.[22] The *Tribune* report mentioned above indicates that the long-standing tradition of inadequate city services in marginal communities is frequently at the root of the perception that these communities have little concern for hygiene and environmental quality. The writer demonstrates how this sets up a vicious cycle in which the victim is blamed for the situation the city and the waste hauling and scavenging companies created.

Community protests have shaped environmental policy from its very beginning. For instance, in the 1880s horse-drawn cars produced a great deal of manure. In Chicago, such sources produced 600,000 tons of manure per year. Generally, horsecar companies would simply store this manure on site in massive pits. Residents' continual protests against these nuisances were the catalyst for the development of new, purportedly cleaner transportation technologies. One of those technologies was the steam-driven commuter train, which produced a great deal of smoke and, not surprisingly, a lot of community opposition. The protests usually focused on single nuisances, such as smoke or waste dumps, so the early environmentalists rarely produced a holistic critique of the root causes of pollution.[23] Opposition to pollution was also generally sporadic and short-lived. But as time progressed, local neighborhood activists and national medical authorities worked directly or indirectly to shape waste management policies in the late nineteenth century. For example, sanitary engineers at this time would not only have to take into account the usual technical aspects of designing a waste management system (quality and quantity of waste, transportation infrastructure, population), but they were increasingly factoring into their planning the anticipated community responses (i.e. protest versus acceptance) to new facilities.[24]

In New York and Chicago during the 1880s and the 1890s, community protests against waste collection and dumping practices were becoming the major purpose of many citizens' groups and civic organizations.[25] And, while many contemporary EJ activists frame environmental issues as human heath issues, this is nothing new. In many major cities, during the 1880s and the 1890s and later, these organizations were mobilizing to secure a clean city and better health for the citizenry. Dozens of "improvement associations" emerged in Chicago during this time to address the many problems with waste disposal and dumping in communities. There were frequent protests against unsanitary and politically suspect dumping practices in Chicago's marginal communities and the greatest push came from women activists (also paralleling the contemporary EJ movement's leadership), who often framed their activities as "municipal housekeeping." Using such terminology, for example, the Municipal Order League of Chicago (primarily a women's group) could place pressure on the city to clean up its act in a way that did not overstep that era's domestic expectations of women. Municipal housekeeping was a way of extending women's traditional roles into the public sphere, thus allowing them to engage in politics while doing so within acceptable boundaries. In Boston, Chicago, Duluth, and New York, civic organizations led by women sought and obtained new legislation to strengthen waste collection and disposal regimes, pollution standards, and the like.

In the first decade of the twentieth century, major cities like Chicago and New York continued to experience a garbage crisis, having fewer designated spaces for waste dumping. Political cartoons in the *New York Herald* depicted the character "King Garbage" as a symbol of how solid waste ruled that city. Chicago began filling clay pits, swamps, and wetlands to meet the need for more landfill space and, in the process, literally created new land for future development.[26] The Citizens' Association of Chicago's loud protests of these practices as "primitive and unsanitary" helped lead the city to adopt a different technology: *reduction*. The Chicago Reduction Company stewed organic garbage in large vats and separated grease, oils, and fats and other materials for sale. Soon, reduction (almost always under private contract) became the most common method of waste management in large cities. Needless to say, this "solution" was met with protests by residents. It also endangered the lives of workers—for example, in 1908 an explosion and a fire at Chicago's Reduction plant killed ten men.[27] Thus, from the earliest days of waste management, community and worker health and safety were linked.

In 1913, Alderman Willis Nance told the City Club of Chicago that the city should consider shifting toward the use of waste-burning incinerators. First, he explained, the expert wisdom of the day was that incinerators were "practically odorless in their operation" and constituted "the ultimate sanitary phase of the problem." Second, he noted that such a clean and odorless operation "means much in a city where there is so much prejudice against the location of a disposal plant in any neighborhood."[28] At the same meeting, Mary McDowell echoed some of Alderman Nance's words: "Such neighborhoods as I represent, the forgotten neighborhoods, the back yard of the city, have had to go through such experiences with the dumps that there is immense prejudice against almost anything that you offer. Some people say we ought to have a plant put way out on the edge of town. Well, human beings live way out on the edge of town and Chicago hasn't got such low standards on the edge of the town that you can afford to put anything unpleasant there. People won't tolerate it any more and they are going around with injunctions in their pockets."[29]

Alderman Nance was certainly correct about the widespread resistance to disposal sites, but he failed to see that the same movements that protested against the city dumps and reduction plants would also target incinerators because they were also (and remain) a threat to human health, despite his claims that incineration technology was safe. Again, this is strong evidence that community protests against environmental injustices were having a real impact on the city's policy making and the development of waste technologies.

Already the reader should be noticing the following pattern: (1) A waste management or other polluting technology is introduced. (2) Strong and vocal opposition by community activists follows. (3) The city and/or the industry introduces stricter regulations and/or new, purportedly "cleaner" technologies. I call this *the movement-policy cycle*.

Popular resistance to waste and polluting facilities was widespread in immigrant neighborhoods and in communities of color. These movements had far-reaching impacts. For example, at the 1914 annual meeting of the American Public Health Association the preeminent Sanitarian Samuel Greeley put it mildly when he told the audience that the recent "location of a garbage disposal plant in a large city received much public discussion."[30]

Interestingly, many protests against dumps led community groups and the city of Chicago toward creative solutions, such as covering the wastes with soil and building public facilities over them. For example, many pre-1950 dumps became parks or school grounds.[31] This "creativity" is ironic insofar as many environmental justice and anti-toxics movement protests in the 1980s and the 1990s concerned new revelations that parks, schools, and entire communities of color were built atop old waste sites. (See chapters 3 and 4.) So instead of the typical protest against the siting of a waste facility *in* a community of color, these protests were against the fact that the community itself had been placed *on top of* the waste! This is an example of how history plays a role in EJ conflicts. Before 1950, a well-placed school or playground could convert a waste dump into a productive space (and the waste would be out of sight and out of mind). Decades later, however, scientific knowledge about the negative health impacts of waste on drinking water, the discovery that *all* landfills eventually leach, and the widely disseminated finding that race, class, and waste are highly correlated produced an entirely different understanding and reaction in regard to the same plots of land.[32]

Much of the waste ended up in neighborhoods of color when African Americans moved into white ethnic communities that previously hosted

LULUs and/or when waste was shifted wholesale into the Black Belt (the South Side) as a result of successful protests in other communities. For example, in a classic NIMBY ("not in my back yard") turned PIBBY ("put in blacks' back yards") fashion, many pre-1950s protests against dumps in communities on the North Side (particularly white communities), combined with industrial expansion near Lake Michigan on the South Side, led to the concentration of ethnic populations (seeking work) and waste dumps in the latter regions.[33] People of color were housed in racially segregated communities and placed next to all manner of LULUs. Some African Americans were in fact "housed" in even stricter ways that exposed them to environmental racism: in prisons. When we think of environmental justice struggles, the image of prisoners and jails probably never comes to mind. But for the first half of the twentieth century there was a huge city dump in a quarry pit at the Chicago House of Corrections. In many ways this type of environmental injustice is one of the most extreme in that the "residents" of this "community" were literally shackled in place and had no voice or decision-making power in the location of this dump.

In this section I have provided short sketches of several environmental justice conflicts during the late nineteenth century and the early twentieth century in Chicago and elsewhere. These struggles were largely focused on facilities that produced an abundance of smoke or solid waste, or on entities that failed to satisfactorily collect such wastes from communities. Each case illustrates the environmental justice framework I introduced in chapter 1. First, the importance of *history* is clear in that these struggles strongly resemble those of late-twentieth-century and early twenty-first-century EJ conflicts (which indicates that history is repeating itself to some degree) and in that earlier conflicts helped to shape later struggles. Second, each conflict noted above involved many *stakeholders*, not just a perpetrator and a victim or target. The media, community residents, workers, businesses (some of which were at odds with each other, as in the case of the packing-house waste example), and the city were involved to some degree in each of these battles. Not only do these stakeholders often have distinct interests; their interests sometimes overlap and often change, and frequently we see divisions *within* stakeholder groups (for example, residents often disagree over the value of pollution as a tradeoff for jobs).[34] Third, *institutional inequality* characterized these struggles, particularly regarding the traditional way of doing business between the city and polluters. That is, it was understood that one does not "rock the boat" when it comes to much needed economic development, *and* the least costly disposal strategy is to dump on the poor and ethnic populations. Fourth, these cases illustrate time and again that community resistance shaped the face of environmental injustice by producing results in the form of media investigations, city government action, changing company practices, and even the development of new technologies. Environmental inequality is therefore a process that requires eternal vigilance on the part of those groups who would protect their communities from hazards. Environmentally hazardous workplaces were even more difficult to protect.

## Race, Ethnicity, and Labor

Alice Hamilton, a medical pioneer associated with Hull House, became a champion of occupational health around 1900. Conducting extensive research in "the dangerous trades," she studied the epidemiology of many diseases and located their growth in poor sanitation and hazardous work conditions. That era was also marked by the collaboration between activist-scholars like Hamilton and advocacy groups. Although a medical doctor by training, Hamilton drew on the social sciences to shed light on the nature and extent of occupational disease in the United States. She and others were framing occupational disease in a broader context that pushed the boundaries of the restrictive biophysical world view shared by many medical professionals.[35]

Florence Kelley, also of Hull House, linked the problem of degraded physical environments to workplace health issues. She conducted research on the "sweating system" (or "sweat shops") —workplaces, often located in tenement houses, that "maintained some of the worst imaginable working and living conditions."[36] In one report on the sweating system in the garment trades, Kelley wrote: "The dye from cheap cloth goods is sometimes poisonous to the skin; and the fluff from such goods inhaled by the operators is excessively irritating to the membranes, and gives rise to inflammations of the eye and various forms of catarrh."[37] These workers were immigrants from Russia and Italy, and their children labored in dangerous industries as well. In the same report, Kelley explained: "It is a lamentable fact, well known to those who have investigated child-labor, that children are found in greatest number where the conditions of labor are most dangerous to life and health. . . . In addition to diseases incidental to trades, there are conditions of bad sanitation and long hours, almost universal in the factories where children are employed."[38]

Like many immigrants and people of color, children are marginalized and have minimal political voice (especially if the legal voting age is 18). Thus it should come as no surprise that their jobs were among the least desirable, lowest-paid, and most unhealthful. These children existed at the margins of their communities and were therefore less able to gain access to cleaner working environments. This political problem was exacerbated by the fact that children are much more biophysically vulnerable to environmental illness than adults. Common diseases and injuries that working children in Chicago's factories contracted during the early twentieth century included nicotine poisoning in tobacco factories, throat disease from frame gilding, spinal curvature and pelvic disorders from buttonholing and machine stitching in sweat shops, lung disease from dust in boilerplate, cutlery, and metal-stamping works, and deafness from all manner of jobs.

Florence Kelley's work aided in the formation of a legislative commission of inquiry (in 1893) into the sweatshop sector, where immigrant women and children often worked. Eventually this effort led to the passage of legislation that established factory inspection agencies and standards such as the eight-hour day and better sanitation conditions in home workshops.[39]

A decade later, more legislation was inspired by popular fiction. Upton Sinclair's 1905 novel *The Jungle* was based on his field work in the Chicago meat packing and slaughterhouse industry, and the ensuing public outcry led to the passage of the Meat Inspection Act and the Pure Food and Drug Act of 1906. Sinclair—also closely associated with Hull House—later lamented this superficial legislative approach because its focus was limited to preventing unsanitary food packing practices while ignoring the broader question of labor exploitation. He was quoted as having said "I wanted to touch Americans in their hearts, but instead I touched their stomachs."

The turn of the twentieth century was a watershed for a number of reasons. The labor movement was gaining momentum with the formation of the Knights of Labor, but elites fought back at the Haymarket Riots in Chicago.[40] The panic (or depression) of 1893 had thrown the American economy into a spin. While most working-class Americans struggled to make ends meet, African Americans were enduring additional hardships. Lynchings of African Americans skyrocketed as the post-Reconstruction South sought to reassert its white supremacy. As if to punctuate this sentiment of white Americans, the US Supreme Court handed down the *Plessy vs. Ferguson* ruling in 1896, giving life to the "separate but equal" doctrine that plagues race relations and environmental policies today. Most African Americans were living in rural areas and therefore largely working in agriculture, as they had been since their forced immigration some 300 years earlier. Sharecropping and tenant farming were prevalent. As Dorceta Taylor argues, this coercive relationship between African Americans and the land may have resulted in the ambivalent feelings some African Americans reportedly have with respect to nature that persists today.[41] In urban centers like Philadelphia, African Americans worked in the lowest-status, lowest-wage "menial employment" and lived in "unhealthful homes, usually on the back streets and alleys."[42] In 1900 in the city of Chicago, nearly 65 percent of African American men and 80 percent of African American women worked as domestic or personal servants.[43] By 1920, most African American women in Chicago were still employed as domestics, and this was the second-highest-ranked occupation among African American men as well.[44] African American and Mexican American men were also concentrated in Chicago's steel mills, stockyards, and railroads, where they invariably worked harder, were paid less, and occupied positions that offered "little or no chance of promotion away from the least skilled, heavier, and more unpleasant tasks."[45] There were drastic differences in pay between African Americans and whites, and marked differences in unemployment levels.[46] In many industries, managers reported that they relegated blacks and Mexican Americans to the most dangerous work for biological reasons. For example, African Americans were concentrated in the cancerous coke ovens of the steel industry in large part because management reported that they were better suited to hot conditions.[47] Many paint manufacturers in Chicago placed blacks in the lithopone and lead departments (the most hazardous positions) because "they were less susceptible to skin diseases."[48] Perhaps these justifications soothed the consciences of white managers and owners as they concentrated certain people in occupational sacrifice zones. In many industries, African Americans were "a distinct labor group."[49] Labor conditions in the meat packing industry were generally unsavory; for African Americans they were horrific. The many sources of institutional and informal racism that African Americans experienced showed few signs of abatement. As late as 1948, according to a special report on employment opportunities, 86 percent of the black work force in Illinois was listed as "semi-skilled" or "unskilled."[50]

Living conditions for both African Americans and Mexican Americans were deplorable. According to one study, aside from overcrowding, unsanitary conditions, and a lack of fresh air (due to an absence of windows), these two groups actually paid more for rent than their white counterparts.[51] The "Black Belt," where African Americans were concentrated on Chicago's South Side was a "metropolis in itself."[52]

Compounding these conditions, the racial intimidation and outright violence directed at African Americans at work and in communities was legendary. Since the late nineteenth century, African Americans were often used as strikebreakers, and soon thereafter all African Americans were popularly condemned as a "scab race."[53] Beatings of African Americans by workers, residents, and even women and school children were especially intensified during strikes and the many race riots Chicago has seen.

Thus, in both rural and industrial settings, the environment that most African and Mexican Americans lived and worked in was unhealthy and of low status. They endured these hardships and environmental inequalities because they were formally and informally denied access to legal, social, economic, and political resources. Other stakeholders—whites of all classes, the state, and corporations—successfully withheld these coveted resources from them, and this had enormous impacts on the life chances and the health of people of color.[54]

### Immigrants and the Waste Trade

While also enduring great hardships around 1900, other immigrant groups generally fared better than Mexican Americans and African Americans, often achieving greater levels of class mobility and ownership of property and businesses. These groups included Italian, Dutch, Danish, and Jewish immigrants, all of whom played an important role in the history of waste management during the nineteenth and twentieth centuries. Opportunities for these groups arose for two principal reasons. First, as cities, industries, and residential populations grew and generated more solid waste, better collection and disposal methods were needed. Second, garbage collection was and remains "dirty work" that carries a social stigma. As new arrivals near the bottom of the social ladder, immigrants were both drawn to and pushed into the business of hauling garbage.

Harm Huizenga, the principal "forefather" of present-day Waste Management, Inc. (WMX), was a Dutch immigrant who arrived in Chicago during the 1893 World's Fair. Huizenga and his sons began hauling garbage at $1.25 per wagonload and built a thriving business through ethnic and familial ties.[55] The Huizengas were able to work hard, be American, and still stay Dutch. Hauling garbage required little communication, a plus for new immigrants.

There is evidence that some immigrant groups also benefited from the emergence of political machines in Chicago.[56] Political machines in this city were infamous for providing jobs in exchange for votes and other forms of political support. These practices raised the ire of some observers. In 1910, for example, the Citizens' Association of Chicago protested: "It is notorious that the 700 or more teams employed by the Street Department [for waste collection] constitute the most important item of political patronage that remains at the disposal of a City administration; and it is well known that this form of patronage has been used by every City administration as a weapon in aldermanic and mayoralty elections."[57]

Italian Americans in San Francisco were hauling trash at the same time. Competition was fierce even during this early period in the history of waste management: "A horse, a wagon, and a gun were standard equipment for many a San Francisco scavenger."[58] In 1912 the daily wage for Italian immigrant scavengers in San Francisco was $2.50. Like other immigrant groups, the Italians moved into the trade, often working with family members or friends, until they could accumulate enough money to purchase their own horse and wagon. Then they would often strike out on their own. This independence and entrepreneurialism are almost totally absent from the solid waste industry today, as larger companies, including transnational corporations, have taken over most of the business. Ironically, the industry began to take on this more rationalized, corporate form in the 1950s and the 1960s—just when African Americans and Latinos were breaking into the business as workers. The irony of the success of the civil rights movement is that it allowed many people of color to enter the door of the private sector as major industries were either declining or undergoing massive consolidation. As a result, today the solid waste industry is marked by a bureaucracy that maintains a racial division of labor, with few people of color in management or ownership positions.

## Labor, Waste Reuse, and Waste Disposal

It is important to contrast how solid waste was managed before World War II with contemporary practices. Waste reuse and source separation were routine components of garbage hauling in the early days. Source separation today involves separating garbage from recyclables, but as early as 1895 residents of New York were required to separate garbage (food, organics), rubbish (non-organic trash), and ashes into different receptacles. Typically the rubbish and garbage would go to the incinerator while noncombustibles (ash, etc.) would go to the city dump. Colonel George Waring, New York's sanitation commissioner, built a rubbish sorting plant (the first in the United States) that sold salvageable goods and returned the revenue to the city.[59]

Like source separation, waste reuse was a much more common form of solid waste management a century ago. For example, a private organization of Italian American scavengers in San Francisco—the Sunset Company—had incorporation papers that included this job description for employees: "To gather, remove, dispose of, buy, sell and otherwise deal in garbage, swill, bones, scrap iron, bottles, sacks, boxes, waste paper, and other waste materials."[60] Relative to most industrial processes, reuse activities generally require "greater use of lower-skilled human labor. Workers sort, move, rework, reclassify, and rethink how to reuse discarded production and consumption by-products."[61] In Chicago, when Jewish peddlers engaged in junk dealing, they used old mattresses and pillows and other sleeping equipment for reuse; however, when synthetics replaced natural fibers such as wool, cotton, and jute, "the scrap from the soft goods could no longer be effectively reprocessed," thus placing this group of ethnic workers in jeopardy.[62]

Although reuse was common, other forms of solid waste disposal were predominant, particularly incineration. During the 1920s, as in previous

decades, community activists launched protests against incinerator operators for emitting tons of pollutants into the local air. In Chicago, "air
cleanup campaigns" began in the 1920s but would not be successful for
another 50 years.[63] In San Francisco, the Scavengers' Protective Association
faced a citizen's lawsuit against its incinerator in 1932. The SPA decided to
adopt the sanitary landfill, at the time a "cutting-edge" technology. This
was different from the traditional open dumps to which many neighborhoods were accustomed. A sanitary landfill was covered with dirt each
evening to create a much more benign, less unsightly appearance. Although
citizen actions had a direct effect on waste management policy, this was a
classic shifting of waste and pollution from one medium (air) to another
(land): a variation on the "out of sight, out of mind" theme.[64] It was also
another example of the influence of community resistance on the development of a "new and improved" and purportedly "cleaner" technology. The
use of "sanitary landfills" continues today. By law in many states, their
operators must cover the refuse with a certain amount of earth at the end
of each workday. Thus, the volume of pollution did not decrease when cities
shifted from dumps to incinerators, or vice versa; the waste technology simply changed form. This is a pattern of industrial response to movements
and regulation regimes we observe throughout the twentieth century.[65]

## Labor and Occupational Safety in a Changing Industry

The twin phenomena of consolidation (i.e., mergers and acquisitions) and
worker exploitation common in many of today's large industries were evident in the waste management sector more than 80 years ago. In 1918 San
Francisco's City Council convened a special committee to deal with the dis-
organized garbage disposal system in the city. At that time, many collection
routes overlapped, charges to residents varied greatly, and communities
resisted these changes. While garbage collection was privatized, services
were provided by small family businesses whose labor costs were kept down
by "family enterprise practices among the immigrant scavengers. . . . Even
pre-teen sons could drive the wagons while their fathers hoisted the
refuse."[66] This practice of "self exploitation" was common and has been
crucial to the survival of immigrant businesses throughout this country's
history.[67] Unfortunately, the uniformity of services and costs—not child

labor—were the issues of concern for San Francisco's City Council. In 1921, when the city of San Francisco announced that it was seeking bids from "competent private companies for contracts to pick up refuse in city-outlined collection districts," many scavengers further consolidated into an Italian American venture called the Scavengers' Protective Association. Further consolidation took place in the years following the SPA's formation. In 1932, for example, 36 waste hauling companies competed for permits to provide services in 97 collection districts in San Francisco. However, by 1935 only two large companies remained in formal competition. As waste companies grew, familial and ethnic relationships gave way to formal and rational-legal structures.[68]

As professional as the white-collar side of the waste business may have appeared, the reality of occupational injuries remained constant. Timothy Jacobson, a present-day waste industry consultant, explains: "Actually doing the job, and not just talking about it, was nasty but necessary work. . . . [But, as the garbage man] gets tired toward the end of a day of heavy hauling, he is more prone to making mistakes, and is easier prey to accidents. His thoughts run to the hot shower and supper ahead, and less to the job still in front of him. His efficiency declines."[69]

Around 1900, garbage haulers using a horse and cart understood the hazardous nature of the work, regardless of how alert employees were: "The work of getting on and off the cart with the trash was very hazardous not only because of the heights at which one carried the weight but also because the biggest fear was the horses—that they would move."[70]

As companies consolidated, the by-laws and regulations were changed to protect the company from any legal liability for injuries. The Sunset Company's 1934 by-laws on work injuries explicitly stated that all injuries could be attributed to the worker's own negligence. There was also no sick leave at the Sunset firm. Still, scavenging was viewed as honest, steady, and hard work.

Waste hauling was not the only hazardous job associated with trash management. Street cleaning (a seemingly innocuous task) was perhaps even more dangerous. For example, in New York during the year 1917, eight out of ten street cleaners were physically disabled on the job—5,484 disability cases in all. Accidents, pneumonia, sunstroke, intestinal disorders, and neuralgia were common and were the impetus for frequent labor

strikes.[71] Work in incinerators and reduction plants was also quite dangerous. As I have mentioned, a 1908 explosion at the state-of-the-art Chicago
Reduction Plant killed ten workers. In the 1950s, Baltimore's 800-ton-per-
day incinerator needed cleaning every week. This required that workers go
deep into the machine (after turning it off) with shovels and wheelbarrows,
facing deadly temperatures and respiratory hazards from ashes.[72] While
generally hazardous, in many ways waste-related work was getting easier
with technological changes, and the pay was good.

Throughout the 1930s, innovations were being sought in garbage
collection to reduce costs and improve performance. For example, the
"Dempster Dumpster" was introduced in 1934. It was a "large steel container fully enclosed with a curved steel top, entry doors, and dump release
bottom . . . designed to be hoisted mechanically onto a truck for transport
to the dump site."[73] The Dempster Dumpster and the hydraulic mechanism
used to empty it are said to have eased the back and arm strain many scavengers experienced regularly; however, they also signaled the beginning of
the displacement of labor by automation in garbage hauling.[74] Scavenging
work was about to undergo further changes as the United States entered
World War II and its population continued to grow and consume more.
These changes occurred alongside a maturation of the waste management
industry and the environmental movement.

# 3

# A Social History of Waste, Race, and Labor, Part II: Waste Management and Waste Conflicts, 1940s–2000

### The State Organizes Recycling Efforts

The volume of solid waste being generated in urban areas was rising rapidly on the eve of the United States' entry into World War II. During that war (as was the case during World War I), citizens' consumption was rationed to conserve valuable food reserves. It also quickly became apparent that the US military had a shortage of raw materials, so citizens were encouraged to contribute all manner of goods to the war effort. A number of federal agencies were established to promote the conservation and collection of certain raw materials. During World War I, the principal agency in charge of these practices was the Waste Reclamation Service. During World War II, the War Production Board met the challenge. Although most history books recount this tale with patriotic fervor, it actually met with mixed success. On one hand, a great variety of materials were gathered and used for production, including scrap metal. On the other hand, although well funded, the scrap metal campaign was ill informed and poorly designed. The recycling rhetoric from the military-industrial complex was strong: "If you have even a few pounds of scrap metal in your home, you are aiding the Axis," claimed a wartime magazine ad for the Martin Company, a Baltimore-based manufacturer of warplanes. "If you think you have given all your scrap, look again more thoroughly. Think of each piece of metal as guns to defend your home."[1]

An untold story about the US government's efforts to encourage its citizens to recycle is that these programs were largely shaped by racial ideology. First, the US federal waste recovery program during World War II was directly adapted from Adolf Hitler's Nazi regime.[2] Specifically, in 1937 Hitler and Reich Minister Hermann Goering instituted a Four-Year Plan for national development that included the systematic collection of waste products. It was compulsory for German citizens to participate in the program , and the Hitler Youth organizations provided the needed volunteer labor. The United States borrowed from this program and others like it in Britain, embracing a curious mixture of conservation, patriotism, and jingoistic nationalism. Second, during the war, anti-Japanese sentiment was running high and focused on "the enemy" abroad (i.e., in Japan) and in the United States. While all persons of Japanese ancestry were being forcibly evicted from their homes and held prisoner in concentration camps throughout the western United States, white citizens were applying these anti-Japanese sentiments to the war effort in other ways. For example, in Chicago, the Junior Victory Army (a youth organization numbering 40,000) hit the streets to collect scrap iron in order to "Slap the Japs with Scrap."[3] Finally, numerous communities held parades to initiate and celebrate scrap collection drives. In one such parade, the lead banner at the front of the marchers read:

"Get in the Scrap"
American Legion "Jalopy" Drive
Turn In Your Jalopy—We'll Send it to the Japs
In Bombs—Shells—Planes—Ships—Trucks—Ammunition
That Will Make Them Yell—"Sorry Please"[4]

This history (along with examples from chapter 2) indicates that race and racism are sometimes intricately linked with waste management.[5]

After the war, the opportunity for social change presented itself, as millions of workers experienced a growth in disposable income and perhaps more leisure time to enjoy, appreciate, and fight to protect the outdoors. An example was the 1953 conflict over a landfill in one of Chicago's South Side working-class ethnic communities: "In 1953 local groups tried to stop the operation of a city landfill that had opened and proven defective even by 1953 standards. Its untreated runoffs polluted the swamps and Lake Calumet, and the stench sickened and even terrorized residents more than two miles away. The facility was not shut down, but its operating procedures were improved. Continued opposition eventually led to the construction (in 1958) of the Calumet incinerator which is now on the landfills next to Lake Calumet."[6] This "success" on the part of citizen protests reveals the general trend in the movement-policy cycle during the 1950s and the 1960s—a shift from landfilling to incineration.

(1)

*Everything is disposable* ex: Diaper, plastic bottle, camera

However, despite such periodic upsurges in activism, the more general trend among the post-World War II citizenry was to move into the role of the carefree consumer.

## Slipping Back Into Old Habits: The Postwar Frenzy

I should note that during World War II the United States collected and recycled materials for the war machine, not for the environment. And when the war ended, so did waste reduction, reuse, and collective recycling on a massive scale.[7] Immediately, the population, economic growth, and personal consumption patterns began skyrocketing in the heady days of the baby boom, cookie-cutter suburbs, and postwar economic prosperity. "Keeping up with the Joneses" became a popular obsession, while the earlier efforts by industrial psychologists to create "dissatisfied consumers" paid off like never before: "The 1950s and early 1960s saw the beginnings of the highly successful disposable industry, an industry that sold the idea that single-use, throw-away items were absolute necessities of a modern life-style. Disposables began with paper cups and napkins and ultimately evolved to include diapers, razors, cameras, and even contact lenses. 'Use it once and throw it away' became the consumers' national motto, and ease and convenience became two of the most desirable qualities in consumer products."[8]

(2)    Contrary to classical and neo-classical economic theories that posit that consumer preferences determine the contour of markets, this consumer behavior was consciously being shaped by industry. Moreover, this growth in materialism had many negative impacts on the occupational and natural environments.[9] The 1960s was a decade when social change efforts by labor and community stakeholders might have presented a challenge to this "gospel of mass consumption." However, the growth imperative embedded in industrial economies, combined with the culture of status seeking and convenience, precluded this possibility.

## The 1960s: Technological and Social Transformations

One of the watershed events of the modern environmental movement was the 1962 publication of Rachel Carson's *Silent Spring*, a powerful book about the dangers of pesticides used widely across the United States. And as the public became more aware of hazardous chemicals in the food, water, and soil, air pollution and solid waste also became major concerns.

In the 1960s, solid waste was dubbed "the third pollution." [10] The public demanded better ways of dealing with this problem. Since the late 1800s, scavengers in Chicago had difficulty siting landfills and these conflicts came to a head again in the 1950s and the 1960s. Against increasing suburban sprawl and stringent zoning regulations, finding suitable space to place a dump was more challenging. A popular saying in the industry at the time was "Everybody loves the garbage man when he picks it up, but hates him when he puts it down."[11]

The new air control laws that came into effect in the 1960s, combined with a growing public dislike for incinerator fumes, contributed to the enormous decline in the use of incineration during the latter part of that decade.[12] Repeating the policies of the 1920s and the 1930s, sanitary landfills were again viewed as a viable solution. In 1965 the federal government enacted the Solid Waste Disposal Act, "which calls for the nation to find better ways of dealing with trash."[13] More specifically, as the first federal law on the management of solid waste, it "authorized the Department of Health, Education, and Welfare and the Department of the Interior to administer grant funding to public and private agencies for research, training projects, surveys, and demonstrations including the construction of waste facilities."[14] The act was to be renewed and amended several times, reflecting the nation's evolving concern with garbage. Meanwhile, the people working with garbage were confronting yet another round of changes.

In the 1950s and the 1960s, two major technological changes made salvaging and reuse more impractical than ever: the use of automatic compacter trucks and plastic garbage bags. The compacter truck presented a danger to scavengers who could have an arm or leg crushed in seconds if caught in the gears. More devastating to traditional reuse businesses was the fact that a compacter crushed not only trash, but all salvageable items as well. These problems confront both workers and environmentalists today for the same reason and form the basis for conflicts around some recycling programs. (See chapter 6.) Petroleum-based plastic trash bags were also introduced at this time and brought with them new challenges. Plastic bags generally hid the salvageable materials that the traditional system of open garbage cans had revealed. And as the growth of plastic bag use continued, the volume of reusable items retrieved declined.

Other technological changes included the introduction of computerized billing and mailing systems in the garbage industry. Previously in most cities, scavengers were required to collect payment from residents' homes once a week, allowing for considerable face-to-face interaction. This would involve extra house calls in the evening or on weekends. Beginning in the 1960s, automatic billing significantly reduced these relational contacts because scavengers were no longer required to pay extra visits to subscribers: bills were now printed by computers and mailed out to residents.

Pulling further at the traditional bonds of family and ethnic ties in small waste hauling firms, the civil rights movement's success provided opportunities to workers of color who had previously been shut out of stable, decent-paying jobs like scavenging and waste hauling. Although this represented a gain for African Americans and Mexican Americans, their entry into traditionally European immigrant ethnic occupations is credited with contributing to the decline of the latter groups' family business orientation.[15] Additionally, like most other industries, garbage hauling continued to undergo efforts by management to cut labor costs while boosting productivity. *Environmental groups promoted trash incineration in the 1980's*

## Labor Pains: Dirty Work and the Drive for a Lean Work Force

Despite technological "advances" in the 1950s and the 1960s, hauling garbage was still dirty and hard work: "It took strong backs, and sometimes strong stomachs too. At an old medical school on the near [Chicago's] West Side, the men removed ashes that sometimes contained incompletely incinerated human remains, the final end of teaching cadavers."[16]

Workers were up against a strong and growing private sector.[17] Industry leaders, mostly Dutch and Italian and mostly based in Chicago at the time, decided to form a national association to influence municipal, state, and federal agencies, legislatures, and the US Congress. In the early 1950s the local trade association was called the Chicago and Suburban Ash and Scavenger Association (later named the Chicago and Suburban Refuse Disposal Association). Soon the National Council of Refuse Disposal Trade Associations formed in 1962, and at the first meeting the group

*Question 2:*

focused an attack on the Fair Labor Standards Act of 1938 (the Wages and Hours Law).

Dean Buntrock was the president of Ace Disposal, a Chicago-based waste hauler. He was well known for his campaign against high labor costs. Buntrock viewed each garbage truck as a "rolling profit center" and set about realizing these profits by cutting two-man crews in half during the early 1960s. True to the cutthroat reputation of the waste industry, Buntrock was not in the business of creating jobs for people; he believed in "cutting the fat" and making a profit in order to survive and grow.

Buntrock's methods often paid off for him and his investors while working against his employees. While reducing the size of his trucking crews, Buntrock necessarily demanded greater productivity from individual workers. Studies of the labor process have long demonstrated that the faster a laborer is forced to work, the more likely they are to commit errors and possibly endanger themselves.[18] Yet, while demanding greater productivity out of workers, like the Sunset Company years before, Buntrock continued to hold employees accountable for industrial accidents and injuries: "When a man works when tired, he becomes not only inefficient but, in lines of work like trash hauling, dangerous to himself and others. Accidents at the ends of long hard days are probably preventable accidents."[19] This was a case of management and shareholders depriving workers of access to safer labor conditions. Workers often resisted these attempts, but on the whole, had less power and few resources to successfully do so.

By the late 1960s, garbage began to take on an entirely different significance, as the social movements of the era entered into the policy debates about solid waste. During the 1960s and the 1970s, residents of Chicago's working-class and ethnic neighborhoods of Burnham, Pullman, and Hegewisch fought many existing and proposed landfills.[20] Building on this public uneasiness with piling up waste in politically marginal communities, the ecology movement began to view garbage not as waste but as a resource for community-building and as a by-product of a materialist, consumption-crazed culture. The late 1960s and the early 1970s were also a time in which we observed two trends. The first was the rise of multinational corporate control over the waste industry. The second was the beginning of the decline in the standard of living of most US citizens. Solid waste resources were being controlled by fewer, more powerful stakeholder institutions than ever before, and high-paying jobs were becoming increasingly scarce.[21]

## Enter the Environmentalists: Recycling as a Social Movement, 1968–1989

### The Solid Waste Industry and the Energy Crisis

Between the mid 1960s and 1973, the refuse industry was characterized by the predominance of agglomerations—large companies dealing only in one commodity. Small or medium-size firms, often family-run, had previously performed the lion's share of garbage and refuse collection. Although some of these firms still exist, the vast majority of markets had been captured by a small number of national companies beginning in the 1960s, during a frenzy of acquisitions. According to a *Business Week* article, the solid waste agglomerates had become "glamour" stocks.[22] Competition was fierce and smaller companies were always disadvantaged against firms with the economies of scale needed to purchase expensive modern equipment. However, during the OPEC embargo of 1973, the solid waste stocks plummeted, even more than the stock market generally. Efforts were made to ensure greater stability.

By 1969, the solid waste industry was one-half to two-thirds private. One of the trends during this time was the push to stimulate capital improvements in an industry long marked by its labor intensiveness. One way of achieving this end was to move toward more "efficient" methods of trash disposal, such as incineration. The energy crisis of the mid 1970s was perhaps the major catalyst driving both government and industry stakeholders back toward the use of incineration. Community activists had objected to the harmful pollution of these plants since the late nineteenth century, despite public and private officials reassuring us all that incineration was a sanitary method of waste disposal that would destroy all impurities.[23] However, issues of air pollution and public health took a back seat to "energy conservation" during the OPEC embargo. The US government promoted the use of incineration as a means to a goal of energy self-sufficiency and national security.[24] Not only were many new incinerators more popular than landfills, they were now called "resource recovery" facilities where, "in addition to disposing of municipal garbage, they could separate out any valuable materials, and even provide energy to nearby homes and businesses."[25] "Resource recovery" allowed for recycling, reuse, and energy production to take place in one operation. However, three problems persisted.[26] First, incinerators militate against waste reduction, as they depend on a constant volume of trash to keep them running. Second, incinerators generally cost taxpayers far more money than landfills and recycling facilities. And third, the smoke and ash from modern municipal waste incinerators are toxic and therefore hazardous to human health and ecosystems. A handful of socially conscious individuals and organizations preferred more progressive ways to handle refuse via recycling.

### Intra-Movement Differences and Conflicts Concerning Incineration

One way in which this book's focus on solid waste conflicts brings to life the irony of environmental racism is that, not only did communities and workers suffer from environmental neglect, but those populations living in and working near waste management facilities suffer from policies intended to protect the environment.[27] Although many EJ activists seek to name a wide range of industrial activities as the driving engine of environmental inequality, the EJ literature has traditionally focused on a more limited set of targets. This literature typically centers around the proliferation of locally unwanted land uses in poor and people of color communities.[28] LULUs generally include waste-to-energy (WTE) incinerators, landfills, hazardous waste dumps, and polluting factories. What is interesting here is that no distinction is made between incinerators, hazardous waste dumps and landfills, on one hand, and polluting factories on the other hand: they are all generally lumped together into the LULU category. Although all these practices are parts of the same socially and economically exploitative market system, the historical subtleties are crucial with respect to the environmental justice movement. Few if any studies have explored the history of incinerators, landfills, and recycling in relation to social movements. This gap in the research is significant because these forms of waste management emerged historically in large response to environmental and public health movement agitation.

From sewage systems to garbage dumps, urban solid waste disposal practices were one of the principle targets of Progressive Era and reform movement leader Jane Addams.[29] Uncontrolled urban refuse was linked to public

Question. 3

health epidemics around 1900 and spawned the concern of professionals in the engineering and medical communities. Today we nonetheless see "landfills" (no longer called "dumps") scattered across the United States. These modern garbage dumps have been regulated increasingly as pressure from the environmental justice contingent, or "third wave" of the environmental movement, mounted during the 1980s and the 1990s. Landfills are now regulated so that they are "sanitary" and are supposed to prevent leaching (i.e., leakage of toxics) into water tables, precisely because activists and public health officials recognized the actual threat to human health that such dumps presented (although we now know that all landfills eventually leach).

Contrary to popular perception, environmentalists were not always opposed to incinerators. In fact, many environmentalists proposed and endorsed the WTE incinerator industry as a way of converting trash into a resource. WTE incinerators were coupled with waste recycling, reuse, and energy recovery, so it is perhaps not surprising that many environmental organizations viewed this technology as the "cutting edge." A member of a Chicago-based environmental organization admitted to this unflattering chapter in her organization's otherwise proud history: "We were with the incinerator people. We thought incinerators might be an OK way to get rid of waste. My group, the Coalition for Appropriate Waste Disposal (CAWD), was with the incinerator people, because at that time the idea of burning garbage for energy was kind of an OK idea."[30]

CAWD emerged in the early 1980s, as landfill conflicts were coming to a head on Chicago's South Side. In fact, CAWD supported (although not without some reservations) the reopening of the Southwest Supplementary Fuel Processing Facility (SSFPF), a WTE incinerator that would be located on the Southwest Side, a part of the city with a large working-class Latino population.[31] Robert Ginsburg, CAWD's chairman during the 1980s, told me: "You have to understand the historical context and the nature of the available technology at the time. Incinerators were everywhere because not as much was known about their environmental effects then as is known today."[32] Echoing this point, Robert Gottlieb writes:

. . . many of the [incineration] sites or facilities were a direct outgrowth of the existing environmental policy system's focus on managing wastes and disposing of them in a more environmentally acceptable manner. But the community groups learned to be skeptical of the claims of that system, particularly with incineration strategies, which had emerged as the preferred high-tech waste management option in an era of growing conflict concerning land filling. . . .With local governments, the EPA, the increasingly powerful waste industry, and "more responsible" environmentalists (as one consultant characterized certain mainstream groups) touting incineration as one solution to the waste crisis, the anti-toxics groups found themselves challenging an important new component of environmental policy.[33]

Gottlieb indicates some of the potentially divisive implications of incinerator endorsements by "more responsible environmentalists" in relation to anti-toxics and environmental justice groups.[34] However, this endorsement of "waste-to-energy" incineration went much deeper and therefore has even more disturbing potential for conflict within the entire environmental movement. For example, CAWD did an about-face on the incineration issue between the late 1980s and the early 1990s because environmental justice organizations with whom CAWD was allied (and sometimes in conflict) were fighting those same facilities. It was becoming more and more difficult for CAWD to claim that its mission was environmental protection and "appropriate waste disposal" when 80 percent of the city's waste was being sent to Chicago's heavily African American South Side.

Another part of this history is the co-optation of the struggle to safely dispose of post-industrial *hazardous waste*. During the 1960s and the early 1970s, many environmentalists, industrialists, and policy makers struggled with the question of proper treatment, disposal, and recovery of these often lethal wastes. Environmentalists hoped to achieve recycling and waste recovery *within* the production process, but in 1976 industry secured a victory with the passage of the Resource Conservation and Recovery Act (RCRA). RCRA only required proper disposal and treatment of hazardous waste at the "end of the pipe."[35] What this meant for communities was an overnight proliferation of treatment, storage, and disposal (TSD) facilities around the United States, including hazardous waste landfills and incinerators. This legislation shifted the burden away from industry and toward consumers and communities—particularly communities where people of color and the working class lived. However, these LULUs sparked the anti-toxics and environmental justice mobilizations. As in the case of landfills and incinerators, the confluence of efforts by mainstream environmental organizations, the state, and industry produced negative outcomes for the poor and for communities of color everywhere.

When we think about the management of solid and hazardous wastes from this historical perspective, we can view recycling as the next chapter in this saga that began with city dumps, reduction (remember: garbage stewing, not source reduction), incineration, and landfilling. More pointedly, realizing that environmental and public health activists endorsed landfilling and incineration as methods of environmental protection, one can view much of the environmental justice debate quite differently. That is, the anti-toxics and environmental justice movements emerged largely out of a concern over the public health ramifications of living next to LULUs like landfills and incinerators—both previously promoted by middle-class ecologists as "environmental protection" measures. The implications of these findings are damning with regard to the already tense relationship between environmental justice activists and the more traditional, white, middle-class environmental organizations. I will discuss these conflicts in greater depth in chapter 4. Although these decisions were made principally by corporations and governments, this amounts to a searing indictment of the public health and mainstream environmental movements and their complicity in maintaining the status quo. Given this perspective—this fresh look at the environmental movement's history—we must rethink and reframe the entire environmental justice debate. We can now move beyond a story of ruthless corporations acting alone while middle-class ecologists fought them valiantly to a more complex scenario wherein environmentalists, the state, and industrialists worked together to shift the externalities and effluents of industrial capitalism into the air, land, and water of poor neighborhoods and communities of color. The present state of recycling warrants historical and sociological scrutiny as the next stage in solid waste management policy and as workers and communities become the latest targets of environmental inequality.

### Recycling's Humble Beginnings

Organized recycling began around the first Earth Day in 1970 as a social movement response to the war in Vietnam and the ecological disorganization in urban areas (with centers opening in Ann Arbor, Berkeley, Boulder, and Chicago). Centers were organized mostly on the basis of volunteer labor and a non-profit motive, as recycling was and remains hardly profitable. Unlike the rhetoric espoused by recycling's contemporary advocates, the push by Ecology Action groups for recycling centers being built in the 1970s was decidedly anti-establishment and anti-corporate. As Gottlieb notes, activists were spurred on "with a mission of personal transformation and environmental consciousness-raising rather than the development of a viable recycling business."[36]

For the most part, however, despite increased public awareness of the rising volume of solid waste, recycling was "little more than a footnote to solid waste management in the 1970s and early 1980s."[37] Garbage disposal was still fairly inexpensive, so municipalities and state governments had no motivation to seek out other forms of waste disposal. In certain regions of the country, materials of value to the private sector were recycled. These materials included corrugated cardboard, tin and aluminum cans, glass bottles and newspaper. Beginning in the 1970s, aluminum giants like Reynolds and Alcoa set up extensive buy-back networks to save on the costs of extracting primary resources (e.g., bauxite) and to gain public relations points. Buy-back centers are non-profit or for-profit facilities where residents can exchange recyclables for cash. Typically these operations receive mostly aluminum because of its high market value.

More prominent at the time were the anti-litter campaigns, sponsored by large businesses and trade organizations like Keep America Beautiful.[38] The slogan "Give a hoot, don't pollute" emerged from this reformist approach to solid waste management. Citizens were urged to "pitch in" by "putting trash in its place"—the waste basket. Seattle, often hailed as a model city in the recycling movement, passed the first anti-litter legislation in the United States in 1971, taxing litter to create a recycling fund. That same year the state of Oregon passed a law requiring a deposit of 5 cents on beverage containers. In 1972 the first buy-back center was established in Washington State, accepting bottles, cans, and newspapers.

This was a time of great excitement among environmentalists as environmental legislation continued to be proposed and be made into law. This was an example of the power of civil society and social movements to force the state to react, rather than vice versa. Stakeholders from communities were gaining access to state resources that only political mobilization can exact. In 1970, the US Environmental Protection Agency was established and the 1965 Solid Waste Disposal Act was amended, creating the Resource Recovery Act (RRA). The RRA required the federal government to publish waste disposal guidelines. Although it would appear that this was a heyday for ecologists, many industry and trade group stakeholders were actively campaigning against progressive legislation like the "bottle bills" and efforts to enforce recycling within manufacturing processes. The best example of the latter is the fate of the Resource Conservation and Recovery Act of 1976. The bad news about RCRA was that it led to increased waste dumping on communities of color and poor neighborhoods. The good news was that the anti-toxics and environmental justice movements grew strong as a result.

### The Anti-Toxics and Environmental Justice Movements: Waste Wars

From the late 1970s through the 1980s, the proliferation of LULUs ignited a populist movement response in many poor, working-class, and mostly white communities. Since Lois Gibbs made national headlines in 1978 fighting the Love Canal disaster, many public interest and neighborhood organizations took up the call for environmental protection. These activists shared an understanding that the dumping of solid, toxic, and hazardous wastes in communities was not only a crime against the environment but also a crime against citizens and human beings. The National Toxics Campaign, the Citizens Clearinghouse for Hazardous Waste, and many other national and regional networks and organizations sprang up to address the solid waste crisis that was most evident in people's back yards. Industry and media critics disparagingly labeled these activists NIMBYs who were alleged to be unconcerned about where the waste ended up, as long as it was not in their particular community. Although these criticisms may have had some merit in certain conflicts, they did not apply to significant arms of the movement, which were much more proactive and pushed for pollution prevention and toxics use reduction in industry.[39]

In the 1980s, another movement, paralleling the anti-toxics cause, began to take hold with a stronger social justice orientation, largely informed by the civil rights and labor movements. In Jim Schwab's words, the movement took on "deeper shades of green" as people of color began to articulate a more grounded environmentalism in what soon after became known as the environmental justice movement.[40] I will detail this movement's origins and impacts in chapter 4, but suffice it to say that one area of agreement among environmental justice, anti-toxics, and mainstream environmentalists was the necessity for national and community-based recycling programs. Each of these segments of the environmental movement played a large role in this struggle and promoted recycling, as it appeared to be a sensible alternative to building more landfills and incinerators. Problems particular to communities of color and poor neighborhoods, such as high unemployment and the proliferation of LULUs, made recycling even more attractive.[41] Paralleling many of the anti-drug campaigns of the time, many environmental justice and anti-toxics activists were urging communities to "just say no" to LULUs—particularly incinerators—and to "say yes" to recycling. "Ban the burn" was the slogan adopted by movement opponents of incineration. One popular T-shirt read "God recycles, the devil burns." Between 1991 and 1994 at least 71 incinerator projects were cancelled across the United States.[42] Recycling was the easiest activity to build support for, as the government and the solid waste industry soon became involved in the practice and lent public service and financial assistance. In the wake of RCRA, the environmental movement's mass mobilization precipitated a "landfill crisis" by rendering the siting waste of facilities nearly impossible.[43] In response, 8,000 municipalities passed laws mandating curbside collection and recycling.[44] Here again we see that the environmental justice framework of chapter 1 applies to recent struggles over landfills, incinerators, and recycling. Stakeholders on all sides (particularly industry and communities) were becoming more organized and powerful. The waste trade was a transnational industry by the 1980s, and the anti-toxics and environmental justice movements were becoming transnational as well.[45] This historical transformation changed the face of the conflicts while building upon past struggles. Social movements, companies, the media, and the government each had a stake in waste management and disposal—revealing a multi-stakeholder conflict. Institutional racism and classism played a role in positioning poor neighborhoods and communities of color as the targets of noxious facility siting. And finally, the debate (and eventually policies) changed as a result of actions by communities that were the targets of LULU sitings.

### The Solid Waste Crisis

It would seem then that the political process had opened up to the environmental movement, with all major stakeholder groups supporting recycling. Unfortunately, as with the Resource Conservation and Recovery Act and the bottle bills, industry exerted considerable influence to undermine the most progressive components of recycling. Environmental activists in

Question 4: The number of landfills dropped due to guidelines that were created.
- They did not know where to put the waste
- They cited potential landfills in land of poorer countries.

large part acquiesced in the neglect of many social justice and environmental protection goals originally embodied in recycling.[46] The 1980s was a time when the environmental movement successfully used the media to frame ecological problems as national and global crises warranting immediate attention. The public remained very concerned about toxic and solid wastes as the environmental movement continued to raise the alarm, and as the media reported sensational "eco-events." One of these was the journey of the Mobro 4000 "Garbage Barge." In 1987, a garbage barge filled with municipal waste from New York sailed down the East Coast, through the Bahamas, to Belize and Mexico, being denied entry at each port. After 6,000 miles of sailing, the ship returned to New York. Its cargo was buried on Long Island, where it had originated. In another media event, a ship called the *Khian Sea* traveled a similar journey, this time with a cargo of toxic incinerator ash from Philadelphia. The *Khian Sea* traveled from the US East Coast to the Bahamas, the Dutch Antilles, West Africa, and finally to Haiti. The untold story that these two incidents reveal is that the problem of environmental racism operates on an international scale, as all the ports at which both ships attempted to dock were in the Global South.[47]

Although the media warned us of the "solid waste crisis," industry's use of disposable convenience products and multi-layer packaging continued unabated.[48] A report by the National Council of Public Works Improvement noted that between 1960 and 1984 the average per capita rate of waste generation in the United States increased from 2.32 to 3.08 pounds per person per day, a rise of 33 percent.[49] With the continued political difficulty of siting LULUs, however, there were sudden sharp increases in disposal costs, wreaking havoc on municipalities already burdened with declining tax rolls.

In response, states began to establish recycling programs and agencies to implement them. In New Jersey, for example, a state whose solid and toxic waste problems are legendary, a mandatory recycling law was passed in 1987. At the federal level, the Environmental Protection Agency published its model of integrated waste management in 1989. Titled The Solid Waste Dilemma: An Agenda for Action, this plan was designed to encourage the United States to use several approaches to solid waste management.[50] Known widely as the "hierarchy of solid waste management," these recommendations called for source reduction, recycling, waste combustion or incineration, and landfilling, in that order.

Question 5: Consumption habits did not change as much

Recycling policies appeared to be the answer to the public zeal and "cultural mandate" to address the solid waste crisis. And while most of the recycling industry was being built and controlled by the garbage hauling and solid waste companies, several non-profit recyclers remained in operation in the 1980s, in the 1990s, and into the new millennium. These firms and cooperatives stressed labor-intensive production, the use of local markets and workers, and waste reuse for community development.[51] The Resource Center, a non-profit recycling center featured in chapter 5, is a prime example of this type of innovation. Nonetheless, these more socially and environmentally progressive practices were the exception.

The environmental policies of the 1980s must be placed against the backdrop of the Reagan-Bush assault on environmental protection, labor, and civil rights during that decade. Environmental protection was often pitted against job protection, with the familiar "jobs versus environment" slogan, popularized around the controversial effort to protect hundreds of endangered non-human species, like the Spotted Owl. However, both Reagan and Bush also actively opposed progressive policies that might have provided more gains to US workers, thus betraying both labor and environmentalists. The continuous recessions of the 1980s added fuel to this fire, as union busting and ecological destruction were given green lights by the Congress and the White House. Union busting was so effective that during fiscal year 1982–83 the pay of the average non-union worker was actually higher than that of the average union worker.[52] This pro-growth zeal laid the foundation for the transformation—by the private sector—of waste from a natural resource to a pure commodity. And for activists in communities of color, this was a bleak time: President Reagan vetoed every civil rights bill that came across his desk.

In Chicago, however, people of color fought back and elected Harold Washington, the city's first African American mayor. Washington worked directly with community organizations in Latino, Asian American, ethnic European American, and African American neighborhoods in an innovative populist fashion. During this time and since then, Mexican American, Puerto Rican, African American, and Asian American politicians and community leaders have gained strength in neighborhood politics and through winning seats in the city council and the US Congress. But as much as historians and activists laud Chicago's reputation as "a city of neighborhoods," those neighborhoods are as racially segregated today as they have ever been. Furthermore, environmental racism in the form of waste dumps and other polluting facilities has actually increased in severity in recent years.[53] And, as in the old days, waste collection services are starkly uneven, particularly in African American neighborhoods.[54]

## Capital Regains the Stage: The Victory of Waste as a Commodity over Garbage as a Natural Resource, 1990–Present

### Recycling Gains More Support

Environmental and community organizations were again successful at sparking reactions from industry and government stakeholders. This opening of the political process appeared to bode well for the movement's future. The federal government continued to pass laws and spend resources on promoting environmental protection through recycling. This support for environmental movement goals invigorated activists, who were gearing up for a milestone. In April 1990, environmentalists celebrated the twentieth anniversary of the first Earth Day. Many activists lamented the continued toxic dumping in rural and urban areas and the assaults by the federal government and multinational corporations on precious flora and fauna around the globe. However, the majority of activists steered clear of targeting the structural roots of these problems in their approach.[55] Students around the country (at UCLA, the University of Tennessee, and Vanderbilt, for example) were organizing environmental audits of universities and persuading these institutions to ban the use of polystyrene (styrofoam) products and to establish recycling programs. Several major corporations (notably McDonald's) phased out their use of polystyrene, and campus and municipal recycling programs introduced a new occupation: the recycling coordinator.

The following year, the EPA published new and stricter guidelines for siting, maintenance, monitoring, and closure of sanitary landfills in the *Federal Register*. These new guidelines, now well known in the solid waste industry, are known as Subtitle D of the Resource Conservation and Recovery Act of 1976. The intent of Subtitle D was twofold. First, its stricter standards were intended to provide for a cleaner environment and better public health. Second, by closing unsafe landfills and raising the costs of operating those landfills in compliance with the law, the new guidelines provided incentives for individuals and industries to place more emphasis on the other three components of the integrated approach: waste reduction, recycling, and waste combustion or incineration.

### Problems Remain: Consumption and Labor

In addition to being commodified by transnational corporations and regulated by the government, recycling actually does very little to challenge consumption habits. With the rise in the amount of packaging in retail items, US consumers continue to generate more solid waste per person. The US Environmental Protection Agency predicts that per capita waste generation will continue to rise, from 3.5 pounds (in 1995) to 4.8 pounds per person per day by the year 2010, even as recycling rates are also expected to rise.[56] So it actually matters very little how many tons of waste we recycle if we continue to increase our consumption, thereby extracting more natural resources to create the goods in the first place.

In addition to these larger ecological issues, an often unnoticed problem in the changing nature of consumer waste is not just the volume, but the content. It is widely recognized that consumer product packaging now constitutes the majority of household waste, but a more significant problem is household *hazardous* waste. The changing nature of housework has paralleled the introduction of chemical household cleaners—often hazardous and toxic—to the American home. Coinciding with the rise in dual-income households, these hazardous cleaners (Pine-Sol, Comet, Ajax, and various bleaches, to name a few) were marketed to working mothers as a quick and convenient way to get through what the sociologist Arlie Hochschild called the "second shift"[57] —the housework that generally remains undone until the wife or mother arrives home after leaving her day job. The average household discards about 20 pounds of hazardous waste a year—things like "paint, drain cleaner, pesticides, antifreeze, used oil, and more"—and therefore has a disproportionate impact on the health of homemakers (mostly women).[58] The ecological and human health dangers household cleaners present are enormous. The US Environmental Protection Agency estimates that, on average, residents are exposed to four times the amount of toxins inside their homes as they are outside their homes. What this means for both home workers and garbage and recycling workers is the very real risk of lethal exposure. For example, in the fall of 1995 three employees at Newell Recycling of Denver, Inc. were badly burned in an explosion at the plant.[59] In November 1996, a New York garbage man was killed from exposure to acid that sprayed forth from a battery that was being compacted in his garbage truck.[60] In another potentially lethal incident, sanitation workers in Brooklyn found a small jug of hydrofluoric acid in the back of their truck as they were emptying garbage cans in December of 1996. And in December of 1997, a shipment of aerosol cans fed into a baler caused a fatal fire at a recycling facility in Paterson, New Jersey. The blaze killed a Polish immigrant worker and critically injured a Latino worker. To provide a historical perspective on this topic, we must remember that, for scavengers and garbage men who "carried the can" before World War II, hazardous waste from households was extremely rare.[61] In addition to dangerous work, the garbage and recycling worker of the 1990s and beyond faces de-skilling and threats to job security from new technologies.

### Working in Solid Waste and Recycling in the 1990s and Beyond: High Tech, Low Pay

Industry experts often point out that the private sector's goal for both recycling and refuse collection is the same: using "fewer people and trucks to collect more material from more stops in a given day."[62] In fact, no industry today is viewed as "competitive" unless it is cutting its labor costs. A recent article in a solid waste trade journal makes this point in no uncertain terms:

Ask just about any hauler what contributes to their costs and the answer is virtually universal: labor. To reduce that big-ticket item, the solution is to make collection more efficient and, consequently, more automated. A look at several areas around the country confirms that haulers want to do more work with less manpower. . . . But whether it is for recycling or solid waste, the drive toward more automated collection on truck bodies is prevalent in almost all areas of the country.[63]

Increased automation is evident in many cities. In Albuquerque and in Boulder, I have witnessed automated trucks in action. A very clean, sleek garbage truck hums up and down the street and stops in front of garbage bins. At each stop, a mechanical arm reaches out to hook onto the garbage bin, pulling it up and over the top of the truck and emptying it. The arm then rapidly replaces the bin in the exact spot in which it stood just seconds before. The truck then moves on to the next bin, all the while with the driver never leaving his seat. In a quarterly newsletter to its customers, Western Disposal Services spins this new device into a "win-win" scenario: "By switching to an automated kart system that has the machine—not the worker—lift the trash all day, Western increased its pool of potential drivers. Employee longevity is also increased. The new karts also allowed Western to minimize any effects of draft OSHA legislation that would prohibit trash collectors from lifting more than 20 lbs. manually."[64] This statement is instructive because it is clear that the motivation behind automation is not only increased efficiencies and profit, but reduced liability. Western also cleverly sidesteps the issue of downsizing by claiming that the machines have increased the number of "potential drivers."

Recyclers and waste haulers such as Western Disposal are publicly stating that not only are they saving money through automation; they are also saving workers from more injurious situations. The manager of SunShares, a large non-profit recycler in Durham, North Carolina, claims: "We were getting a number of knee and leg injuries. . . . We've since [begun to use automated lifters and] reduced our workers' comp costs, and the guys love it."[65] For Charlotte, North Carolina, the principal objective of automation is "preventing back and foot injuries" incurred when the driver jumps off the truck or lifts a trash container. The argument being made here then is that innovations in technology produce healthier profits and workers.[66] That may be the case, but the cost for worker and community stakeholders is less employment generation from such a capital-intensive apparatus. I pursue and problematize these claims by industry in chapters 5 and 6.

In keeping with the information revolution, the solid waste industry has also wholeheartedly adopted new, computer-based technologies in recent years. In billing, accounting, decision making, collection, processing, labeling, and shipping, the solid waste industry has begun to use labor-saving, time-saving robotics and expert systems.[67] Some programs in France outfit collection bins with silicon chips that computers on collection trucks can recognize for automated pickup and deposit. From conveyor belts to air classifiers and semi-automated sorting, the manual labor "on the line" in the recycling facilities continues to be rationalized and reduced. One trade journal article reported: "This efficient separation [process] . . . reduces the amount of manual sorting required, which is still essential as a final stage."[68]

The ominous implication here is that soon most manual labor may not be required. These trends are consistent with a central goal of Schnaiberg's model of the treadmill of production: to displace and de-skill human labor to achieve greater profit with less risk of collective resistance from below (i.e., by labor and/or communities).[69]

## Why Labor Matters: Work and the Labor Process as a Non-Issue

### Workers on a Treadmill of Production
In earlier studies, my collaborators and colleagues (Allan Schnaiberg, Kenneth Gould, Adam Weinberg) and I drew on the "treadmill of production" model to represent the political-economic dynamics of local, regional, national, and transnational environmental conflicts.[70] That model provides a useful conceptual link among the environment, the economy, and the workplace. The logic of the model is as follows: As corporations and individuals invest and reinvest capital in markets to seek maximum profit and economic growth, there are strains on the ecosystem and the social system. Economic growth is fueled by the continual withdrawal of natural resources for industrial feedstocks. Industrial production and individual consumption practices create waste and other pollution, producing further ecological disorganization. Capital intensification and automation become the most profitable path in most industries, resulting in increased worker underemployment and unemployment. The ecological and social strains place pressure on the state, communities, workers, and corporations to address these ills—often, ironically, through more pro-growth policies. Each stakeholder group operates under the assumption that advances in public welfare are achieved primarily through economic growth.

The concept of the marketplace as a treadmill of production highlights the fact that in a capitalist framework managers of corporations are under continual pressure to produce more profit and increase shareholder value. This pressure places economic, environmental, and social goals in conflict, as managers, workers, and communities each have needs the others fail to meet. Continued corporate restructuring (which the market rewards, despite the disruption of ecosystems, workplaces, and communities) and the growing number of underemployed and unskilled workers laboring in contingent and unsafe jobs at longer hours best exemplify these dynamics.[71] Thus,

• Withdrawl Resources → Economic growth ↘ Waste and other pollution ↓

• Corporations maximize →

Address problems w/ pro-growth policies ← Strains on ecosystem and many proposals or actions leading organizations and economies toward sustainability are met with fierce resistance. Likewise, policies and practices that challenge the logic of rationalizing production through maintaining unsafe and low-paid occupational environments for the working poor and people of color incur the wrath of both the public and private sectors.

One of the principal stakeholders in the treadmill model is labor, a group that contends with the needs and wants of producers and often with those of environmentalists. Labor, producers, and environmentalists often battle over access to natural resources. Industries wish to maintain access to ecosystems for raw material industrial inputs. Environmentalists generally seek to slow down or reform the treadmill. Workers (and communities) have dual needs— as residents and employees they wish to maintain secure and safe employment and clean neighborhoods. These needs often conflict with each other, as (1) producers—through routine production—pollute both local ecosystems and workplaces where laborers live and work, (2) environmentalists often wish to regulate industry while neglecting labor's interests, and (3) workers seek decent-paying jobs, which may pollute the external environment and place limits on producers' profit margins. One significant difference here is that, unlike producers and environmentalists, lower-skilled workers tend to occupy lower socioeconomic categories and are more likely to be people of color. What workers *do* have in common with environmentalists is their desire for cleaner local ecosystems, while both workers and producers generally support sustained economic growth. However, most environmentalists and producers have little sustained interest in the prevention of workplace hazards or in the redistribution of wealth and political power. This sketch of each stakeholder's interests illuminates the many conflicting and cross-cutting allegiances and motivations that make environmental policy making and movement action difficult. This complexity of stakeholder interests also often produces and ignores environmental inequalities that impact the working class, low-income persons, and communities of color.

Thus, the vision of workers laboring on a treadmill of production allows us to understand that any progressive components of policies like recycling are likely to be undermined by the private sector's interests in efficiency, profit, and shareholder value—business as usual. Business as usual also includes maintaining nearly racially distinct low-wage jobs characterized by unsafe occupational environments.

More generally, there are several major dilemmas confronting workers today: threats to occupational safety, wage declines, increases in hours on the job, and growing underemployment and unemployment. The issue of occupational safety and health has been all but neglected by policy makers in recent years. Publicly acknowledging that millions of workers are injured and thousands killed each year might constitute a threat to established powerful interests. Beyond that, why and how have the safety and health of US workers remained non-issues, particularly within the environmental community and in movement mobilizations around recycling and waste management? There are four major reasons.

First, most environmental organizations strongly support recycling and have done so for a long time. And, in recent years, attacks by journalists and others on the financial viability of recycling have led environmentalists to dig in even deeper and reject virtually all criticism of this industry.[72] It is also likely that many ecologists might argue that the price of a hazardous occupational environment several thousand people face is far outweighed by the collective benefits society enjoys from recycling.

The second reason why occupational hazards in the waste industry are a non-issue for most environmentalists is that these issues are, like the waste itself, "out of sight, out of mind" once they leave the curbside. Environmentalists often feel that the real task is convincing consumers to recycle and securing agreements from municipalities and companies to do the same. What happens after that is not as important. After all, we're recycling, aren't we?

The third reason why workers are left out of this debate might be the widespread socioeconomic disorder that has long plagued communities of color and poor neighborhoods. As social inequality in the United States continues to grow, the ranks of the working poor, the unemployed, and the underemployed become an army that is often grateful when offered jobs of any sort. The municipalities and states in which these marginal populations live are likewise engaged in a "race to the bottom" for almost any kind of economic development. Under these conditions, recycling centers, with their image as "environmental businesses," are likely to be welcomed from time to time.

The fourth and final reason why it has been so difficult to shed light on the labor issue in waste management is the time-honored tradition of pitting economic growth against environmental protection.[73] Presidents Ronald Reagan and George H. W. Bush stand out as superlatives in the category of politicians most likely to veto environmental protection legislation (and civil rights legislation, for that matter). Both administrations were also at the forefront of the deregulation movement, gutting environmental laws in addition to preventing new ones from passing. Recycling therefore constitutes a "win-win" scenario for government and private companies because, in truth, it actually speeds up the treadmill of production and it meets the desires of businesses, consumers, and middle-class environmentalists.[74] Recycling has a real multi-stakeholder quality, as a wide range of interest groups pressed for its adoption nationwide. In this context, with this clustering of interests, shedding light on recycling's occupational dangers would likely anger powerful stakeholders.

These factors rendering laborers invisible are part of the larger problem of the workplace/environment divide that maintains artificially constructed barriers between environmental issues on the job and those in communities. This divide therefore keeps environmentalists and labor advocates from recognizing and mobilizing around their common interests. Chicago labor and environmental activists have periodically attempted to bridge these gaps, but have frequently met with ignorance, stubbornness, or political conflicts within environmental organizations, labor unions, and COSH groups. For example, recent attempts to produce Good Neighbor Agreements with polluting auto plants in Chicago have revealed a lack of sophistication on the part of environmentalists and a lack of vision and power on the part of labor unions. In another example, environmentalists in favor of a Chicago-wide recycling system paid no attention to the occupational health hazards that this program produced. (See chapter 6.) Robert Gottlieb explains:

Overcoming the work/environment divide is perhaps the most difficult and contentious question facing the future of the environmental and labor movements. So much of the jobs-versus-environment debate or the promotion of labor and environmental alliances suffers from fundamental limitations associated with both labor and environmental discourses. If how we work is an environmental question, it has yet to enter the language of environmentalism. If what is produced at work as well as how it is produced represents a labor question with significant environmental and social consequences, then those considerations too have been largely absent from the language of the labor movement—and of environmentalism as well. A new, integrated language of work and environment needs to be developed.[75]

Ultimately, without addressing the workplace/environment divide, Chicago's environmental justice movement will be severely limited.

## Conclusion

This chapter and the previous one are efforts to recount some of the rich history of community conflicts over solid waste management in Chicago and the United States. These stories are useful for constructing a better understanding of how environmental inequalities are produced in our society. The struggle among different stakeholders for valuable resources—like solid waste, decent jobs, profit, and a clean environment—can often pit workers or communities against the state, industry, and environmentalists. At other times, workers and industry stakeholders may struggle against regulations imposed by the state and environmentalist stakeholders. These different combinations of interests and alliances can only be explained by a framework that pays attention to local variations in the struggle for valuable resources and the struggle for and against environmental justice.

Thus, any study of the driving forces behind environmental injustice must include a historical analysis of environmental conflicts. Much of the current research on environmental injustice implies that it is a new type of inequality, largely rooted in the 1976 RCRA legislation that led to the proliferation of LULUs in poor and people of color communities. In fact, however, environmental inequalities have always been a distinctive feature of the social landscape of urban and rural communities.[76] The passage of RCRA was simply another spike in this otherwise long-standing trend, this traditional battle between communities and those who would place garbage at their doorsteps and toxics in their workplaces. The historical and contemporary terrain of solid waste management represents a complex drama of environmental racism. But environmental inequality also has many faces. This is the subject of the next three chapters.

# 4

## The Movement for Environmental Justice in Chicago and the United States

In the South . . . a philosophy is insisted upon which says . . . "You must have mud-sills to society. You have got to have the Negro down where he cannot have power, because all society that is worth anything has people of that sort, people on whom you can wipe your feet, people who do the unimportant work, people whom you attend to and who have no right to attend to themselves"[1]

### Chicago

Hazel Johnson has been described as a soldier in the army fighting against environmental racism. Since 1982, her organization, People for Community Recovery (PCR), has been leading the battle for environmental justice on Chicago's South Side. Ms. Johnson is more than a local neighborhood activist—her reputation and influence extend throughout the Americas. She stood with civil rights activists when Martin Luther King came to Chicago in the 1960s. She stood with human rights, women's rights, and environmental activists at the United Nations Conference on Environment and Development (the Earth Summit) in Rio de Janeiro, Brazil in 1992. And in 1994 she stood with EJ activists at the White House as President Clinton signed the Executive Order 12898 (discussed below). Hazel is "Mama" to many children and adults in her community and has come to be known as the "black mother of the environmental movement."

Hazel Johnson's home is Altgeld Gardens, a public housing community. For most of us, just knowing that this is a housing project on the South Side of Chicago would be enough to draw several conclusions about what kind of place it is. High rates of crime, unemployment, and poverty come to mind, and sadly, one would not be too far off the mark in making these assumptions. But that is not the half of it. And this is why environmental

racism is so insidious—because it exploits and exacerbates existing problems to produce an even unhealthier environment. Built on a landfill in 1945
on the edge of an old industrial and "sanitary" dump (or "sewage farm"),
Altgeld Gardens is now home to 10,000 residents. The neighborhood is 97
percent African American, 62 percent of whom live below the poverty level,
and is surrounded by more than 53 toxic facilities, including landfills, oil
refineries, waste lagoons, a sewage treatment plant, cement plants, steel
mills, coke ovens, and incinerators.[2] Forty-two sites have been evaluated
and considered for the federal Superfund program, and 36 are regulated as
hazardous waste facilities under the federal Resource Conservation and
Recovery Act (RCRA).[3] The South Side has been a popular dumping ground
ever since heavy industry moved there in the 1870s and the 1880s.[4] In 1940,
the city opened a 300-acre municipal dump there, "giving official sanction
to the Far South Side's use as a waste depository for the entire metropolitan
area."[5] Today, residents of this area breathe in an estimated 126,000 pounds
of toxic pollutants emitted into the air each day and are surrounded by the
most landfills per square mile in the United States. A 1983 study of the
Southeast Side "turned up cancer rates double those in the rest of the city."[6]
This is one of the 20 Chicago communities with the highest percentages of
low-birth-weight infants, the highest rates of infant mortality, the highest
percentages of lead-poisoned individuals, and the highest rates of cancer
mortality. This is a textbook case of environmental inequality, one that Ben
Chavis, the former director of the United Church of Christ Commission on
Racial Justice, called "the worst case of environmental racism in the country."[7] A prominent geographer has called the region "one of the greatest
ecological disasters in the history of North America,"[8] and Hazel Johnson
has often charged that environmental racism in her community is "another
form of genocide."[9] Regarding more basic needs, Johnson once told a
reporter: "This is a forgotten area. . . . We don't hardly get city services. It's
like we were a little island unto ourselves."[10] Johnson is not exaggerating.
In 1986 her organization succeeded in acquiring water and sewage service
for the elderly residents of the Maryland Manor community—an annex to
Altgeld Gardens. The irony of playing host to the city's sewage treatment
plant while not receiving sewer service is stinging.

   People for Community Recovery has put the Southeast Side of Chicago
on the radar screen for activists and policy makers around the United States

who are concerned about environmental racism. Activists from all around the United States and from other nations come to visit in order to meet and learn from PCR and to take a "toxic tour" of the area. Cheryl Johnson, Hazel's daughter, has worked with the organization since the beginning. She says: "We call this area the 'Toxic Doughnut' because everywhere you look, 360 degrees around us, we're completely surrounded by toxics on all sides."[11]

Hazel, Cheryl, and others have worked hard to document the harsh reality they face on a daily basis. Through health surveys of local residents and studies correlating race and income with toxic releases, PCR and other Chicago environmental organizations have done their homework. Studies demonstrate that of Chicago's 162 toxic "hot spots," 99 are in zip codes that are at least 65 percent people of color; of the six zip codes with the highest toxic releases, five are more than 79 percent people of color; of the 10 community areas with the highest incidence of lead poisoning among children, all are at least 70 percent people of color; and the 24 city wards that are 65 percent or more people of color account for nearly 80 percent of the illegal garbage dumped in the city.[12] But studies and data are never enough; they do not speak for themselves. PCR quickly learned that if they were ever going to improve the community's situation, they would have to mobilize and create a political force to challenge the state, corporations, and white residents who helped produce the toxic witch's brew engulfing their homes and invading their bodies. And, as I discuss in chapter 6, PCR would also need to do some soul-searching to uncover their own mistakes in the complex drama that environmental injustices in Chicago have become.

Altgeld Gardens residents have a lot to say about the state of their community. One resident, Regina Roberts, explained:

I've been to St. Francis Hospital [for my son's asthma] so many times I feel like I live there. It's so many kids out here with asthma. You can't grow vegetables out here and you can't keep flowers out here. It don't grow. You know it's something in the air when you get a sour stomach when you get on the highway. It's like a shit smell with acid flavor. At the hospital they asked me how long has my baby been sick and I said "well he was sick when he was born."[13]

A young African American man put it this way:

I feel they put us in one group with all these factories around us and they know sooner or later that you going to die. You don't live long when you stay out here— not by somebody killing you—mostly you would die by chemicals.[14]

One resident who has volunteered at PCR for a number of years stated:

When I go to the store and talk about the environment, people get so excited that I'm talking about it because they say "everyone we know is dying of cancer." You don't have to go outside to get shot; you can get "shot" sitting right in your house.[15]

Altgeld residents have also done quite a lot to clean up the area, attempting to create community gardens, attending rallies protesting pollution, and supporting recycling programs.

Several organizations mobilizing around toxics issues on Chicago's Southeast Side predated PCR's emergence. Irondalers Against the Chemical Threat (IACT), the United Neighborhood Organization (UNO) of Southeast Chicago, the Committee to Protect the Prairie, and Hegewisch Organized to Protect the Environment (HOPE) were groups that battled the local CID (Waste Management) landfill, proposed designating the entire Southeast Side as one massive Superfund site, and combated threats to the Lake Calumet Wetlands in the late 1970s and the early 1980s. When PCR's work came to public attention, there was a great deal of coalition building occurring among these groups, and a few conflicts as well. Citizens United to Reclaim the Environment (CURE) was one such coalition (comprising many of the above-mentioned groups); it helped block the creation of a landfill (at O'Brien Lock and Dams), got the permit for another landfill (the Paxton fill) revoked, and opposed Waste Management's plans to locate a dump on a marsh in the area's wetlands. Unfortunately, because of internal conflicts and differences over issues like the location of a third Chicago airport in the area and the issue of allowing limited landfill expansion along with incineration, these organizations "failed to produce a more powerful, multi-racial, political force that could have pushed for much broader environmental change in the Chicago area."[16] There was frequent disagreement among these groups—particularly between PCR and others—over access to funding sources, turf, and issue priorities. And there were splits within and between environmentalists and EJ groups over the value of incineration. Specifically, following the recommendation of Mayor Washington's Solid Waste Task Force report, the Coalition for Appropriate Waste Disposal, Citizens for a Better Environment, and the United Neighborhood Organization felt that limited landfill expansion, along with a shift toward incineration, would be acceptable; while groups like People for Community Recovery and Hegewisch Organized to Protect the Environment firmly disagreed because they had been inundated with waste from both sources for years. This is all the more unfortunate because UNO was a Latino organization that could have made strategic alliances with local white ethnics through HOPE and with the African American community through PCR.

## Assessing National Progress: Environmental Justice in 2000

On February 11, 1994, with Hazel Johnson by his side, President Bill Clinton signed Executive Order 12898, which required all federal agencies to incorporate environmental justice concerns into their mandates. The order was officially titled Federal Actions to Address Environmental Justice in Minority Populations and Low-Income Populations. This meant that these agencies would work to ensure that vulnerable populations would not be unfairly burdened with environmental hazards.

Executive Order 12898 represented a milestone in the movement for environmental justice. On the sixth anniversary of the executive order (2000), several environmental justice organizations and citizens (including children) came to Washington to present their evaluations. Their report was unflattering and urgent. They told the press that communities of color and low-income populations remain under siege, battling what one activist termed "toxic terrorism" at the hands of polluting federal facilities and chemical industries. The negative human health consequences of these activities are increasingly visible, as adults and children continue to suffer from a range of cancers, respiratory diseases, and nervous system and reproductive disorders, to name only a few. Equally disturbing, the political process these communities hoped to access appears to be closing. Damu Smith, the environmental justice coordinator for Greenpeace, noted: "When I looked at what was happening around the country, it became clearer that the forces behind the movement to *undermine* environmental justice are very organized, very powerful, and are part of a nationally organized strategy to take away protections for people of color. . . . [We must] do battle with the sinister forces in the nation, out to totally dismantle the environmental justice framework that we have worked so hard to achieve."[17]

Dr. Mildred McClain, Executive Director of the People of Color and Disenfranchised Communities Environmental Health Network (PCDCEHN), was also present at this event and criticized the Departments of Energy and

Defense for completely ignoring the issue of environmental justice with regard to the cleanup of toxic federal sites. The US Environmental Protection Agency was also implicated in the lack of progress on the executive order's implementation. This inaction with regard to environmental justice policy is nothing new, in view of that agency's history of corruption and complicity with polluters.[18]

## Moving Forward

The struggle for environmental justice is one of the most exciting and comprehensive movements for progressive social change to emerge in several decades. From urban to rural areas, linking the built and the natural environments, from degraded housing stock in the Midwestern United States to the canopies of the Amazon rain forests, from Native American reservations in the United States to the sacred lands of aboriginal peoples the world over, from the streets and highways of the megalopolises on both US coasts to the logging roads of the Pacific Northwest and dirt roads throughout the Global South, from the human "sacrifice zones" of African America to the hazardous waste havens of Africa, and from the sweatshops in Chinatown to the sweatshops in China, the EJ movement has touched people from every continent on the planet. This movement is both local and global in scope and purpose. Its composition is multi-issue, multi-ethnic, multi-racial, multi-cultural, multi-class, and multi-national. Its impact is evident in the mobilization of both supporters and detractors in communities, government, and corporations around the globe. The EJ movement also has much greater hope of bridging the gap between the labor and environmental causes than any previous effort. This movement has effectively demonstrated that while vulnerable populations do indeed bear the greatest burdens of military, industrial, and consumer excesses, no one is immune from these hazards. Finally, some scholars and activists are linking the struggle for environmental justice not only to other contemporary movements but also to a long history of socio-environmental inequality between racial and class groups around the globe. Therefore, the problem of environmental inequality is not rooted in activities that began during the 1970s or the 1980s. The historical record indicates that since the time of the first civilizations refuse, effluence, and detritus in cities have always been concentrated in the quarters where the poor and/or ethnic minorities were housed.[19] Likewise, the struggle for environmental justice is as old as struggle itself. Thus, we must begin to reinterpret all of human history through the lens of environmental justice and inequality. In this way, we can begin to see historical continuity between ancient and current conflicts and begin to come full circle to our origin within and dependence upon the natural environment.

In this section, I discuss some of the many watershed events in the movement for environmental justice in the United States.

In 1982, the same year that Hazel Johnson founded People for Community Recovery on Chicago's South Side, a major protest took place in Warren County, North Carolina. Several hundred protesters, mostly African Americans, ministers, teenagers, homemakers—many of them high profile civil rights activists and congresspersons—were arrested. But this was no ordinary civil rights mobilization. These activists were calling for an end to the expansion of a PCB landfill in this African American county. Although the protest failed to close the landfill, the activists were successful at sparking the movement for environmental justice. They were also successful at convincing the US General Accounting Office to conduct a study of environmental racism in the South a year later, in 1983, which determined that African Americans in that part of the United States were losing the garbage war; one-fifth of the population was hosting 75 percent of the region's hazardous waste.

That same year saw an unprecedented gathering of labor, racial, and environmental justice advocates in New Orleans for the Urban Environment Conference's "Taking Back Our Health" Institute. Participants in this historic event sought to frame the struggle against toxics as one of power, class, and racial inequality. The publication that emerged from this conference stated that the gathering was "a positive response to the alarming toxics threat sweeping through minority communities. For the first time at the national level, it [the Institute] brought together people of color who are facing this threat daily with unionists, health experts and other activists."[20] This view of pollution and environmental problems was a stark departure from the mainstream environmental and conservation movement's message. During the Reagan-Bush era, the "Big Ten" national environmental organizations were busy either trying to regain a foothold within lobbyist circles in Washington or pushing officials to take our existing endangered species and forest conservation policies seriously.[21] All of this was important work, but, as EJ activists pointed out, it overlooked the fact that there were other "endangered species"[22] living among us—people of color fighting environmental racism in the cities and rural areas.

By this time, the movement was moving forward, with scores of battles against incinerators, landfills, and other LULUs occurring annually.[23] In 1986, for example, Concerned Citizens of South Central Los Angeles and Mothers of East Los Angeles (MELA), successfully stopped a major incinerator project and several other LULUs in that city. These victories sent a surge of pride through many Latino communities and were a needed shot in the arm for the EJ movement. Equally important, it sent a message to polluters that communities were not going to take toxics lying down. The industry had already gotten wise to the EJ and anti-toxics movements and was commissioning studies like the Cerrell Report, which profiled the demographics of those communities least likely to resist a LULU siting. This is a classic example of the environmental justice framework I introduced in chapter 1 in that, between the movement and the industry, we see a give and take, a game-like interaction. The movement-policy cycle unfolds as industry develops a method of waste management that communities resist and label an environmental injustice; industry responds by commissioning studies to find the "path of least resistance" and/or developing new, allegedly cleaner technologies. But to profit-hungry industry leaders and community residents whose health was on the line, this was no game; it was a war.

The next major event that hit the EJ radar screen was the 1987 release of the study *Toxic Wastes and Race in the United States*.[24] Beyond its major accomplishment of formally putting the issue of environmental racism on the policy map, this study was catalyzed the movement and the regulatory agencies. The movement gained a great deal of steam as a result of the attention being paid to environmental racism. Another important impact of this study was the emerging cooperation and alliance building between university scholars and community-based EJ activists. One of the most notable of these community-university collaborations was the 1990 Michigan Conference on Race and the Incidence of Environmental Hazards. Several activist-scholars attended this event and came together to present and debate the evidence for or against environmental racism. Bunyan Bryant and Paul Mohai published *Race and the Incidence of Environmental Hazards* as a result.[25]

That same year, as white middle-class environmentalists were preparing to celebrate the twentieth anniversary of the first Earth Day, there were major developments in communities of color. The Gulf Coast Tenants Association (GCTA) was making headlines battling polluters from its home base in Louisiana's "Cancer Alley." In Albuquerque, the Southwest Network for Economic and Environmental Justice (SNEEJ) was formed. Both of these groups placed a major media spotlight on the problematic relationship between the "Big Ten" (mainly white and middle class) national environmental organizations and the EJ movement. In January and March of 1990, several environmental justice, faith-based, human rights, and civil rights organizations signed on to scathing letters from the GCTA and SNEEJ directed at the "Group of Ten" environmental organizations. These letters took the Group of Ten to task for perpetuating a monocultural perspective on environmentalism, for a lack of racial and ethnic diversity in their membership, staff, and boards of directors, and for ignoring the plight of people of color struggling against environmental racism. The following excerpt makes the point:

There is a clear lack of accountability by the Group of Ten environmental organizations towards Third World communities in the Southwest, in the United States as a whole, and internationally. Your organizations continue to support and promote policies which emphasize the cleanup and preservation of the environment on the backs of working people in general and people of color in particular. In the name of eliminating environmental hazards at any cost, across the country industrial and other economic activities which employ us are being shut down, curtailed or prevented while our survival needs and cultures are ignored. We suffer from the end results of these actions, but are never full participants in the decision-making which leads to them.[26]

Even more damning than these sweeping critiques was the documentation of politically problematic practices by mainstream environmental organizations. For example, the Nature Conservancy and the National Audubon Society opposed a sustainable economic development initiative among traditional Hispanos[27] in northern New Mexico on the grounds that their sheep were grazing on "protected" lands. The letter also disclosed the contradiction between mainstream environmental organizations' stance in

favor of ecological protection and their receipt of support from major polluting corporations like GE, DuPont, Dow Chemical, Exxon, IBM,
Chemical Bank, ARCO, British Petroleum, GTE, and Waste Management.
Not only were these corporations funding Big Ten organizations, but in fact
many of these firms had representatives sitting on the boards of directors
of these environmental groups. This was particularly hurtful to EJ groups
because each of these corporations has had a hand in creating environmental injustices in communities of color around the world.[28]

In Chicago, People for Community Recovery (like many EJ groups)
protested the domineering practices of the Big Ten environmental organizations wherein they would monopolize funding sources or "use" EJ groups
to leverage greater resources without sharing the benefits. PCR's Hazel
Johnson put it this way: "We don't need white people to speak for us. We
speak for ourselves. . . . We ain't going to participate if they come in with
their own agenda. We want our own agenda. The Sierra Club and the
Wildlife Federation use information from grassroots groups like us and take
it back to their offices and get grants and we don't get any of the money."[29]

These unsettling relationships were also a major part of the debates and
discussions at the First National People of Color Environmental Leadership
Summit. This conference, held in Washington in October of 1991, brought
together hundreds of EJ activists from around the United States and other
countries to forge a coherent vision of their platform, embodied in "The
Principles of Environmental Justice" (see the appendix). One of the goals
of this conference was to advocate for more powerful and cohesive EJ
activism in the form of regional and ethnic networks. These networks
sprang up over the next several years in the form of the Asian Pacific
Environmental Network (APEN), the Indigenous Environmental Network
(IEN), the Northeast Environmental Justice Network, the Southern
Organizing Committee for Economic and Environmental Justice, the
Southwest Network for Economic and Environmental Justice (SNEEJ,
already formed by this time), and the Midwest/Great lakes Environmental
Justice Network. In this way, different regions and ethnic groups could
place the necessary emphasis on their own particular struggles while coor-
dinating larger efforts with networks around the Americas. For example,
APEN could focus on the needs of Korean immigrant workers being
exploited in West Coast sweatshops and on the health conditions of

Vietnamese immigrants ingesting dangerous levels of toxins as a result of fishing in San Francisco Bay. The IEN would continue the long-standing battles between indigenous peoples and their former colonizers over treaty rights and sovereignty issues. And SNEEJ spearheaded campaigns against "English only" legislation, the North American Free Trade Agreement (NAFTA), and the ecological, economic, and occupational health impacts of locating an Intel computer chip plant in New Mexico.

One of the leaders of the EJ movement is Luke Cole, an attorney with the California Rural Legal Assistance Foundation. Cole was a poverty law attorney by training, but quickly found himself gravitating toward cases that were pushing the boundaries of poverty law and environmental law. In 1991, Cole represented the California group El Pueblo para Aire y Agua Limpio [People for Clean Air and Water] against ChemWaste, a subsidiary of the world's largest waste hauler, Waste Management (WMX). This grass-roots effort led to a landmark court victory against the company over a proposed incinerator. The law requires that environmental impact statements and public hearings be held whenever a facility like this is proposed. The goal is to have adequate public participation (or at least public dissemination of the news) in this decision. However, in this community, where Spanish was the first language of 40 percent of the population, the fact that all the public documents were printed exclusively in English created a de facto exclusion of many Latinos from participation. The people, therefore, were not being properly informed and were not adequately apprised of the details of this proposal. Cole and El Pueblo won this case to the delight of activists everywhere, particularly in Latino and immigrant communities. This victory and the larger movement against hazardous waste dumping were arguably the main reasons why WMX got out of the chemical waste business.

After the 1991 summit, the various networks strove to secure political and legal victories all around the United States. There were many failures as well. Without a doubt, one of the most important events during this period was the signing of Executive Order 12898 (requiring all federal agencies to work toward environmental justice), an event that has variously been described as the movement's greatest moment, the death knell of the EJ cause, and a piece of policy that has been virtually ignored by those whom it obligates to act. Those observers who view Executive Order 12898 as a victory recognize that when a movement is able to get the attention of the highest political office in the land this represents a major accomplishment. This optimistic perspective, shared by many regulators, also views legislation and its implementation as the pinnacle of achievement. From another perspective (taken by some activists), the public, philanthropic foundations (who provide much of the movement's resources), policy makers, the media, and perhaps community activists themselves began to view the issue of environmental racism with less urgency the instant President Clinton signed the executive order.[30] There is evidence to support this perspective: many non-profit movement groups have gone bankrupt or become inactive, and many activists have experienced "burnout" without the assurance that a new generation will take over the cause. Yet another perspective views the executive order as purely symbolic. This viewpoint also has a great deal of merit, as demonstrated earlier in this chapter, when several EJ groups traveled to Washington to denounce the lack of implementation of the executive order.

Three years after the signing of Executive Order 12898, in 1997, the Pennsylvania community group Chester Residents Concerned for Quality Living was given a green light by the courts to pursue a case against polluters under civil rights law. Visiting Chester in July of 1995, I was amazed as I toured this community of poor and working-class African American and European American folks trying to survive in the middle of one of the most polluted places in the United States. As Zulene Mayfield of CRCQL explained, "every hour of the day, there are no less than 15 trucks coming through this main road carrying waste into our community." Ms. Mayfield introduced me and other activists to community residents whose homes were less than 100 yards from a major medical waste facility. A recycling plant (against which residents had already protested), a medical waste incinerator, construction dumps, chemical plants, and a host of other LULUs were the only business establishments observable in the area. The depths of environmental racism and the degree of human and ecological degradation in Chester are overwhelming. Although the US Supreme Court threw out the case against the polluters, the struggle continues.

Just a year later, in the state of Louisiana, the United States witnessed another battle involving pollution and toxics on a colossal scale. This case was even more important to the movement for environmental justice, as the EPA agreed that this would constitute a test of the disparate impact standard.[31] This standard allows plaintiffs to sue for discriminatory impact rather than requiring the proof of discriminatory intent. Tulane University law professor Bob Kuehn expressed the magnitude of local environmental practices in plain language: "Louisiana has world-class polluters . . . and we have single chemical plants that produce as much pollution as the entire state of Ohio."[32] Kuehn was not exaggerating, and when the Shintech chemical corporation tried to site a $700 million polyvinyl chloride (PVC) plant in Convent (a majority African American community) it only confirmed that polluters in Louisiana enjoy unparalleled access to the political process. Chemical corporations, for example, regularly influence the elections of judges, city council members, and the governor, and they enjoy heavy subsidies and an absence of environmental regulation.[33] Shintech expected to be treated no differently, but got a rude surprise in the form of a national environmental justice effort to oppose the siting process. After the lack of results in the Chester case, many activists and scholars described this case as a landmark in the struggle, as important to the EJ movement as the *Brown vs. Board of Education* decision was to the civil rights movement. Local EJ groups in Louisiana collaborated with Greenpeace and other major environmental organizations and universities, successfully preventing Shintech from siting its facility. Jesse Jackson's Operation PUSH, the NAACP, and the Congressional Black Caucus all supported this struggle. As a result, there was a major backlash. The governor de-funded the Tulane Environmental Law Clinic (an organization whose resources were crucial to winning this battle), and several major African American leaders and organizations joined with business groups and politicians to denounce the EJ movement's alleged negative impact on economic development in the African American community.[34]

Combining many of the features of the anti-toxics, civil rights, labor, and traditional environmental movements, the environmental justice movement is a force unlike any other. Producing a more balanced and more radical concern for the natural and social environments, this movement has united strange bedfellows and exposed divisions within some communities. In the next sections I return to the neighborhoods of Chicago for a closer look at environmental justice struggles that reflect the complexity, the promise, and the dangers within this movement. These "garbage wars" reveal the tensions within the movement and within the African American community over the value of environmental health versus the promise of economic development.

## Environmental Racism as Colonization

Throughout history, one of the most effective ways of controlling a colony was to create hierarchies (or intensify existing ones) between social classes and/or ethnic groups, so that each would have an incentive to focus its energies on the others rather than on the colonizer. Empires would generally appoint local puppet chieftains to maintain immediate control over the masses, to disburse resources, and to report all goings on to the central authority. This arrangement exists in various forms today all over the globe, in the Global South, in indigenous communities, and in communities of color in the United States.[35] Native American communities have Tribal Governments, which were set up for this purpose in 1934. African Americans, Asian Americans, and Latinos are "represented" by politicians who often serve this same purpose (often unwittingly). There are a few progressive political leaders who go against this grain, but they are rare. However, many of them play the role of the puppet with relish and make the most of it. The case studies below are reflective of this dynamic in several African American communities in Chicago. They are also stories of environmental racism that reveal how deeply rooted and complex EJ struggles are. These are not just stories of people of color versus whites, or of a single perpetrator and a single target; they are stories of the powerful versus the weak, of racism, and of resistance from below. These divisions are the core of what drives environmental racism, and they must be among the future targets of the movement for environmental justice.

## Conquering "The Mountain": Operation Silver Shovel, Waste Recycling, and Disrespect of Communities of Color

If someone told you about a hypothetical case where several waste companies illegally dumped garbage in a community, then when this crime was discovered, the polluters were *paid* to clean it up, you would probably exclaim "Impossible!" This hypothetical scenario is not only possible, it is the true story of Operation Silver Shovel and the nightmare that several

African American and Latino neighborhoods in Chicago experienced recently.

Since 1914, the City Council of Chicago has recognized the need for strong legislation against illegal dumping.[36] But before and since that time, there have been frequent scandals over waste dumping and the graft that accompanies this illicit trade in garbage for favors and cash.[37] So this story is not without precedent.

John Christopher was a businessman. He was in the business of "recycling" construction and demolition (C&D) waste and finding places to dump it at the lowest possible cost. Since the late 1980s, Christopher's company, Krisjon, had discovered what every successful polluter knows: that the most profitable path is the path of least resistance. In other words, dump on the poor and people of color and you are a lot less likely to encounter resistance from residents or politicians, the laws are less likely to be enforced, and if they are, they will be applied leniently.[38] Christopher began dumping in working-class and low-income African American and Latino communities on Chicago's West Side, particularly in the black community of Lawndale. In order to ensure that he could get away with these crimes without the hassle of the police or City Hall, he paid local aldermen bribes in cash.[39] Every community where Christopher dumped his waste was majority African American or Latino, and each alderman whose palm he greased was African American or Latino. This section will focus on the African American communities of Lawndale and Austin.

The Krisjon company was allegedly recycling the C&D waste for use in other construction operations. This type of recycling business is actually growing and has the support of many environmentalists for its potential to reduce the extraction of virgin resources to fuel construction projects. However, Krisjon was not actually recycling this waste. Instead, the company was crushing large rocks and concrete blocks and simply piling them up—creating dumps in the neighborhoods. In fact, much if not most of the waste was from city-run construction sites. Local activists soon discovered that Krisjon in fact had no permits for this operation and was therefore in violation of several city ordinances. The Krisjon company was engaged in illegal, or "fly," dumping.

Local neighborhood groups in Lawndale and Austin protested these operations from early on. In 1990, community residents gathered to discuss a site that was being proposed for a C&D dump to be operated by Krisjon. Calling themselves Concerned Parents of Sumner, Webster, and Frazier Schools, they were mostly parents of children who attended those schools within blocks of the dump site.[40] Concerned Parents and several other community groups sent letters to John Christopher requesting dust reduction practices during school hours, the construction of a fence around the lot to prevent children from climbing the mounds of debris, sod planting on the mounds and on parkways surrounding Sumner school, repairs and cleaning of neighborhood homes and streets damaged by the operation, and the communication of information to the public about his "recycling" activities. Christopher never responded and did very little to address community concerns.

His dump sites, however, were bustling and were receiving waste from 96 different locations around Chicagoland. The noise and vibrations from trucks delivering waste was so great that it cracked the streets, the sidewalks, damaged the foundation of nearby homes, and kept residents awake at night. The dust from the operation was so great that it caused severe respiratory and other health problems for residents in these African American communities. One resident told investigators from the Chicago Legal Clinic that he had experienced "coughing, wheezing, short of breath, headache, sinus" and had been "hospitalized six times since the dump been on Kildare [Avenue]." He continued: "I had to remove carpet from floors because of dust and dust flares up my asthma.[41] Another resident, Doretha Griffin, wrote of her son's medical problems, "including a trip to the emergency room in January for headaches, dizziness and difficulty breathing." The emergency services report attached to Ms. Griffin's letter stated that the "community is quite polluted by trucks that dump dirt into air." Ms. Griffin pleaded: "Please stop this illegal operation in our neighborhood."[42]

Even though the Illinois State's Attorney has the authority to bring a legal action against a company when there is "substantial danger to the environment or to the public health," the community received only a noncommittal letter from an Assistant State's Attorney.[43] By this time, one of the sites at Roosevelt Street and Kildare Avenue was 80 feet high. Residents began to refer to it as "the mountain." The city responded by filing a suit against Christopher's operation as a common law public nuisance and as a violation of the Municipal Code prohibiting open dumping. In fact, the

Illinois Environmental Protection (IEP) Act expressly prohibits both open dumping and the operation of unpermitted waste storage, treatment, or disposal facilities. At this and countless other requests, the court denied the motion, allowing dumping operations to continue. There are also requirements in the IEP Act concerning dust minimization and permits. Despite the fact that Christopher's facility violated all of these regulations, the Illinois Environmental Protection Agency issued no citations. This official sanctioning of direct violations of city and state laws in communities of color was stunning.

Community meetings and protests continued. In February 1992, more than 600 people signed a petition calling for the closure of Krisjon's two major sites. The South Lawndale Community Block Club wrote to city and state environmental regulators:

Krisjon is receiving more consideration and respect by the courts than the residents who live and own property in this area. This is an insult to our community.[44]

We are still appalled that this company has been allowed to operate in our area next to our homes, residents and schools with no regard to the rights of the people who reside in our area.[45]

All the while, of course, local aldermen were receiving bribes to allow these acts of environmental injustice to continue unabated. Furthermore, activists were very much aware of the environmental racism dimensions of this struggle. In a letter to the Cook County State's Attorney, one resident wrote: "*The company operates only in minority areas.* We also know that the company poses health hazards, damages our buildings and houses, and decreases our property values."[46] This resident is correct. It turns out that these acts of environmental racism are part of a larger pattern. A study by the Chicago Department of Streets and Sanitation revealed that, of the ten neighborhoods with the most illegally dumped garbage, all are at least 60 percent African American or Latino. And wards where people of color are the majority account for 79 percent of all illegally dumped garbage in the city.[47]

Christopher knew his time would be limited if he failed to play his cards properly, so he began to build community support for his operations. One strategy was to pay off certain residents who had complained about his facilities. "I told John [Christopher] that his dust was a problem covering my cars every day," one resident is quoted as saying. "So he gave me $20.00. I told him that wouldn't pay for a whole year. Earlier he had sent $15.00."[48]

Christopher invited other residents to participate in "beautification projects" wherein he provided grass, flower, and vegetable seeds and offered to clean up debris from certain vacant lots. He also got the support of one of the strongest institutions in the African American community—the church. In 1991, a local pastor wrote a public letter applauding Christopher's efforts to "give back" to the community, and 30 residents signed a petition indicating they "welcome the Krisjon Construction Company into the community and are grateful that the company is involved in a beautification project that will benefit the community and its residents." Whether or not these individuals were paid off or coerced in any way is unknown. But the point is, under any colonial arrangement such as that experienced by poor African Americans, one can almost *always* find local leaders to support even the most egregious violations of human rights.

In 1992 an interesting turn of events took place. The Federal Bureau of Investigation secured John Christopher's cooperation in what became known as Operation Silver Shovel. Christopher became a "mole," working undercover for the US Attorney's Office and the FBI in a plan to uncover political corruption associated with the disposal of C&D debris in Chicago. As he had done in the 1980s, Christopher bribed African American and Latino aldermen to allow him to dump waste in their wards. The only difference was that in 1992 he was secretly videotaping the transactions. The public was not informed about this sting operation until 1996, when the media broke the story. The story was repeatedly told as "another case of those corrupt Chicago politicians taking their constituency for a ride." Not once did the major media report the fact that this was also a classic case of environmental racism. By this time, the dump site at Kildare Avenue contained an estimated 700,000 cubic yards of debris. Also, hazardous waste materials were discovered in nineteen large drums at one of the sites.

Community residents were incensed at these developments. Jesse Jackson and his Operation PUSH got involved in the effort to clean up the sites. Jackson told reporters: "These dump sites must be removed. They bring property value down with rats and roaches. . . . They're health hazards. If you live in those areas call PUSH and fight back or they'll keep doing it."[49]

Activists were successful, ultimately, at getting the city, the Illinois EPA, and the US EPA to take action, including developing a community policing program specifically for illegal dumping, strengthening the city ordinance regulating dumping, and cleaning up the waste at each of the sites. Proposed city ordinances in Chicago included jail time for illegal dumpers and the barring of contractors convicted of illegal dumping from future eligibility for contracts. The city instituted a new surveillance system near illegal dump sites and other vacant lots and began vigorously prosecuting and fining dumpers.[50]

In the meantime, Christopher successfully dodged all city citations, fines, and other charges because, in addition to declaring personal bankruptcy and seeing the Krisjon company involuntarily dissolved by the Illinois Secretary of State, the FBI gave him prosecutorial immunity. Christopher never paid any fines, never served any jail time, and in fact committed crimes with permission of the city, the state, and federal governments (via the sanction of his illegal operation and his work with Operation Silver Shovel).

Johnnie Baker, an activist with the United Concerned Citizens, sums up her feelings about this scandal from her vantage point as a homeowner and a parent:

Before Christopher started dumping, our neighborhood was stable. Our kids grew up there. It was a good community. The dumps changed all that. Christopher and his companies literally tore up the neighborhood—the alleys, the streets and our homes. We couldn't keep our houses clean because of all the dust. Our basements flooded from the runoff. At one point Christopher promised to put black dirt in the vacant lots. Instead, he left dirt mixed with crushed concrete. Nothing will grow there now.[51]

Jacquelyn Rodney, a representative of the South Lawndale United Block Club Council, put this event into a political perspective that many African American communities share:

This made us look at the legal system and our country totally differently. We fought for our rights as hard as we possibly could. But no matter what we did, Christopher was allowed to operate in our community. It makes us feel the justice system is unfair. No matter how well we tried to do for our community, we were still abused, even by our own government.[52]

The final insult to the Lawndale and Austin communities was the settlement agreement between the city and the waste companies guilty of dumping in these areas to allow them to recoup some of the cleanup costs by recycling and selling the debris *and* the decision to allow them access to city-owned dump sites at deeply discounted rates.[53]

Operation Silver Shovel, an egregious case of environmental racism, can be analyzed using the EJ framework I introduced earlier.

First, the *historical* dimensions are important to understand how Lawndale, Austin, and other communities got into this mess. Illegal dumping in Chicago is more than a century old and has been one of the principal battlefronts in that city's garbage wars. So what was happening in the Lawndale and Austin neighborhoods was part of a long-standing and larger pattern of dumping in communities of color around the city.

Second, there were many stakeholders involved in this conflict. The community residents and the waste dumpers were just two of the players. The aldermen in these communities allowed this dumping to occur as long as the polluters were willing to give them cash bribes. The most corrupt alderman, William Henry, was later voted out of office by angry constituents. Many residents and community leaders also accepted payoffs for this purpose, thus dividing the community over an issue that was negatively impacting everyone who lived there. The *Chicago Defender* and local community newspapers covered this case from day one, informing and mobilizing residents. The network media also deserve credit for breaking the story of the FBI operation. The other major stakeholders were the various levels of government, each of whom was complicit in allowing these acts of environmental injustice to go unchallenged, despite their obvious illegality. The courts allowed the dumping to continue despite the violations, and the state failed to issue any citations for several years. The federal government is easily the most culpable actor here, having actually engineered an undercover operation that produced more waste in these communities of color. The feds emerged unscathed and were able to place the blame on the aldermen and John Christopher. To its credit, the city government eventually went after the polluters. Unfortunately, these different approaches produced unproductive finger pointing among the city, the state, and the Illinois EPA.

Third, Silver Shovel has everything to do with institutional racism. This type of locally unwanted land use is not likely to appear in middle-class or affluent white communities. It was clear that Krisjon and the FBI targeted these communities because of their vulnerability, their lack of political power, and the presence of politicians willing to sell the communities out to the highest bidder.

Finally, this was a defining moment for the power of the grassroots to change a tough situation. The community fought back repeatedly and, with almost no official support, was able to initiate governmental action, regulatory enforcement, and a cleanup of the waste. In this way, even the most dispossessed and disenfranchised communities in this nation can shape and even reduce the impacts of environmental racism.

Operation Silver Shovel and the conflicts surrounding it overshadowed another conflict in the West Side neighborhoods of Lawndale and Austin. This was the battle over the operation of a garbage-recycling facility in this African American community. In 1993, as Chicago's West Side was struggling over Silver Shovel and "fly dumping," a related form of environmental injustice was in the offing. C&S Recycling, Inc. had requested a permit to expand its operations to build a waste transfer station. By this time, Chicago's Department of Environment and mayor's office had been hammered with community complaints and protests over illegal dumping in the area by Krisjon and other companies, so they were not about to make the same mistake twice. Department of Environment Commissioner Henry Henderson immediately denied C&S a permit, on the ground that "C&S has demonstrated a lack of respect for this community."[54] Specifically, after taking into account extensive comments from the community, the city learned that C&S had a history of rodent infestation, excessive traffic, and was operating without a permit near the Webster Elementary school. In fact, the company had knowingly lied about its operations in documents it had provided to the Zoning Board of Appeals. If anyone had doubts about the role of community power in this victory, Commissioner Henry Henderson commented, "the on-the-spot reaction from the community helped lead to the (department's) decision."[55]

But the conflict continued. C&S Recycling changed its name to Flood Brothers and successfully pushed Alderman Jesse Miller to change the zoning to allow their transfer station to be built legally. The community was outraged. A progressive alderman named Michael Chandler (one of the few who apparently were not in the polluters' pockets) helped organize Citizens In Action (CIN), a community group whose major purpose was to challenge this polluting facility. Chandler and his organization mobilized hundreds of residents to protest Flood Brothers/C&S Recycling and to vilify Alderman Miller for allowing this facility to expand in North

Lawndale and "sell the community right down the drain for a few pennies."[56] One protest involved more than 200 people—many of them young African American men, the last demographic group that most experts would expect to exhibit concern for the environment. At another event, more than 150 residents came to a public meeting to speak out against these problems. ACORN (Association of Community Organizations for Reform Now), a veteran community organization, also got involved; its Lawndale representatives worked on the case. The local community newspaper referred to this as a case of "environmental racism" and noted: "In poor areas of Chicago where toxics dumpers, solid waste treatment companies and others see large profits to be made from garbage and industrial waste [they] attempt to gain footholds with the cooperation of greedy, corrupt, and stupid elected officials. Apparently, the first battle-ground is North Lawndale."[57]

The embattled Alderman Jesse Miller reportedly claimed that "everyone in the community favors this project," but residents continued to picket the site. Prayer meetings were held at local churches, and the priests and parish councils of Precious Blood and Presentation (two Roman Catholic congregations) wrote to Mayor Daley to condemn the plan.[58] Not surprisingly, the more seasoned and powerful Alderman Miller reportedly threatened to have Chandler fired from the City Council "if he didn't back off."[59] Alderman Miller eventually publicly changed his position on the rezoning issue after the media criticized his heavy-handed tactics.

But this was not the end of the battles against waste in Lawndale and on the West Side in general. In 1994, Citizens In Action teamed up with groups fighting the Operation Silver Shovel sites to protest what they called an attempt to build a "second mountain" in the neighborhood.[60] The same zoning changes that Alderman Miller had made the previous year allowed Niagara Enterprises to propose opening a "rock reprocessing facility"—in other words, another construction and demolition debris dump. CIN and ACORN led this battle and stopped the siting process in its tracks. But they had to continue their fight against fly dumping, often using non-traditional methods such as waiting for dumpers to appear at a site and making citizens' arrests of truck drivers.

The divisions and betrayals within the West Side communities went much deeper than the misdeeds of corrupt politicians and immoral businessmen.

In fact, according to one report, local gangs in the Austin community were found to be regulating the fly-dumping trade and were said to have charged as low as $5 per ton of waste on dumping grounds.[61] Austin and Lawndale are two communities in desperate need of sustainable economic development, so politicians and residents are often easy prey to bribes or temporary jobs involving illegal waste dumping. For example, in December of 1997, a number of Austin residents employed by a North Side remodeling company, Design 41, were cited for illegally dumping debris in the community. "You have companies and residents, bringing garbage from the suburbs back into their own neighborhoods," one observer commented.[62]

As a result of this and the Operation Silver Shovel conflicts, US Representative Cardiss Collins (of Illinois) introduced a bill intended to outlaw environmental racism. Although this bill eventually died, the African American residents of Lawndale were able to put environmental racism on the agenda at the US House of Representatives for some time.

The battles over environmental justice on Chicago's West Side reveal that environmental racism is much more complex than simply a scenario wherein a polluter targets a community for waste dumping, unloads the garbage, and moves on. In fact, several stakeholders within and outside these communities had much to gain and lose over the struggle against C&D and garbage dump operators and "recyclers." It is interesting that many white environmental organizations (and scholars) assume that African Americans are not interested in participating in environmental activities like recycling.[63] These struggles against waste "recyclers" reveal that communities of color are very concerned with this type of "environmental behavior" because it frequently negatively impacts their health. Thus, we can see recycling as one more example in a long line of purportedly "environmentally sound" technologies that fall far short of the promise of being "clean and sanitary" and whose negative impacts are placed on communities of color.

**Divide and Conquer: The Fight For and Against the Robbins Incinerator**

One morning in 1992, when I was working as a volunteer for People for Community Recovery, I walked into the office and heard an unbelievable story about Robbins, an all-black community that was begging a company to locate a waste incinerator in its borders. My response was typical: "How in the world did that happen? Is that environmental racism or not?" These are two of the many perplexing questions this case raises.

In 1987, as the United Church of Christ was making headlines with the release of *Toxic Wastes and Race in the United States*, anti-toxics and EJ groups around the nation were blocking landfills and incinerators. The Illinois legislature, fearing a sudden exhaustion of landfill capacity, passed the Retail Rate Law, providing significant tax subsidies to incinerator companies that choose to locate in the state. This was the state's way of saying "We're open for business and we'll pay you to burn trash here." Not surprisingly, this legislation sparked an enormous growth in incinerator proposals in Illinois.[64] This is yet another example where the EJ and anti-toxics movements were influencing (if not driving) policy, although the shift from landfills to incinerators is both an unintended consequence of the anti-LULU movement and a trend we saw in the 1890s and in the early 1900s. (See chapter 2.) In 1987 there was only one burner in the state: the Northwest Incinerator. And the irony of unintended consequences gets even thicker because this proliferation of incinerators occurred in the South suburbs and nearby communities, which were heavily African American and/or poor (like the earlier shift from Chicago-wide dumping to a concentration of landfills on the South Side that occurred after the 1950s—see chapters 2 and 3). The proposed or existing burners included a tire-burning incinerator in Ford Heights, a medical waste incinerator and two municipal waste incinerators in Harvey, a medical waste incinerator in Stickney, a municipal waste incinerator in Forest View, a municipal waste incinerator in Southeast Chicago, a municipal waste incinerator on the West Side, and of course the waste incinerator in Robbins. Ford Heights, Harvey, Southeast Chicago, and Robbins are all African American communities and all poor. Forest View and Stickney have white working-class populations as well. The trash incinerator proposed for Summit is the only example of a burner that was being placed in a Northern Illinois town that was neither poor nor African American. So, of these nine proposed and constructed incinerators in the greater Chicago area during the late 1980s and the early 1990s, seven were in African American communities and two were in working-class and/or white ethnic neighborhoods. African Americans constitute only a fraction of the state's population, so any observer of Illinois' incinerator siting practices would likely conclude that this pattern did not emerge by chance. Class and race intersected to position people of color and working-class and low-income populations as the most attractive candidates for incinerator siting.

Robbins, founded in 1917, is the oldest city in the Northern United States governed entirely by African Americans.[65] Today, unfortunately, this village of 7,000 is also one of the poorest communities in the US. In 1989, Robbins was the fourteenth poorest suburb in the country, with a per capita income of $7,037 per year. It faces mounting financial debts, including a $1.3 million unpaid water bill owed to the city of Chicago. The village has also had a history of problems retaining its public employees on the payroll.[66] In 1987, scores of village workers walked off the job, protesting lack of payment. Others continued to work for no pay after the village's funds were seized to ensure payment of a lawsuit.[67] In 1988, Cook County cut off $1.2 million in federal block grant funds to Robbins because the village was three years behind in accounting for previous grants. Since the 1980s, the city has held charity drives to raise funds for its own management![68] This is a ghost town as far as most businesses are concerned, a barren landscape with few prospects for economic development. In fact, the major economic activity in Robbins consists of a nursing home, liquor stores that open at 8 A.M., mom-and-pop convenience stores, and the illicit trade in drugs and sex. Like many municipalities, Robbins experienced a mass exodus of both businesses and residents (one-third) during the period between 1970 and 1990. Since that time, each mayoral administration has courted all manner of businesses, to no avail. Until now.

It turns out that Robbins had been working for some time to attract *any* sort of waste management facilities. In the 1970s, the administration developed a plan for an "energy park," where a waste-to-energy incinerator and several ancillary industries would be sited. That idea languished for a while because landfilling was cheap and even waste firms had reservations about the level of poverty and destitution in the village. Finally, in 1986, while a major incinerator battle was raging in Los Angeles, the Illinois Senate approved a measure to acquire land for an incinerator in the village of Robbins.

The deal that Robbins struck with the Reading Energy Company and with Foster Wheeler Inc. was as follows: With the taxpayer subsidy from the Retail Rate Law, the companies could boost annual profits from the burner to $23 million and would pay the village nearly $2 million in rent each year.[69]

This proposal immediately spawned a major campaign against the incinerator. People for Community Recovery and the Human Action Community Organization (African American EJ groups from the South Side), Citizens for a Better Environment (the oldest environmental organization in the state), the Illinois Environmental Council (a legislative watchdog group), the South Cook County Environmental Action Coalition (a savvy, mostly white South suburban organization), the Sierra Club, Greenpeace, and many others coalesced around this issue. A few strong-willed residents and leaders within Robbins stood up against the burner as well. These groups built a coalition with the many citizens' and environmental organizations that had already formed to oppose incinerators throughout the Chicago area. They even flew the world-famous anti-incinerator activist Paul Connett out to speak at a rally in Robbins. In a memo written by Citizens for a Better Environment and PCR, these organizations outlined the environmental dangers of incineration and the environmental injustice of locating this burner in Robbins:

Minority and low income communities have long been the favorite dumping ground for society's pollution. Recently, there has been a growing movement demanding environmental justice. To that end, we should oppose facilities such as Robbins that wish to add pollution to our already overburdened populations. Although our communities need additional jobs, this cannot be justification enough for exposing our families to a considerable health risk. . . . Ironically, it has been certain African American politicians who seem to have blocked an effort to repeal an Illinois law enacted in 1987 (the Retail Rate Law) that subsidizes the construction and development of incineration facilities like Robbins using Illinois tax-payers money.[70]

In flyers, speeches, and letters to newspapers, the EJ coalition sent a message to the public that an incinerator burning 1,600 tons of refuse per day would release dangerous levels of mercury, dioxin, and other carcinogens into the air. This would not only impact the health of people in Robbins, but also put people in adjacent communities at risk. Also, many of the 80 jobs Foster Wheeler was promising to Robbins residents would be hazardous and low-wage (and probably less than a dozen in the final analysis) while any white collar jobs would go to non-Robbins residents. Taxpayers would pay several hundred million dollars for this facility, and that figure alone catalyzed a lot of support for the anti-incinerator cause. The coalition also pointed out that incinerators are hazardous operations because they routinely experience a high rate of accidents.[71] With regard to solutions, the movement argued that recycling initiatives would be much more economically and environmentally sound, and could produce many more jobs with less funding.

This was a case of environmental racism, they argued, not because the company had targeted the community, but because the community was in such dire economic straits they felt they had no choice but to court an incinerator. Jim Schwab of the American Planning Association told a group of activists at a conference in Chicago: "Asking the question 'Is this environmental racism?' *begs* the question as to *why* Robbins would seek an incinerator. When you answer that second question, you have to confront the fact that racism had everything to do with the current position the village finds itself in."[72] It is incredible to think that this town could not attract a drug store or a grocer or any major development whatsoever, but an incinerator company was more than willing to do business there.

Activists were successful at urging Attorney General Roland Burris (a progressive African American) to file suit against the incinerator developers in 1992 because they did not properly notify residents near the proposed area. The controversy steamed on, however, as the developers continued to press forward, gathering the support of the Illinois Environmental Protection Agency, the *Chicago Tribune*, and the South Suburban Mayors and Managers Association. At a hearing later in 1992, scores of incinerator supporters (outnumbering opponents) showed up, wearing painters' caps that read "Yes, in my backyard," "Don't trash jobs," and "Right 4 Robbins." Incineration opponents wore shirts that read "Ban the burn" and "Over our dead bodies." The *Chicago Tribune* was staunchly in favor of approving the Robbins incinerator, printing editorials decrying anti-burner protests and the regulatory hurdles placed before the facility's developers.[73] In 1993 the incinerator received a green light when the Illinois EPA awarded the operators a permit.[74] But the movement against the facility moved forward.

At another rally organized in opposition to the facility, Reverend Adolph Coleman, an African American pastor from Robbins, informed the audience that many Robbins residents opposed the incinerator and viewed opponents from outside Robbins as "saviors" rather than "outsiders," as the mayor had portrayed them: "This kind of pollution knows no boundaries, no race. . . . If permitted, it will poison the air for miles around. . . . It's going to be on your doorstep. I don't blame you for standing against it."[75] As with the anti-toxics and EJ movements around the United States, the anticipated negative human health effects of the incinerator were a driving factor in the opposition to this burner. Early on, administrators at the St. Francis Hospital and Health Center joined efforts to stop the Robbins incinerator in a public letter referring to the project as an "enormous" threat to the health of the hospital's patients and the community.[76] That same year, the American Public Health Association announced its support for a ban on the construction of garbage incinerators in areas that failed to meet Clean Air Act standards, and Chicago was one such place. This was evidence that momentum was building in support of a ban on incineration in the area, and activists could almost taste victory.

The movement against the incinerator used a two-pronged strategy: First and foremost, put the spotlight on the Robbins facility and frame it as environmental racism. Second, repeal the Retail Rate Law, because without it Foster Wheeler and other incinerator companies would lose profits. So I and other PCR staffers (working with Sierra Club lobbyists) were dispatched to the state capital (Springfield) immediately, to meet with state legislators about this pressing issue. There were two main responses from African American legislators: "Wow, I've never heard about this. I'll look into it" and "Well, I think you need to be dealing with Robbins and not worrying about what's happening [in Springfield]." This failure of African American leadership on EJ issues was disappointing. However, in 1993 the movement achieved a major success, as nearly a dozen south suburban municipalities passed resolutions opposing the Robbins incinerator. This meant that the potential sources of trash to fuel this burner were dwindling rapidly. These resolutions were made possible because of the predominance of incinerator foes voted into office during the 1991 council elections. So the anti-incineration movement in the Chicago area was successful at placing supporters in positions of political power.[77]

The movement against the incinerator was a coalition of groups outside and inside Robbins, but it was difficult to mobilize any significant mass of Robbins residents for this cause. Some clergyman joined the protest to criticize the exploitation of a down and out town, but they were often drowned out, as were we, by the hundreds of incinerator supporters. Robbins police intimidated and harassed anti-incinerator activists as well, with a number of unprovoked arrests. Robbins Mayor Irene Brodie, the person leading the campaign to court the burner, was therefore able to frame this conflict as one stirred up by "outside agitators," thereby potentially rendering our position as environmental justice advocates illegitimate. The mayor also quite cleverly used the observation that whites were universally against the incinerator as "evidence" that white folks did not want to see an all-black town pull itself up and out of poverty. Furthermore, she claimed that if activists prevented Robbins from building the incinerator, that such an outcome would constitute environmental racism![78] In what some activists have called a "twisted logic," Brodie proudly proclaimed: "There's always been environmental racism. We're just making it work for us for once."[79] To her credit, the promise from Foster Wheeler for twelve college scholarships for Robbins students came through. Some activists would call this blood money.

Foster Wheeler's reaction to the anti-incinerator movement was predictable. Like incineration proponents a century before, they claimed in billboard and newspaper ads and in trade journals that they planned on constructing a state-of-the-art facility that would be clean and safe[80]: "Pollution emissions will be low, especially carbon monoxide and nitrogen oxide. The amount of residual ash will also be held to a minimum. . . . The plant's environmental impact on air quality should be minimal and well within permissible limits. . . . Waste-to-energy facilities that recover materials for recycling are viewed more favorably by an environmentally minded public."[81]

The above claims regarding the Robbins Resource Recovery Facility are age-old and should come as no surprise in view of the cycle whereby a polluting technology is introduced and public opposition spawns a "cleaner" technology—a cycle that has been witnessed since the 1880s. As Mayor Brodie put it: "Strangely enough, the opposition was good in that it assured us that the best possible equipment would be installed to control pollutants that we might have overlooked."[82] So not only was the industry promoting this technology as clean and safe, but government did so as well. In addition to Mayor Brodie's boosterism, the Illinois Environmental Protection Agency approved the permits for the facility, and the US EPA upheld this decision, stating "the facility would not have a significant impact on ambient air quality and that the health effects would be negligible."[83]

As with Operation Silver Shovel and the C&S (Flood Brothers) Recycling fiasco in Lawndale, Robbins was a case of a vulnerable community of color whose leaders were willing to make a tradeoff that others might not make or be forced to make. In Reverend Coleman's words, "leadership gets bought out."[84] Having been arrested for merely passing out anti-incinerator flyers, African American activist and Robbins resident Gloria Scott ominously commented: "Our officials have sold us out. It's too late for us. Don't sell your people out."[85] State representative William Shaw, a powerful and often reviled African American leader, publicly stated his suspicion that the incinerator opponents were envious of the "money and jobs" the burner would provide Robbins, and wanted it for themselves.[86]

The Robbins Resource Recovery Facility finally opened in 1997. Its white smokestack stands 37 stories tall and, in the sarcastic words of US Representative Jesse L. Jackson Jr., is "like the Washington Monument [of de-development] in Chicago's south suburbs."[87] The facility began processing garbage from twelve cities around the Chicago area. The plant is called a "resource recovery facility" because workers were expected to separate out recyclables from the garbage *and* sell 50,000 kilowatts of electricity to the utility company by burning the leftover garbage. When the facility was finally built, environmentalists did not cease their efforts to shut it down. Several groups stepped up an earlier campaign to encourage residents in communities with contracts with the incinerator to send their garbage elsewhere.

Despite our inability to keep the incinerator in Robbins from opening, environmental and community activists finally repealed the Retail Rate Law in 1997 (the same year the facility opened), a landmark achievement that sent a strong message to incineration proponents and the waste industry.[88] This turn of events threatened to halt the taxpayer subsidies going to Robbins and the other burners that had been built since 1987—which would have been an estimated $360 million by the year 2007. "Taxpayers were paying for their own poison," Jeff Tangel of the South Cook County Environmental Action Coalition stated. Foster Wheeler was losing $1 million per month, thus offering Robbins $600,000 less than they had promised. As a result, the village of Robbins is arguably worse off today than it was before this saga began.

Environmental justice activists' claims that the facility was dangerous were borne out several times. The Illinois Environmental Protection Agency disclosed that the incinerator had violated the conditions of its operating permit by allowing excess air emissions 779 times in 6 months.[89] The state of Illinois filed a suit against the company for exceeding the legal pollution limits. Illinois Attorney General Jim Ryan commented: "We want to assure residents living in the region that the state will act aggressively in making sure the incinerator operates safely and cleanly."[90] In view of the number of carcinogens, heavy metals, and other toxins linked to respiratory ailments, cancer, birth defects, and immune system damage emitted from even the seemingly most benign burner, it is highly unlikely that any waste incinerator could ever meet the standards of "clean and safe."[91] However, that was just the beginning of the troubles. Even more dramatic were the two serious fires that erupted at the facility in one month. In both instances, several towns had to call out their fire departments to extinguish the flames. After the second fire, Mayor Brodie downplayed the incidents, reaffirming her unwavering support for the incinerator and stating that it was likely either the result of worker carelessness or sabotage. Each of the neighboring towns without incinerators in their borders called for the facility's closure. In 1999, the decision was finally made to shutdown the Robbins Resource Recovery Facility.

Thinking back to those days, Mayor Irene Brodie recalls: "Everybody got all in an uproar when we said we wanted to bring Foster Wheeler in here. They said it was bad for the environment and all. . . [But] didn't nobody ever come out and protest the fact that we were poor. How come nobody ever protested that?"[92]

Returning to the environmental justice framework I suggested earlier, we must understand the history of incineration and the context in which this individual struggle took place. Above all, what makes the Robbins case stand out was that this was an all-African American village that was vigorously courting the waste industry, not a situation where the industry was targeting the community. This irony does not negate the argument that environmental racism is at work; rather, it forces us to take a hard look at the roots of social inequality in African American communities to understand why and how the village of Robbins could find itself in this unenviable position in the first place. Historically, African Americans have been treated as second-class citizens at best, and as sub-humans at worst. Having moved north during the Great Migration of 1915–1940, African Americans remained relegated to the dirtiest neighborhoods and the dirtiest work and were politically marginal for most of the twentieth century. The existence of all-black towns like Robbins may instill pride in African Americans, but they are also peripheral to society, receiving fewer federal funds and scarce business development and enjoying little or no political influence in state politics. Compounding the situation was the recent growth of incinerator proposals in the state of Illinois, shifting waste management solutions from landfills to burners. As in previous eras, this change occurred on the backs of the poor, the working class, and people of color, shifting and/or maintaining the waste inside their communities. Robbins was caught in the middle of these historical currents. The stakeholders in this conflict are too numerous to name, but it is clear that environmental justice struggles are much more complex than battles only between whites and people of color, or perpetrators and victims. This struggle divided people within a community and within the Chicagoland region. It also raised a fundamental challenge to the movement for environmental justice when African Americans were recruiting a polluting industry rather than the other way around. Institutional racism and classism were certainly at work in this case. For example, the pattern of incinerator siting in Illinois is clear: African American, low-income, and ethnic communities remain the most likely candidates for the location of a waste facility. So the Robbins conflict was just one of many struggles against environmental racism in the area. The capacity of disempowered people to change this situation was demonstrated time and again here. For example, the repeal of the Retail Rate Law was a major victory for the EJ movement and was evidence that, even after a facility is sited, the struggle is not over. Activists fought the facility from the day it was first proposed until after it was built, and finally won. It was just a matter of time before the incinerator would close down. I should emphasize that the very passage of the Retail Rate Law was a legislative response to the anti-toxics and EJ movements' success at blocking the siting and expansion of landfills. This is an excellent example of how activists can shape the contours of environmental racism (even in unintended directions) over time.

The movement for environmental justice has been forged over more than a century of struggle against a range of artificially constructed hazards imposed on poor and working-class neighborhoods and communities of color. This movement has undergone dramatic changes in its resistance against corporations, governments, the white environmental movement's racism, and even internal division and betrayal within communities of color. The comparison between environmental racism and colonization is real and underscores that there are many levels at which this phenomenon is at work, and that it is deeply rooted in the history of exploitation of Third and Fourth World peoples by those in the First world. Three things are clear: (1) Environmental racism is not just about correlations between hazards and populations. It is about the power dynamics that produce these inequalities and the power of the grassroots to challenge and reverse them. (2) Environmental racism is not just about people of color versus whites. Racism plays an ever-present role in these conflicts, but class dynamics, political power, and intra-racial divisions matter a great deal too. (3) Until we understand how and why certain environmental organizations and people of color are more than willing to court environmentally unsound development in communities of color, we will never truly understand environmental racism and therefore be ill-equipped to move toward environmental justice.

In the next two chapters, I will explore what happens when organizations move beyond protest and actually implement development plans for environmental justice. This is the case of recycling, the latest technological promise in the evolution of the garbage wars. And I will make a special effort to get "up close and personal" with recycling by going to the source—the workplace. This takes us to another, critical level of environmental justice struggles—at the point of production.

# 5

## Working for the Movement: Recycling Labor at the Resource Center

The environmental justice framework I introduced in chapter 1 makes it possible to explore the role of different actors and institutions in the production of environmental racism. This chapter is a case study of how different stakeholders—the government, recycling workers, and environmentalists—produced and challenged environmental inequalities at one of the nation's first community-based, non-profit recyclers: the Resource Center (RC). In the struggle for two valuable resources—post-consumer waste and good jobs—environmentalists, the recycling industry, and governments collaborated to produce many benefits for the community. The RC is a pioneering organization that has done a great deal to improve the state of low-income communities of color. In this chapter I problematize these benefits by placing them against a backdrop of environmental hazards communities and workers face as a result of the location of recycling facilities and the dangers that lie within their walls.

I examine the recycling industry in this chapter and in chapter 6 because recycling is the latest development in the evolution of solid waste management and because recycling developed as a direct response to the environmental movement. I emphasize the role of workers in this industry because they are on the front lines of environmental hazard exposure and because EJ scholars and activists must pay more attention to the links between community-based environmental struggles outside and inside the workplace. Indeed, it is in the workplace that hazards are first produced and people are first exposed.

In the case of the recycling industry, where workers often labor in hazardous conditions and residents are exposed to pollution, there are three factors that produce and challenge environmental inequalities. First, there is a convergence of interest among community groups, environmentalists, industry, and the government in support of recycling. Although often at odds with one another, these stakeholders have collaborated to sustain an ideology in support of recycling's environmental and economic benefits that shifts attention away from the pollution and the dangerous work required to recycle post-consumer waste. Second, there are decisions made by managers at recycling firms that can directly contribute to or improve dangerous work conditions for employees and produce a range of pollutants and waste in communities. And third, the nature of worker independence in these plants allows for different expressions of resistance against those managerial decisions that may contribute to work hazards.

The central contradiction embodied in recycling is the deep disparity between its ideology of pro-environmentalism and the fact that nearby residents and recycling workers confront a wide range of environmental injustices, including physical and psychological hazards. This disparity is especially instructive for two reasons: (1) It is the result of efforts by environmental organizations, community groups, the state, and industry to frame recycling as a "win-win" solution. (2) Recycling is a green industry, which suggests that it is environmentally responsible.

It must be noted that there certainly are documented benefits that many recycling programs have provided communities, workers, and ecosystems. In many cases, recycling has led to job creation, the reduction of property tax increases, and the removal of solid waste from community streets and landfills. However, the data I have marshaled for this chapter and the next will assess these benefits against the social outcomes of recycling.

What I find interesting is that, while social scientists studying environmental racism have continued to call for cleaner communities, improved economic development, and sound waste management policies for the poor and people of color, few have suggested an examination of existing environmentally oriented firms involving community economic development for unskilled workers of color.[1] Such firms do exist in the form of private, municipal, and community-based non-profit recycling centers. As communities that are overburdened with pollution and unemployment begin looking to stable, cleaner employment and economic development opportunities, recycling centers may present strong alternatives. In fact, if the principal concerns of the environmental justice literature can be summed up as the unequal distribution of waste and its effects on the poor and on people of color, then the waste recycling industry—a sector that employs working-class people of color to divert waste that might otherwise be dumped in these communities—might be an ideal place to look for solutions.

Environmental justice research has acknowledged recycling's potential for reducing the volume of solid waste that might otherwise be dumped and/or incinerated in politically powerless communities, but few assessments of recycling practices, costs, and benefits exist.[2] Sociologists have conducted significant research on attitudes toward and participation in recycling programs.[3] A number of social scientists have praised the benefits of consumer-resident recycling as a positive civic and "pro-environment behavior."[4] This chapter places a more critical focus on recycling and demonstrates that, in some cases, there are many anti-environmental dimensions of this practice.

Recycling is the label applied to a variety of practices involved in recovering and adding value to post-consumer and post-industrial waste (i.e., garbage and scrap). The three arrows usually associated with the recycling emblem symbolize the three principal processes required to recycle waste: collecting and sorting, remanufacturing, and purchasing. Collection and sorting are done by non-profit, private, or municipal waste haulers who pick up the waste at residents' curbsides or from commercial buildings, and transport it to materials recovery facilities (MRFs, pronounced "murfs") where the non-recyclables are sorted from the recyclable materials. The recyclable materials are then baled and shipped out to end users who remanufacture them. Remanufacturing is the industrial process whereby recyclable materials are mixed with virgin materials to produce new products for market. Purchasing occurs when consumers, private industry, or governments pay for goods with recycled content. Thus, it should be understood that, unless a product is simply reused, it will be physically transformed and new materials will be added to it in order to produce "recycled" goods. This observation is important because it underscores the fact that recycling is both an industrial process and an activity that, by its very nature, produces pollution. When observers notice pollution in the recycling industry, it is usually within the remanufacturing stage. For example, one environmental organization completed a study using 1990 census data indicating that pulp paper recycling mills, which emit enormous amounts of poisonous effluents like dioxin, are disproportionately located in poor neighborhoods and communities of color.[5]

The focus of this chapter and the next is the MRF—the site where workers and machines sort and bale recyclable materials. The MRF is important because it is the site where the consumer, laborer, and remanufacturer intersect and it is there that we find a variety of "green" claims by industry. In addition, the great proliferation of MRFs in the last decade resulted from a strong social movement led by citizens and supported by the state and industry. These multi-stakeholder origins of recycling represent several interest groups' efforts to engage in "win-win" policy making.

**Recycling Proponents and Their Claims**

Advocates typically frame recycling as a policy that provides environmental, social, and economic benefits to cities. Neighborhood groups, government, industry, and environmental organizations have touted recycling as a policy that can meet one another's needs. Producers wish to maintain access to natural resources for input into production; environmentalists seek to reform or slow down production processes that pollute; citizens and community groups wish for job creation for their residents; and the state wishes to balance these often conflicting needs while maintaining its own authority and legitimacy. Recycling would appear to meet each of these stakeholders' needs.

Environmental movement organizations have supported recycling for years and continue to promote its virtues. For example, a recent article in a Citizens Clearinghouse for Hazardous Waste publication was titled Recycling: A Modern Day Success Story.[6] Another example was a statement a Chicago Recycling Coalition board member made during an interview with the author: "It's important to do recycling as part of sound management of your resources. Socially, I think it's kind of a metaphor for taking responsibility for what you generate. I think it's a powerful image for the way you should live your life."[7]

Proponents have frequently measured the benefits of recycling against other waste management practices. Job creation has been one of the main themes. For example, one study indicated that, compared to the remanufacturing sector, MRFs, or "recycling programs which only process or separate wastes appear to generate even higher employment figures."[8] Environmental organizations have made similar comparisons:

... taxpayers will pay double for incineration.... It also becomes clear that a recycling alternative has lower costs, as well as additional benefits of job creation and lower pollution.... Recycling creates more jobs than conventional waste disposal methods. Reuse and recycling operations are often labor-intensive and can be a source of entry and skilled level positions. Additional jobs can be created locally by attracting industries that will turn recovered materials into finished products.[9]

The Natural Resources Defense Council, a national environmental organization, compared the job-creation potential of landfilling versus recycling:

Far from strengthening local economies and producing jobs, landfills actually produce very few jobs, the least of any waste management option, and a review by the EPA of the socioeconomic impact of landfills concludes they hurt established local economies. Also, the jobs produced by landfills involve exposure to many workplace and environmental hazards. By contrast, recycling has proven to be the greatest jobs producer of any waste management option, and many of the most prosperous communities in the United States have the best organized recycling programs.... The utopian vision of simple, cheap, and environmentally safe landfills helping to finance schools and libraries is an exceptionally rare phenomenon and logically inconsistent. It is precisely because of the documented adverse environmental, economic, and public health threats caused by landfills that so few communities want them. It is for these reasons that developers of landfills have had to pay for community benefits such as schools and computers to those very few and very poor (and often minority) communities forced to consider land filling as an economic-development option.[10]

It is ironic that the above statement actually raises the issue of occupational safety, and makes the assumption that recycling jobs represent clean work. This quote from the NRDC also makes the observation that poor neighborhoods and communities of color are often forced to host landfills. However, the NRDC implies that hosting a recycling facility would not be viewed as equally problematic. The examples of C&S Recycling and Operation Silver Shovel reveal that a range of recycling businesses exists and many of them meet with strident opposition from communities. (See chapter 4.)

Government agencies have also lauded recycling as a job generator. A study commissioned by the state of Illinois reported that one recycling firm, the Resource Center, "estimates that the recycling industry can support at least 1,000 jobs in the city at a 25 percent recycling level," and that this estimate is "based on the Center's own experience with its labor-intensive recycling program, which supports 16 jobs by moving 8,000 tons of residuals (one job per 500 tons), potentially creating 1,500 jobs in the city at the 25 percent mark."[11]

Promoting its new "Blue Bag" recycling program, the city of Chicago has stated that its new sorting sites—which are "dirty MRFs" (MRFs that accept garbage along with recyclables, as distinguished from MRFs that only accept recyclables) —are "Good for the Community . . . and [will] be clean and environmentally friendly to their host communities."[12] During the 1980s, the Coalition for Appropriate Waste Disposal (CAWD) wrote letters to several Chicago aldermen stating that "recycling is non-polluting"[13] and also claimed that "recycling does not endanger public health."[14] Although often stated, this is possibly the most problematic claim—that recycling processes are "clean" or sanitary. This is especially problematic for "dirty MRFs," where the amount of garbage generally outweighs the volume of recyclables. As one industry observer put it: "A dirty MRF means garbage in, garbage out."[15] The myth of recycling as a clean process is most likely an extension of the symbolism recycling invokes around the simplistic notion of "cleaning up the environment." But this claim should come as no surprise to the reader who has seen that incinerator, reduction, and landfill proponents have and continue to make similar promises about their respective technologies. (See chapters 2–4.)

## The Resource Center: A History of Stakeholder Cooperation in Communities of Color

It is often difficult to distinguish between the Resource Center and Ken Dunn, because Dunn is such a charismatic leader in the recycling movement and the RC is his baby. For more than 30 years the RC has successfully served consumers in several of Chicago's neighborhoods, while providing dozens of jobs for low-income, low-skilled men and women of color. It is the oldest non-profit recycling center in the United States. Dunn, a legend in Chicago's environmental movement and community development circles, came to Chicago in the late 1960s as a University of Chicago graduate student in philosophy. Having grown up on a family farm in Kansas, he had a deep appreciation for the ecosystem and a passion for hard work. In 1968, at the height of some of the most radical and disruptive social movement mobilizations in modern US history, Dunn started the Resource Center. Every summer he would go home for the wheat harvest and bring back a ton of grain to make bread at the RC's bakery. In the bakery, Dunn and his employees would also cook pizzas and other food from locally grown ingredients. This was just one of many enterprises in the RC's expanding web of eco-ventures. Dunn employed low-income African American men, who had been disenfranchised and marginalized as Chicago began to de-industrialize: "His first project, organizing homeless men to pick up bottles and cans for recycling, has expanded . . . to include a variety of projects, including planting gardens and cleaning up vacant lots on the city's South Side, an extensive recycling program for the whole city, a bicycle shop where children can repair or build their own bikes from recycled and donated parts, and the Creative Reuse Warehouse."[16]

It should come as no surprise that this type of business practice is not terribly profitable. Indeed, the point of community-based recycling is to create social and environmental change through education and action, rather than focusing on the "bottom line."

Community-based recycling emerged as a social movement in Chicago in the late 1960s, as an attempt by environmentalists to change the "system," to implement a tangible alternative to the established way of doing things. Recycling was viewed as one such alternative. It was founded on a "mission of personal transformation and environmental consciousness-raising rather than the development of a viable recycling business."[17] The first community-based centers sprang up in Ann Arbor, Berkeley, Boulder, Chicago, and other college towns around this time. But, unlike many social movements of the 1960s, recycling quickly became institutionalized and accepted.

By 1984, the RC was the nation's third largest non-profit recycler. Ken Dunn was famous for referring to garbage as "a resource out of place."[18] Dunn was often quoted for believing that there is no difference between "a pile of junk and a pile of valuable resources."[19] While many ecologists espouse such romantic values, Ken Dunn actually puts them to work. Working as a volunteer alongside Mr. Dunn and his employees, I immediately recognized that he is a tireless, down-to-earth individual whose rough and stained hands and wind-whipped face are testimony to his commitment. The RC also had a very practical vision of how recycling could be a part of a thriving, sustainable regional economy:

The Resource Center's philosophy is that recycling can be a part of the solutions to several major urban problems at once, to turn liabilities into assets: garbage to resources, unemployed people to employed people, disposal costs to earned revenue, and new enterprises where business and industry have fled. The idea is to put to best use the resources we already have, i.e., human potential, energy-rich scrap raw materials, and available revenues, to foster what Jane Jacobs calls the "regional economy." For example, rather than import raw materials at ever-increasing cost and risk, we can harvest them from the waste stream. Or, rather than drain tax dollars out of the city to distant landfills, the dollars can continue cycling locally through Chicago-based recycling/reuse/manufacturing jobs and industries.[20]

Unlike many large for-profit recyclers, the RC has a much higher rate of recycling and reuse of the materials it collects. The reason for this is that the RC has a "source separated" system: its employees collect only recyclables and leave garbage for the waste haulers. This means that workers at the recycling facility are sorting through and processing only recyclables for which they have markets. As the director of the RC's Uptown facility put it: "We recycle 99.5 percent of what we collect. . . . We're not in the garbage business."[21]

Some time later, the government became involved with funding support and provided new opportunities for entrepreneurs and the industry to stabilize recycling businesses. And environmentalists were already encouraged by the passage of many laws, ostensibly intended to protect the environment. These included the Solid Waste Disposal Act of 1965 (later amended as the Resource Recovery Act of 1970), the National Environmental Policy Act (NEPA), and the founding of the US Environmental Protection Agency (EPA) in 1970. While increased air pollution was on the minds of many city dwellers and urban planners, solid waste was being dubbed the "third pollution" and was recognized as a serious urban problem.[22] Responding to these crises, environmentalists developed local drop-off or buy-back recycling centers to convert trash into cash and produce something out of nothing. The benefits and possibilities of community-based recycling seemed abundant and boundless.

The Resource Center is credited with producing a number of positive environmental, economic, and social changes in Chicago's poor neighborhoods and communities of color:

Each ton . . . residents divert from the waste stream by recycling saves the city—that is, all of us who pay taxes and/or garbage collection fees—$100 in disposal costs. That means that in 1983, patrons of the Resource Center's collection service have already saved the city $94,200. In fact, over the life of the Resource Center, the total volume of materials recovered through its many recycling services has saved Chicagoans $1.9 million.[23]

Not only was the RC located in low-income communities of color, but unlike many recycling businesses who feel that these communities are not interested in recycling and are best used solely as a processing site, the RC actively sought out participation in recycling from these residents. For example, RC staffers regularly visited community block clubs, churches, and civic organizations in the African American, Latino, and Southeast Asian communities in which they worked.[24] They also distributed several thousand bonus coupons for recyclables at the annual Bud Billiken Day parade (a major African American event in Chicago). These coupons gave bonus money for each pound of recyclables brought to the site. The middle-class African American community of Beverly became one of the RC's hallmark collection areas, with participation rates higher than virtually any recycling program in the United States. And prominent African American politicians, like Black Panther-turned-alderman Bobby Rush and Mayor Harold Washington, went out of their way to support the Resource Center on the City Council floor and through various city agencies.[25] In 1985, the Resource Center and CAWD successfully urged Mayor Washington to provide a subsidy for each ton of waste diverted from landfills (called a "diversion credit") and to modify zoning laws to allow recyclers siting flexibility in neighborhoods. These were major victories for the recycling movement in Chicago. By 1986, the RC had successfully made inroads into the African American community of North Austin. The RC expanded dramatically and was providing recycling services to 17 Chicago neighborhoods with a total population of 300,000.[26]

The Resource Center was not just successful in terms of its own growth, but it also produced many spinoff recycling businesses. The Uptown Recycling Station (URS) and the South Shore Recycling Station were both outgrowths of the RC.

Finally, the RC hired many of its employees from the communities in which it operated. This included local residents who were looking for work, and others who had recently been downsized. Additionally, many homeless and indigent folks made their living by collecting recyclables and exchanging them for cash at the site. Ken Dunn refers to these individuals as "alley entrepreneurs" rather than the less flattering term "scavengers." For example, Johnny worked for RC after being laid off at another plant: "That's how I got this job. The big meat company I worked for went out of business. I started recycling cans and I ended up getting a job here after Ken knew me and hired me."[27]

Jason, another employee, manages the aluminum can baling machine. He was hired on after being downsized at one of Chicago's many closed steel mills. And Bill, an alley entrepreneur who describes himself as "the homeless man on 53rd Street," has been exchanging recyclables for cash at the RC's buy-back center since 1986. He stated, "I think I'm very good friends with Ken on an employer-employee basis. I'm a scavenger and I go to him for my livelihood."[28] Bill's statement underscores the economic multiplier effect that we might miss if we simply view the RC's formal employees as the only persons benefiting from this facility's operation. In a very real sense, the alley entrepreneurs like Bill are, in his words, "employees" as well. They work all day to collect recyclables and deliver them to the center and get paid for it. These materials constitute a significant percentage of the volume of waste processed at the RC and contribute to its revenue (and therefore the wages of its formal employees).

In the mid 1980s, the Resource Center purchased a site in Uptown, which served a community unlike any other in the city. "At that site we are providing income to about 450 multi-ethnic neighborhood residents, including many East Asian refugees, and recycling 50 tons of materials per month," Dunn stated in a newsletter.[29] During the 1980s, there was a major influx of refugees to the Uptown neighborhood from Southeast Asia. Laotians, Vietnamese, Cambodians, and Hmongs were foremost among these groups. Some of the RC's workers came from these groups, but many more were "alley entrepreneurs" trying to make ends meet with recyclables from the street. At one of the Resource Center's South Side recycling yards there was a significant contingent of Guatemalan workers, also refugees. Many of these refugees were hosted and supported by churches involved in the Sanctuary Movement of the 1980s. This was a nationwide network of organizations set up to provide peaceful immigration and a new life in the United States for refugees from war-torn nations, particularly those where the CIA was active in terrorizing civilian populations. The RC's Uptown Recycling Station (URS) paid out over $167,000 to local residents during the first 17 months of operation. One resident of the North Side told WBEZ radio that "the buy-back station makes it possible for him to earn 'pocket money' for soap, razor blades, and incidentals that he couldn't otherwise afford on his public aid allowance."[30]

Jobs are hard to come by in the City of Big Shoulders. Chicago had been rocked by continuous recessions since the late 1960s. Job losses in Chicago's manufacturing sector were especially hard. One study found that 203,700 manufacturing jobs were lost through industry closures in Chicago between 1977 and 1981, with another 132,000 jobs lost due to corporate decisions to shift investments outside the region.[31] The result was that Chicago lost one-quarter of its factories in the 1970s. Like many older industrial cities, Chicago's economic foundation was linked to manufacturing. De-industrialization changed all that, and was accompanied by rising crime rates, unemployment, and social decay.[32] So the city and its neighborhoods were desperate for virtually any type of economic development. Recycling held a great deal of promise for that reason alone. Any environmental benefits that came along with the jobs would be "gravy."

One of the RC's many sites is a buy-back center in Grand Crossing, a struggling African American neighborhood on the South Side. Much of this chapter is devoted to environmental inequalities *within* the recycling workplace, but one cannot help but take note of the environmental hazards in the surrounding community. Grand Crossing is 99 percent African American, with a third of its residents living in poverty. It hosts several public housing projects and still bears the wounds of its bout with urban renewal during the 1950s. Like many Chicago neighborhoods, Grand Crossing became all-black almost over night. Between 1950 and 1959, as 50,000 African Americans moved in, 50,000 whites moved out to other neighborhoods in the city and suburbs. Today this community is what William Julius Wilson terms a "new poverty area," which means that "a substantial majority of individual adults are either unemployed or have dropped out of the labor force altogether."[33] In this single neighborhood, there are hundreds of vacant lots and contaminated "brownfields" from previous industrial activity.[34] Illegal ("midnight") dumping is rampant and abandoned factories and homes produce a blight that many residents wish could be redeveloped. In this neighborhood, while the local currency exchange, a liquor store and a small grocery market are all absentee-owned and staffed, RC is virtually the only organization that employs local residents and—through materials buy-back—brings dollars into the communities in which it operates. It is also one of the only institutions with origins at the University of Chicago that grew with—rather than over—the surrounding community.[35]

Earlier I indicated that environmentalists and non-profit recyclers were able to garner the support of the city to pass a waste management plan that included a subsidy (diversion credit) for recyclers. In addition, RC was also instrumental in getting the city to pass an ordinance mandating curbside recycling. This ordinance was first introduced by Mayor Harold Washington and Bobby Rush and was later taken up by Mayor Richard Daley, who argued that by supporting recycling he was acting on the cultural mandate it had become. Daley declared, "People basically want recycling."[36] Thus stakeholders in environmental and neighborhood organizations successfully sparked a supportive response from the government for what were also the goals of a social movement.

So environmentalists, community organizations, the RC and the city all viewed recycling as a policy that would address solid waste problems while creating employment opportunities. Recycling lies at the intersection of each stakeholder's interests. This coalition appeared even more legitimate because it was the institutionalization of a social movement's goals, and industry and government would benefit as well—a "win-win" policy.

In this section I have documented many of the benefits the RC brought to communities of color in Chicago. However, recycling is not as pure and cost-free as many ecologists might believe. The gains detailed above must be weighed against the often hidden environmental inequalities that workers and nearby residents confront. The next section highlights the many community concerns with recycling centers.

### Unintended Negative Consequences of Recycling: Facility Siting and Pollution

Resource Center advocates remained largely oblivious to the negative impacts of recycling, creating unfortunate blind spots. For example, at the RC's 1984 Annual Meeting, one Board member was quoted as saying: "Unlike other issues, which have pros and cons, recycling has no disadvantages."[37]

As I noted in chapters 2–4, social movement groups often unwittingly support new waste management plans and technologies that produce their own environmental injustices. The RC is no exception. In 1983, the RC and the anti-toxics movement in Chicago were successful at pushing a one-year moratorium on the construction and expansion of landfills in the city.

This new legislation—coupled with the revelation that Chicago's waste collection and disposal costs were the highest in the United States that year—created an immediate sense that new waste management options would be needed.[38] Thus, as we saw in chapter 4, the region began to look toward the construction of *new* incinerators in the 1980s and the 1990s. This change also had the effect of diverting more waste to *existing* incinerators, such as the Northwest Incinerator, located on Chicago's heavily African American West Side.

That same year, the RC co-sponsored (along with the City Department of Streets and Sanitation and the Bethel New Life Community Development Organization) the expansion of recycling services into the 37th Ward. This project was part of a pilot program to test the feasibility of a citywide collection service. The Resource Center actually provided the labor and performed the collections. The interesting twist is that this project was coordinated in cooperation with the Northwest Incinerator. As Gretchen Brewer, the RC's recycling coordinator put it, "[t]he hypothesis is that diverting non-combustibles like cans, glass bottles, and bulky metal goods will improve plant operation and reduce the cost of land filling incinerator residue."[39] In other words, like the Robbins Resource Recovery plant, the Northwest Incinerator began separating out much of the waste it received, to be sent to recycling plants. The Northwest Incinerator was a monstrous facility spewing out all manner of toxins in communities of color. The Coalition for Appropriate Waste Disposal (CAWD), of which the RC was a member, supported this recycling-incineration scheme in order to accommodate the waste no longer going to landfills. (CAWD also included People for Community Recovery, the Sierra Club, and Citizens for a Better Environment.) The logic was that, in addition to creating ground water pollution and other hazards, landfilling municipal waste also offered no opportunities for recycling or future use. Incineration, while carrying its own associated pollution problems, would allow for recycling at the front end of the process and, through burning the garbage, would reduce the volume of trash to ash (which would then be landfilled). So, given these limited choices, the environmental movement and recyclers pushed for the "lesser of two evils."

As Mayor Harold Washington and the City Council were debating a new waste management ordinance in 1984 and 1985, the Resource Center, the

CAWD, and other environmental organizations pressed for several policies to be considered in this plan, including (1) the establishment of a financing mechanism for recycling, such as a waste diversion credit, recognizing recycling as disposal and as a cost containment measure, and (2) improved citizen access to recycling services in all Chicago communities by allowing centers of appropriate size, appearance, and noise level to locate in commercial and residential areas.[40]

The City Council agreed to both of these requests. This new waste management plan demonstrated the power of the environmental movement and community-based recyclers to influence city policy. It also indicated the progressive nature of the Washington administration, which had a reputation for working with neighborhood groups.[41] The diversion credit was quite a boon to recyclers because it required that the city pay them for each ton of waste recycled, as this was waste being diverted from landfills. The payment made sense because the city would have had to pay the landfill operators a "tipping fee" if the trash had been sent to the dump. The diversion credit recognized recycling's role as an ecological benefit and compensated recyclers for it.

The second request listed above, was perhaps less progressive. The CAWD's intentions may have been noble, but changing city ordinances to allow recycling centers to locate in residential neighborhoods produced problems later on, because noisy, polluting, and dirty recycling operations did in fact proliferate in Chicago's communities of color. For example, in chapter 4 we saw how virtually *any* business referring to itself as a "recycler" was allowed to locate in African American and Latino communities on the West Side. From Krisjon's construction and demolition debris "recycling" facility to the C&S (Flood Brothers) recycling operation, recycling was producing enormous environmental health risks among residents and destroying their neighborhoods. Some activists called this another example of environmental racism. And in the 1980s, there were even protests against the Resource Center itself for its unsightly trash, unwelcome noise, and tendency to attract homeless and indigent clientele, and vermin. It may have made good business sense to seek out low-cost solutions for recycling, but this was a political mistake for CAWD. For example, in a 1984 proposed revision of the city's Waste Ordinance, CAWD suggested that the city "rent or lease at below market rates unused, city-owned vacant lots to not for profit community based recycling organizations to be used as low-cost operating sites for recycling activities."[42] Since the majority of Chicago's estimated 80,000 vacant lots are in poor and people of color communities this proposal was inherently problematic for environmental justice reasons. But CAWD learned from this mistake and three years later, seeking to shape the city's next waste ordinance, the group urged that recycling "sites should be equitably distributed throughout the city" and that the "community should be thoroughly informed on siting."[43]

However, years later, in 1993, several major Chicago and Illinois environmental organizations pressed Illinois State Senator Alice Palmer to propose an environmental justice bill. Senate Bill 188 would help create recycling businesses in low-income and people of color communities. Senator Palmer reportedly "said the recycling facilities will reverse the treatment that many communities have received from garbage in the past. Citing high numbers of toxic waste facilities, incinerators and landfills in low-income communities, Palmer said the garbage brought into neighborhoods under this bill will be sent out at a benefit."[44] Unfortunately, this measure, like the Chicago waste management plan the RC and the CAWD helped pass, would open the doors to more waste facilities in communities of color. On the face of it, one can see the logic of promoting recycling in communities hard hit by environmental injustices. And while sustainable development should be part of any environmental justice vision, recycling operations in residential neighborhoods will bring additional trash, noise, and odors that residents are likely to resist. Environmental groups like the RC and its CAWD partners were in a tough position: they either promote the status quo or policies that might offer a few benefits. However, locating recycling facilities in these communities might be viewed as "two steps forward, and two steps backward" at best.

Once again, we have an ironic tale: When environmentalists try to resist environmental injustices or implement environmental justice projects, they sometimes help spawn new forms of environmental inequalities because affluent communities, industry, and government limit their choices. So, for example, the CAWD would never have been able to locate a similar recycling facility in a politically powerful, affluent, white community. Furthermore, providing jobs is a benefit that some activists might view as outweighing the costs of further burdening communities with more waste.[45]

In the next section I take a closer look at how environmental inequality operates in the workplace—a community-based recycling center.

### Recycling Work at the Resource Center

The RC's main site is a large outside yard where workers manually sort through piles of recyclables that are dropped off by collection trucks. There are several stations throughout the yard where the different materials are dumped, crushed, and sorted by hand, including cans, cardboard, several grades of newspaper and junk mail, glass and plastics. RC management has a policy of only accepting source separated recyclable materials—this excludes the municipal solid waste (MSW) some MRFs allow. This policy is important because those MRFs that receive MSW have far greater occupational dangers (due to the range of hazardous materials contained in garbage).

Ken Dunn oversees a staff of several dozen laborers who work either in the office or in the recycling yard. The RC typically hires people who, to quote a manager, "would otherwise be considered unemployable."[46] Some of the workers have criminal records, substance abuse problems, and live on the fringes of homelessness. The RC accepts referrals from churches, friends, and community organizations for job candidates who are struggling and need a helping hand. Except for two white male volunteers (from Volunteers in Service to America [VISTA] and the Lutheran Volunteer Corps), all of the recycling workers are men and women of color: Guatemalan, African American, and Southeast Asian.

While some workers are intensely sorting recyclables by hand, others negotiate prices for people who bring recyclables to the yard. They receive hundreds of people each week who stand in line to have their materials taken out of shopping carts to be weighed, and paid for at the going rate. The following is an excerpt from my field notes:

All employees at the RC do multiple tasks: trucking, fork lifting, weighing, crushing, baling and sorting. Carlos and many of the workers in the yard are Guatemalan. He is friendly and popular with the clientele. He speaks heavily accented English to the customers and Mayan to some of his co-workers. This is a place where families come to work. Three Guatemalan girls are helping their mothers sort and stack newspaper in a big garage in the yard. They are separating cardboard and other paper from newspaper and putting them into piles. A little

Guatemalan boy with a bike who has a flat tire approaches Carlos who fixes it. The kids find shoeboxes and other items from the many piles of recyclable materials checkering the yard and play games with them. They are all children of the workers and come here when school is out during the summer.[47]

The only machinery used here are collection trucks, scales, and baling machines. Everything else is done by hand. This labor-intensive production is the result of a negotiated process at the end of which management agreed to use what Ken Dunn calls "low tech" or "appropriate technology"; after employees complained about the pace of the work and the physical strain caused by the use of machinery like conveyor belts. In this case, workers had the power to influence decision making about working conditions. Ken Dunn recounted some of this history to me during a field visit at an RC recycling yard. He pointed to an old rusted conveyor belt:

. . . it really worked fast and really worked great but everybody [my employees] hated it, and so I actually started working on it for a while, and there is something about a monotonous activity being all the same. The worst of it is that the stuff is coming along the conveyer at you and you have to kind of spot it there and follow it a little bit, and it gives you a headache to have to keep adjusting the eyes like that. It's standard that that's what everybody [in the industry] does is have everybody sort on a conveyor . . . and when I saw they [my employees] didn't like it and I sensed why they didn't like it, they said "could we go back to what we were doing before?" This is what they were doing before [he motions toward several employees manually sorting piles of newspaper and cans]. So what they do is sort at their own rate, wading through the piles, picking up things. And it's much more labor, but I don't know how much more expensive because there is no machine maintenance, no electricity [and he doesn't exactly keep strict accounting]. It's a curious thing you discover, that the latest technology is sometimes inhuman.[48]

Technology and its introduction, use, and abuse, have been at the heart of struggles between labor and management throughout the last two centuries in the United States. In most cases, technology is introduced not only to increase production, efficiencies, and profits, but to control the work force as well. The so-called Fordist system of production and its trademark assembly line is the classic example of managerial control over workers. Automated production technologies also helped reduce the labor force size because machines could do much more work than human beings.[49] Occupational safety advocates have also corroborated Dunn's observations that the repetitive motion and the eye strain of assembly line work produce a range of hazards for laborers.

So while the lack of capital-intensive automation and the presence of a cooperative work culture may have their benefits, recycling workers at the RC also confront numerous occupational hazards every day on the job. I detail some of their experiences in the next section.

### Hard Work, Low Status, and Occupational Hazards: Laboring in Recycling Centers

Although members of Chicago's environmental community are well-intentioned, they cannot be exempted from the responsibility of producing and ignoring environmental inequalities in recycling firms. I had a conversation with Josephine Dennis, a board member of the Chicago Recycling Coalition, on the subject of supporting recycling and other "progressive causes." When asked why she thinks recycling became so popular in the 1980s and the 1990s, she replied: "Because I think people are generally concerned about where we live in our environment. I think the polls show that over 80 percent of the people are concerned about the environment. And recycling is a real proactive thing that someone can do and see some results from. But when you're supporting a group that's stopping the destruction of rain forests, you can't really see that."[50]

Dennis's words are a stark example of the irony that an environmentalist in the United States can view rain forest protection in the Global South as "out of sight, out of mind," but remain oblivious to the hidden hazards in the recycling centers in her own city.

One of the resources workers seek is good-paying jobs. However, RC often falls short of paying its workers well. Executive Director of RC's Uptown operation, Jim Burris, admits: "Our technology has traditionally been more low tech, which has a positive effect for people of modest income because it provides a few more jobs. But frankly, it's hard to provide a living wage with hand sorting materials, given the fact that we are now essentially in a competitive industry as opposed to a social movement."[51]

Workers are paid on a day labor basis, in cash at the end of each shift. Most of them are from families where all able-bodied persons work and come home to cramped, overcrowded quarters in some of Chicago's most undesirable neighborhoods. Workers at the RC face a tough work environment and are not fully compensated for it through their monetary wages.[52] Working poor in a low-status, dangerous job is difficult and often unrewarding. For volunteers—generally middle-class white college students—this type of labor is worth the hardship because of its perceived ecological contributions (volunteers can come and go as they please). A VISTA program participant had this to say about the work at the RC: "The labor that is required is hard and dirty, but necessary in order to remain true to the attempt to restore the ecological balance of the world."[53] Full-time workers at the RC paint a less romantic picture of the work, as they are not volunteers. And as members of the lower classes, they have little choice but to labor in dirty, dead-end jobs, whether it be at a recycling facility or any other establishment. Below is an excerpt from my field notes at the RC's South Side site. They give the reader a feel for how physically taxing recycling work is:

Melinda is working in the sorting area. She grabs four bottles and throws them into a big container. She is alone on bottles while Guillermo is carting the materials Melinda accumulates back and forth to the truck [they are both Guatemalan]. They do a lot of bending and are constantly rubbing their backs and taking breathers, in what looks like exhausting work. Melinda is crouched somewhat precariously on and around hundreds of commingled containers and cans that one could easily slip on, so she has to continuously shift her weight to maintain her balance. It is now 10 A.M. and she leaves her pile to take a break [they've been working since early that morning]. She and Guillermo sit down against the barn and eat sandwiches. They regulate their own breaks. I walk to the sorting area where Melinda was just working. There are four bins in the area, one filled with recyclable cans, another with tins, another with glass and the last with cans again. It smells like strong, sour vinegar over here. With a lot of gnats, flies and bees swarming around the pile getting their fill, this alone is enough to turn one's stomach and potentially result in a sting. The temperature is in the mid 90s.[54]

Make no mistake, this is hard work. Sorting, crushing, and composting are challenging. RC workers also experience hazards on the streets, during collection times. Below is an excerpt from my field notes when I accompanied workers on the RC's "mobile buy-back" route. This is a program in which employees go into Chicago public housing developments with a truck and collect recyclable materials from residents and pay them for it in return. This program was initiated in 1996 because the city and Waste Management, Inc. agreed that poor neighborhoods and communities of color would participate in recycling more enthusiastically if given an immediate economic incentive. Thus far the program has been a major success, with entire families turning out every week with piles of cardboard, bags of aluminum cans, and stacks of newspaper. Unfortunately, there are hazards to both workers and customers here. One of them is the constant danger of being hit by passing vehicles as workers and residents mill about in the street. Other hazards arise, too:

> On the RC's mobile buy-back, I was present when seven glass bottles dropped from the truck to the ground and broke. Broken glass was strewn everywhere on the surrounding pavement. This is a work hazard to residents—many of whom are children—and workers. A worker, Angela, sweeps up the mess with a miniature broom and dustpan.[55]

Most of the dangers workers confront, however, are on site. Below is an excerpt from my field notes at the RC's South Side recycling yard:

> I go into the shed where the cans are being baled. This thing creates a hell of a lot of noise. . . . It's deafening and you can't speak to each other when it's operating. Jason, an African American employee, shows me the machine up close. It's a simple feeding system where he takes a shovel and places the cans onto a conveyor and they go down into a little bale-shaped casing. He pushed another button and the metal presses it into a small bale. It produces one about every 50 seconds. Jason gave me some headphone earplugs (like those used on shooting ranges and air runways), yet he didn't use his own plugs.[56]

Noise pollution is a major problem in industrial work and many MRFs regularly violate the law with regard to how much workers are exposed to.[57] After an 8-hour shift in a MRF, one's ears will "ring" for several minutes and maybe hours. Hearing loss can result.

Other hazards abound as well. Chemical substances found in industrial and residential waste are often found on the site, due to contracts the RC has with all manner of commercial and private establishments, including medical facilities. Shavon, one of the RC's Uptown facility employees, explained:

> We have no health and safety plan at Uptown. There are a lot of chemicals like bleach and ink that have been dumped into things we get and have to open up. We get stuff in our eyes and on our hands and because there's no toilet or running water on the site, we can't wash up until we go home.[58]

Shavon provides further details on how the work can be physically injurious: "We had a contract with some medical place and we got stuck with some syringes during that time. [Pointing at his arm] Look there, there, there, and there."[59] On each of his arms there were approximately five cuts, from sorting scrap metal and getting stuck with syringes, he says. Recycling workers must be prepared to routinely handle unregulated toxic household, medical, and industrial wastes.

Because RC employees work in an outside recycling *yard*, they are exposed to the elements with little protection. Freddie, another worker, told me:

The snow, the rain, the cold, the temperature, hot and cold, four seasons a year is bad for us. [He points to one of his index fingers] See that mark? That's from the frost bite I got last winter. Plus the rain just makes you shiver to the bone. It's no use in you bringing a change of clothes to work because if it's raining they'll just get soaked just as bad. Your whole body is like wearing a wet suit and I get colds a lot of times.[60]

However, the RC's Executive Director, Ken Dunn, states:

They work in fresh air. Strangely it would be nice to have this under a roof, and our other facility has that. But you know there is less illness for workers who work out doors. It's a healthy thing to have the fresh air and the variations on temperature.[61]

Dunn may in fact be correct. But, as I have noted above, workers certainly suffer when there is extreme heat or cold, rain or snow. Exposure to climate changes and conditions was not just hazardous to workers' health. As "AJ" informed me, it also impeded the labor process itself:

This winter there were days when it was 48 degrees below zero wind chill factor. The problem is that the gloves that keep your hands warm tear easily and they don't allow you the flexibility and the dexterity to get your job done. But the gloves that do allow you to do your job don't keep your hands warm.[62]

One of the Southeast Asian workers, Vang, told me: "We were only closed one day all last year, when the snow was up to our knees."[63]

There is a range of hazards at the RC, from the benign to the serious. Devon, an African American man, works mostly in the newspaper truck, sorting and stacking different grades of newsprint. In one discussion I had with him, he confessed that the uncertainty about his health worried him:

There is very little ventilation in the shed and the newspaper truck. The particles from the newspaper and the glass really irritate your lungs and throat. No matter what you do, even if you have gloves and face masks, your life will be shortened by working here. That's just a fact. . . .[64]

Research by occupational health professionals substantiates Devon's concerns. For example, one review of studies on this topic found that back-aches, cuts, pin pricks, eye infections, skin diseases, respiratory disorders, and intestinal conditions are associated with working in recycling centers around the world.[65]

In addition to the physically hazardous aspects of the work, there are social dimensions that present their own dangers. RC workers are constantly in contact with customers who either drop off recyclables (usually middle-class whites) or seek to sell them for cash at the buy back (usually indigent immigrants, African Americans, and white alley entrepreneurs). When market prices fall for materials, often times buy-back customers (alley entrepreneurs) become angry at receiving less money for their hard-earned materials. This dynamic sometimes places workers in danger. As Kenny recalls: "Sometimes scavengers have come in and threatened me, with force . . . one person threatened to pull a gun on me. Devon had to help me out and back me up and fight this guy. We had to remove him from the premises."[66]

Thus recycling workers face hazards that we commonly associate with traditional industrial jobs. These are dangers that the industry, government, and environmentalists have ignored (or perhaps they feel such risks are outweighed by recycling's ecological benefits). But the risk to one's well-being is just one of many categories of hazards workers face.

### The Deeper Side of Environmental Inequality: Hidden Injuries

As much as there are physical dangers confronting RC workers, they also face "hidden injuries"—those blows to one's self esteem and psyche that accumulate from living and working at the lower rungs of the class and racial hierarchy.[67] Recycling workers sustain hidden injuries because they perform society's "dirty work"—low-status, socially reprehensible tasks.[68]

Consider the following field notes from a conversation I had with one worker-alley entrepreneur, JC:

DP:  So you do this rain or shine, summer or winter?

JC:  I got to pay my rent, man! I live in a hotel and I pay by the week. I can't get no job and I'm sick. Something's going to blow up, man because it's too many people out here doing this.

DP:  Has it gotten worse as far as the number of people out here doing this kind of work?

*JC:*  Wooo weee! Goddamn, shit! It's so many peoples out here man. I mean it is increasing, you know. Of course! Well who likes doing this? Times are getting rough, now. People are trying to stay out of jail. That's why you see a lot of people do this—trying to stay out of jail.

*DP:*  How long do you think you might do this?

*JC:*  Till I find something else to do. There ain't nothing but this for me now. It hasn't gotten no nicer for me. This shit is hard, man. Don't nobody want to do this shit. These motherfuckers [are] tryin' to make an honest living [referring to himself and his co-alley entrepreneurs]![69]

Like many workers at the Resource Center, JC is homeless. When he says he lives in a "hotel," he is referring to a Single Room Occupancy building (SRO) where many indigent men and women stay on a temporary basis. JC has made it clear that the uncertainties, dangers, and social status in the life of an alley entrepreneur are anything but pleasant.

Another employee, Nate, is a sorter and an all around "handy man" at the RC's South Side facility. He is a white man, a university student on an internship at the RC. He described his job as follows:

. . . basically the bottom of the ladder stuff, you know. Anything that gets brought in and dumped, glass, paper—which includes cardboard, low grade, high grade—so I just go through and sort and separate. . . . It's not the most glamorous work there is. You know, you're sorting through other people's trash, in a sense, you know. It's a tough job, but somebody's got to do it, 'cause it does have to get done. I suppose it could be done a lot more automated, with more machines and stuff. But then that cuts out the employment, you know. So I think that's one thing I think Ken is trying to prioritize.[70]

The above quote highlights Nate's ambivalent feelings about being "on the bottom of the ladder" doing low-status work. The social standing of a person who works as a recycling sorter is very low, he points out, and this impacts his self-esteem. Many workers described their occupation as if it were one step below the category of "sanitation worker." The status level of this occupation is highly problematic with regard to personal esteem. There is evidence that these sentiments are widely held:

In repeated surveys of occupational rankings, Americans have consistently placed the garbageman's work at the bottom. Only shoe shining or street cleaning is ranked lower. The "hidden injuries" of this status system may be linked to the apparent injuries that public health and safety experts can document.[71]

One of Nate's co-workers, Jack, describes the feeling he gets from working a job that "never ends":

Trucks come in pretty much regularly all day, so it's a constant flow. That's one aspect of it that it never ends. I'm sure you've seen the big mound of paper in there [he motions toward the recycling center]. It never ends, never ends. That can be kind of a downer. You don't actually get the satisfaction of completing a project.[72]

Like Nate, some workers speculated about the prospect of having machines do their jobs. On the subject of automation and the possibility of having machines do the "dirty work" of recycling, Pete says:

Well in one sense you know, I guess it's a good idea to have these jobs, because there are a lot of people that don't have jobs that need 'em. On the other sense, it's not very satisfying work for a lot of people. And I don't see how you could just do that all day and just not really enjoy your job at all. I try to make it as interesting as possible. Sometimes I feel like I'm getting exercise out of it (he laughs). I try to have a little fun with it. I would say it's not the type of work that most people would enjoy doing for a living and get satisfaction from it. So in that sense, let the machines do it.[73]

At a low-tech operation like the RC, brawn and muscle power are the main engines of production. However, for Devon, a sorter at RC's Uptown facility, management's exclusive focus on his strength as his only recognized skill bothers him: "It's a damn shame that every time I've been hired for a job it's only been because of my strength. That really can mess with a man's self-esteem."[74]

Recycling centers often operate with informal accounting and hiring practices and are generally non-union. This lack of rules precludes grievance structures for workers and can frustrate, disempower, and wear individuals down. John, one of Devon's co-workers, details this and other parts of his work at the RC that he finds displeasing:

You know that Chi [a Southeast Asian co-worker] and I don't even exist as far as the RC's payroll and records? I figured out that we must be tax write-offs as costs or machinery or as equipment or material. I'm paid in cash every day [like a day laborer]. That's a damn shame that I don't even exist there and that's how [the manager] treats me. He doesn't treat me like I'm a man. The problem with the RC is that I'm treated like a kid. I have skills, I'm intelligent, and I'm not recognized for it. He [the manager] insults my intelligence. He treats me like an ant—he thinks I have the intelligence of an ant as well as the strength of an ant [an insect that can move several times its own weight]. I'm a day laborer who gets paid day by day.[75]

Many other workers corroborated these sentiments that recycling work is not very satisfying. This is partly because recycling work in particular is not terribly desirable, and also because, in general, low-paying, dangerous and low-status work is unsatisfying. Recycling is just one of a growing number of low-status, low-paying, high-risk jobs in the new "service economy" being celebrated in the United States. Many Resource Center workers recounted similar tales of their bad experiences at other jobs. These included jobs at janitorial services, construction firms, factories, and steel mills. Many of these jobs paid more than recycling work, but they were also generally dangerous. As Perry, a can baler at the RC, remembered, "Before this I worked at a place where we treated light posts and telephone poles with creosote."[76] (Creosote is a hazardous chemical that can have severe negative impacts on human health.)

These voices from the front lines of environmental justice detail the vast disparity between the promise of recycling and the reality of recycling work. These testimonies from workers and observations of the labor process challenge ecologists' claims that the work is always fulfilling. This same claim is made by proponents of green industries in general. For example, Tom Chappell, founder of Tom's of Maine, makes the sweeping assertion that work in a green business "takes on a deeper meaning and satisfaction."[77] On the contrary, I would argue that green industries deserve extra scrutiny from activists, researchers, and policy makers precisely because of the eco-responsibility image they enjoy.

This brings us to the next dimension of this environmental justice struggle: worker resistance.

### Worker Resistance: Shaping Environmental Inequalities

The physical and psychosocial hazards in the recycling workplace raise interesting questions about the level of power RC workers might have to resist and shape these conditions. In this section I demonstrate that, despite the many environmental hazards these workers of color confront, they successfully struggle for dignity and independence on the job.

Workers at the RC are generally subjected to what Richard Edwards called "simple control" by management.[78] That means direct, face-to-face supervision over one's labor. At the RC, even the simple control is relaxed. The work is slow and labor intensive, and the employees are allowed considerable independence to do their tasks. In a sense, this affords workers some "safe space" and a sense of turf where they can assert control over the labor process and protect themselves when the need arises. Shavon recounts one such experience:

There are also times like today when this white woman came to drop something off and kept asking me "why can't I put envelopes in the office paper bin?" And I said to her "Well, take a look at the sign, ma'am. It says 'please do not put envelopes in the office paper.'" But she said "Why?" and I said "I don't really know, but you can talk to our site manager." But she kept giving me shit saying "Why this, why that?" and I finally said "Look, I'm sorry, I can't help you. I've got work to do." The problem there is that, in addition to being a worker who's filling up a news truck, I do have to serve the customer. That's my job, to be there for the customers. But when they act like that, sometimes I have to go off on them. I've also had to escort people off the site who have become rowdy or who accuse Vang of cheating them. I've told a few of them they are not welcome back here.[79]

On the subject of independence, consider this excerpt from the field notes I took at the RC:

It is clear that there is very little oversight over workers in a direct sense. You really work at your own pace and do what you can. Carlos leans down while sorting paper and magazines and begins to read a *Sports Illustrated*. A man arrives in a Ford pickup with materials to drop off. Two African American men come in, one with a bag from Aldi's and Goldblatt's [two nearby stores] and the other with very little at all. He has a small air conditioner and aluminum cans. They all approach Carlos, who will weigh the materials and pay them for it. Another man has a plastic cooler that Carlos takes a long look at and finally says "It's not worth anything. We're not taking a lot of plastics because we don't get no money for it."[80]

So not only can workers make decisions about how they do their work and when they take breaks, but they also can make decisions about quality control that directly impact both customers and the RC's revenue. There are other benefits workers gain from being employed at the RC. Shavon told me about one of the "perks" of working in a community-based recycling center:

Me and other workers here always take junk from the morning loads that the RC can't use and we fix it up and sell it. Hell, sometimes I have yard sales to get rid of this stuff. I sell toasters, fans, lamps, lights, cigarettes, magazines, novels, irons, and anything else. The reason why, is I gotta get paid. And if I get paid, I might as well get paid twice. I make 25 cents per cigarette and I made 75 dollars from the yard sale yesterday. The other thing is I fix up bikes that we get. I've already made $800 this year from fixing up and selling bicycles.[81]

Workers engage in these activities to retain some control and security in an occupational environment that is frequently unsafe and unrewarding. Sometimes this resistance took the form of standing up to the boss. Shavon remembers the time he stood up to a manager:

One time James caught me sitting down on the job—which he does every time he comes here. And I had been working hard and taking a break. And I told him, "James, I'm a man, a human, not a machine. There is only so much I can do and I'm doing the best I can."[82]

These acts are all forms of survival and resistance against the servitude embedded in recycling work. These are also acts of resistance against the dominant trend wherein the poor and people of color bear the brunt of environmental policies, whether it be playing the host community to toxics and waste or cleaning them up at work. The independence and control over the labor process that RC workers have are significant because laborers in this market economy are under increased pressure to work longer hours for less pay and are often directly threatened with de-skilling and displacement by automation. Increasingly workers have less control over their jobs. In this way, the Resource Center has resisted many of the trends occurring with widespread acceptance in most labor markets. Environmental hazards and the labor process in which they occur were therefore negotiated by workers and management within a fairly cooperative system, despite the hazards.

I did not anticipate the revelations about the hazards workers face at the RC. I was initially sold on recycling no matter where, how, or by whom it was being done. It is obvious that these men and women face many of the same physical and psychological hazards as do workers in some of the most dangerous industrial occupations. But what makes it bearable is that the work culture at the RC is cooperative. Workers can flex their muscles from time to time if they need to. They have direct contact with and influence over customers, the managers, and executive director. They can negotiate with each other over how the work gets done. These informal practices are flexible and do not require management's knowledge or oversight. There is also the question of turf. When someone threatens workers on the site, they can intervene and remove people from the premises. Workers can, in this way, attain some degree of power and enjoy less alienating work.[83]

## Conclusion

There is certainly much to celebrate about community-based recycling at the Resource Center. Benefits include the many jobs created, the ecological value of recycling, composting, and reuse, and the community building that comes from widespread public participation and business development in communities of color. However, we must temper the positive portrait of the Resource Center with a hard look at the environmental hazards these African American, Southeast Asian, Guatemalan, and white volunteer workers confront every day. As with many environmental inequalities, RC's occupational dangers emerged and were shaped through a struggle among many stakeholders.

There are three principal ways in which stakeholders produced, challenged, and shaped environmental inequalities at the RC.

The first dimension is the process by which social and environmental ideologies were appropriated in the organization. The RC is a classic case of a charismatic leader, Ken Dunn, and his social movement organization mobilizing resources to bring together land, labor, and capital. They were aided in this process by the support of neighborhood and environmental organizations who provided volunteers and contracts, and by the city of Chicago, which paid them a diversion credit, offered a variety of grants, and passed pro-recycling ordinances. A strong environmental and social justice ideology pervaded the organization as multiple stakeholders collectively viewed recycling as a jobs-producing, environmental protection policy. And while this orientation shifted the focus away from the hazardous work, the labor process was made more bearable by a less stringent system of authority and an ideology of cooperation within the RC. Thus, workers at the RC benefited from an ideology of social justice that translated into more ecologically oriented policies, negotiated decision making, and flexible work practices.

The second dimension of the process by which environmental inequalities emerged at RC is decision making. At this level, working conditions at RC were exacerbated or ameliorated by two major policies. The first of these was the choice to accept certain types of waste for recycling, such as only source-separated recyclables. By excluding municipal solid waste, workers labored in a much safer environment than do mixed waste facility (dirty

MRF) employees. The second policy was the use of certain technologies. The decision *not* to use conveyor belt technology was due in large part to the more active role labor occupied in that organization, which may have led to reduced health risks.

The third dimension of environmental inequality struggles at the RC is worker independence and the culture of resistance. The labor conditions I detailed in this chapter are both physically and psychologically damaging, but they are embedded in a social process. And despite the dangerous conditions some RC workers face, they also exercise a fair degree of freedom and power. RC workers can flex their muscles if they need to. And because the hierarchy of authority at the RC is relatively flat, workers have direct contact with and influence over the executive director, the managers, and the customers. They can negotiate with each other over the division of labor and can therefore achieve some empowerment at what might otherwise be an alienating job. The cooperative work culture at the RC gives rise to distinct expressions of resistance by workers. Workers were actually concerned with the plant's productivity and future and were less likely to exit or engage in outright rebellion. They were able to use other forms of resistance like salvaging materials and standing up to management or customers. Workers at the Resource Center therefore shaped environmental inequalities in that, without their resistance, the physical and psychological hazards of recycling work might have been much greater. At the Resource Center, the above decision making usually had a positive effect on the work conditions. So while managerial decisions may have produced or reduced environmental hazards at the RC, they were often successfully negotiated and contested by workers.

I want to make it clear that when I implicate recycling movement groups and EJ organizations in the creation of new environmental inequalities, I am not arguing that they are the principal forces producing these problems. What I am saying, however, is that EJ and environmental groups are not without fault in these processes. And because of the power that industry, government, and affluent communities wield, they can shape and limit the choices of movement groups, who are then forced to accept "the lesser of two evils." So until EJ organizations can seize more power relative to government and corporations, and when they finally pay attention to history, perhaps they can begin to undue the past and move toward an environmentally just future.

The Resource Center was put on notice in the early 1990s that there would be major changes occurring on Chicago's recycling terrain. In fact, well before the city of Chicago handed the contract for a new recycling program to Waste Management, Inc. there were signs that the post-Harold Washington era (under Mayor Richard Daley) was going to be a lot less welcoming of non-profit recyclers. The Daley Administration had a close relationship with Waste Management and the city's Department of Environment was repeatedly accused by the RC's Uptown station of "sabotaging" the center, by funding private recyclers in the area who would compete with the non-profit, for example.[84] When the city's Blue Bag program went on line in 1995, this officially signaled the beginning of the end of the city's support for non-profit recyclers. This shift toward for-profit recycling, under a contract with the largest waste hauler in the world, had dramatic consequences for the EJ movement, for the recycling movement in the city, and for the degree to which workers were exposed to environmental inequalities. This is the subject of chapter 6.

# 6

# The Next Evolutionary Stage: Recycling Waste or Recycling History?

This chapter is a case study of the success and failure of the environmental justice movement to maintain a sustainable waste management system in Chicago. Combining technological trends featured in chapters 4 and 5, this is also a story of incineration and recycling. But this is a much more brutal example of environmental inequality that reaches deep into the unsettling history and future of the garbage wars, racism, labor relations, and the movement for environmental justice. This case is important because it is a window into a currently en vogue stage in the development of waste management. That is, incinerators continue to be built, the non-profit recyclers have largely faded, and privatized, "dirty MRF" recycling has become dominant. The privatized model is characterized by the paradox of more public investment with less public control, by a stronger market orientation for recycling, rather than an ecological value base, and by control and degradation of labor. The struggle detailed herein seeks to explain how the movement's success at closing down an incinerator was overshadowed by the subsequent implementation of an environmentally unjust recycling system. This brings us to the first dimension of the environmental justice framework: history.

## History: Before WMX, Before the Blue Bag

The environmental movement of the 1960s and the early 1970s was successful at pushing anti-pollution legislation. The Solid Waste Disposal Act of 1965 (later amended as the Resource Recovery Act of 1970), for instance, imposed new regulations on landfill operators. Consequently, as we saw during the earlier decades of the twentieth century, incineration once again became the dominant method of waste disposal in Chicago. Since 1956, when the city's first modern incinerator went into operation, the old method of landfilling waste was practically abandoned.

In 1971, the city completed construction of the Northwest Waste-to-Energy incinerator, the first and biggest large-scale, mass combustion resource recovery facility in the Western Hemisphere. This incinerator burned 1,000 to 1,200 tons of refuse daily on Chicago's poor, working-class, and African American West Side. It also used a portion of its combustion heat to produce steam, which was sold to an adjacent industrial plant.[1] Chicago had four incinerators at that time: the Northwest facility, the Medill plant (later converted to a Blue Bag recycling MRF), the Southwest Incinerator, and the Calumet plant.

As with incinerators of the 1910s and the 1920s and much later (e.g., in the Robbins era), proponents heartily claimed the Northwest burner was perfectly safe and sanitary:

When the Northwest incinerator went into service. . . the results were astonishing: 97 percent of pollution particulates were removed. The emission is not only well under the .08 grams per cubic foot set as a goal by the Federal Environmental Protection Agency, but is also well below the new Illinois State emissions standards of .05 grams per cubic foot . . . [It] represents the next step in the evolution of the municipal incinerator; it is a sophisticated power plant which uses refuse as fuel. . . . The incinerator is under negative air pressure which keeps the odors confined within the buildings. . . . Chicago is now able to incinerate 100 percent of its present annual collection of 1.3 million tons of domestic refuse and consequently has phased out its landfills.[2]

The *Chicago Tribune* claimed that environmental health and economic prosperity would be among the many benefits of this burner:

Chicago's new, ultramodern Northwest Incinerator may save taxpayers one million dollars next year and even more in years to come by selling steam and other by-products. . . . The Northwest Incinerator was designed and built to meet the city's tough antipollution ordinances. The triple forced-air combustion system combined with the most sophisticated European-designed and built burning grates assures maximum burning with a minimum of pollutants . . . leaving virtually no odor inside or outside the plant.[3]

The Northwest facility was no ordinary waste burner. From the day it opened, it also salvaged metals from its burned residues and sold them to scrap dealers. During each day of operation in 1971, more than 60 tons of cans were salvaged and sold. All of the city's incinerated cans (from the four burners) were sold to scrap processors for more than $100,000 in a single year.[4] In 1972, a formal recycling program was set up between the Northwest incinerator and a new recycling plant.[5] This might sound innovative, but a closer look reveals some interesting findings. This new recycling plant was to be housed in the Calumet Incinerator building (the same plan later enacted for the Medill incinerator), which was right next to the Calumet landfill at 103rd street and Doty Avenue, in an African American community on the South Side.[6] So, on one city block in the Black Belt on the city's South Side, a landfill, incinerator, and a recycling plant were constructed and operational.[7] A rough calculation of the combined amount of waste sent to these facilities indicates that this African American neighborhood may have been hosting nearly 40 percent of Chicago's garbage at one time.[8]

The honeymoon of waste incineration would last quite a while, but not without some early objections. Here is a sampling of initial signs of resistance.

John Sheaffer, a professor at the University of Chicago, was the subject of a *Chicago Tribune* article a year before the Northwest Incinerator was to be built: "He challenges the assertion that incinerator residue is 'clean.' 'Research has found that incinerator residue, improperly disposed of, does breed flies and rats almost as well as raw garbage,' [he stated]. Sheaffer also contends that incinerator by-products may be a greater peril to the community than dumped raw garbage."[9]

Citizens for a Better Environment (CBE) Illinois and Saul Alinsky's Campaign Against Pollution were founded in 1971 and 1970, respectively. These groups took on incinerators and other polluters and forced these issues onto the public agenda.[10] In 1973, on the eve of the global energy crisis, citizens of Roseland and nearby areas successfully urged the Illinois Attorney General to file suit against the city of Chicago for violations of pollution laws at the Calumet incinerator. An overabundance of fly ash, sulfur dioxide, hydrocarbons, carbon monoxide, and nitrogen oxides were cited in the suit.[11] In 1975, the US Environmental Protection Agency sent a warning to the Illinois EPA (state EPAs are generally unforgivably inactive), indicating that "the Northwest Incinerator, Southwest Incinerator and Calumet Incinerator are in violation of the State's particulate matter and carbon monoxide Regulations Rules."[12] The US EPA warned that if the Illinois EPA did not take action, the federal agency would intervene.

Eventually the Medill and the Calumet incinerators were closed, but the Northwest facility's final day would not come for 20 more years. (The Southwest Incinerator closed in the mid 1970s.) In the meantime, unprecedented developments were ongoing in the regulatory agencies and in environmental movement communities.

The second dimension of the environmental justice framework is the role of stakeholders in these struggles. While there certainly was an environmental justice battle in the making with respect to incinerators, all stakeholders eventually agreed that recycling was the appropriate road to the future of waste management in the city. But the process of getting to that agreement included a major garbage war over the last burner in the city— the Northwest Incinerator.

In 1976, the federal Resource Conservation and Recovery Act (RCRA) produced an increase in the number of landfills around the country in order to handle the growing solid-waste crisis.[13] This new law coincided with— and helped catalyze—the growing anti-toxics and environmental justice movements, which were quite strong in Chicago. For the next several years, the movements battled landfills and promoted recycling. In an ironic twist, the local movement even supported incineration as an anti-landfill policy, particularly when it was coupled with recycling.[14]

The veteran Chicago environmentalist Kevin Greene later reflected: "A lot of us were scratching our heads in the mid 1980s. . . . Initially people had mixed feelings about [incineration]. We thought it might be better than landfills. There was a big rush to it on the east and west coasts where landfill fees were higher."[15]

Interestingly, despite this ironic support of incineration, there is evidence that some members of the environmental community were opposed to the Northwest Incinerator in the early 1980s. In a *Chicago Tribune* editorial, the Resource Center's recycling coordinator, Gretchen Brewer, wrote:

The Environmental Protection Agency may claim that Chicago's Northwest Incinerator emissions are "twice as clean as they need to be," but the absence of EPA standards for much of what garbage burners release into the air makes this an empty claim. Recent studies have shown that emissions from burn plants contain unpreventable levels of dioxins, dibenzofurans, PCBs and heavy metals like mercury and lead. According to one study, "the exhaust plumes that spread downwind of the stacks carry vaporized metals and an invisible cloud of halogenated hydrocarbons, not to mention carbon monoxide and precursors of acid rain."[16]

During the 1980s, white environmentalists were also waking up to the fact that many incinerators were being placed in communities of color. Environmental racism was becoming a hot issue in communities of color, and opposition to these LULUs was once again driving policy and technology development with regard to solid waste. In 1985 the city's Department of Planning reported:

Four fifths (80 percent) of the garbage generated in the City of Chicago is disposed of in sanitary landfills located on the Southeast Side [where a large percentage of African Americans live]. While still the cheapest method of waste disposal, primary reliance on landfills *has become unacceptable to adjacent neighborhood residents,* results in environmental degradation, and is of limited physical capacity.[17]

White environmentalists and EJ groups teamed up to resist hazardous incinerators and landfills during the 1980s. In 1983, a strong environmental movement campaign produced a moratorium on the expansion and siting of new landfills. This ban precipitated a crisis that forced the city to think about future waste disposal plans, such as recycling and incineration. In chapter 5 we saw that Mayor Washington, the Resource Center, and environmental movement groups crafted this moratorium. In 1987, Waste Management, Inc. announced that it would reduce the amount of waste accepted at its Southeast Chicago landfill by 70 percent and during that year landfill tipping fees rose from $10 to $20 per ton.[18] Also, a major legal battle had been brewing that would shape the future of the Northwest Incinerator struggle (and all subsequent incinerator battles). Since 1988, the Environmental Defense Fund and Citizens for a Better Environment had been fighting the city of Chicago in court over whether or not the Northwest Incinerator's ash was hazardous. Tests of the incinerator found unsafe levels of lead, cadmium, and other toxic substances in ash samples.[19] In 1994, the US Supreme Court handed down a decision declaring that Chicago's incinerator ash was not exempt from the Resource Conservation and Recovery Act (RCRA). This meant that the 400 tons of ash waste produced every day at Chicago's Northwest Incinerator (the city's principal waste management system since 1971) were now subject to more intensive regulation. The city was therefore in danger of violating this ruling because, by burying the ash in landfills and quarries, it was not properly disposing of these materials. To correct the situation, the city would have to increase its expenditures for the testing of ash and begin sending it to specially designated hazardous waste dumps.[20] The solid-waste crisis in Chicago showed no signs of subsiding, and by the 1990s, the city was undergoing another transformation in the movement-policy cycle.

In 1993, a major movement was being mobilized against the Northwest burner all around Chicago, but particularly on the West Side. The leading voice in this movement emerged as a coalition of environmental, faith-based, public interest, and social justice organizations called the Westside Alliance for a Safe and Toxic-free Environment (WASTE). WASTE held rallies, public meetings, hearings, marches, circulated petitions, and placed articles in the local media that were critical of the city and the incinerator. As this movement was just gathering steam, the US EPA issued a notice to the city of Chicago for the Northwest Incinerator's "significant violations" of pollution laws. The city did little or nothing to address it. In response, Citizens for a Better Environment wrote a letter to the US EPA on behalf of WASTE. CBE directed the EPA to carry out its mandate and intervene, or face the consequences:

Community residents most directly affected by these emissions want the city to be held accountable for its irresponsible polluting practices. . . . While WASTE recognizes that filing a citizen suit is an available option, it hopes that this alternative will not need to be considered.[21]

In another letter to the US EPA from WASTE Executive Director Fred Friedman, he dispensed with the pleasantries to tell it like it is:

No one asked the community whether the garbage burner should be built in the first place, and now no one is asking the community whether the garbage burner should continue to send poisons into the air. The community believes the garbage burner *should be permanently shut down and replaced with a more viable, jobs-producing recycling alternative.* Since the City and State have failed to take their environmental responsibilities seriously, you must intervene to ensure that the City is doing everything possible to protect the community. . . . The permit [for the incinerator] requires the City to operate the ash handling system in a manner that minimizes emissions of particulate matter. This is a vague requirement that *does not sufficiently protect workers and prevent ash dust from escaping into the community during removal.*[22]

So CBE and WASTE were digging in their heels and urging action at the highest regulatory levels. WASTE's letter also underscored support for recycling and, unlike many mainstream environmental organizations, revealed a concern for the *workers inside* the incinerator.[23]

Echoing Friedman's call for viable alternatives to the incinerator, WASTE coalition member, Center for Neighborhood Technology (CNT), issued a report during the height of the conflict, which concluded:

Jobs are being created in Chicago in companies that either recycle, reprocess or utilize discarded materials. We can use some of that Chicago experience to project how new jobs will be created through an aggressive recycling initiative to replace the Northwest Incinerator. . . . If the City were to invest $30 million . . . the Center estimates that 635 jobs could be created for residents over the next five to ten years.[24]

At the local level, the WASTE coalition was successful at urging 12th Ward Alderman Mark Fary to present a resolution to the City Council that included the following language:

Chicago has a flourishing material reprocessing industry and a mandate to reuse or recycle at least 25 percent of its waste by the year 1996; and . . . incinerators require a dedicated stream of wastes with high heat content, the same materials (largely paper) that are being recycled in ever-increasing quantities; and . . . experience in many cities has confirmed that many more jobs are created by investing in material reuse and recycling than in incineration.[25]

This resolution recommended a thorough analysis of recycling options that would shift waste away from the incinerator toward more ecologically, socially, and economically useful ends. The text of the resolution also reveals that Illinois law requires that Chicago have a recycling plan that would achieve a 15 percent recycling rate by 1994 and 25 percent by 1996. This plan, and Chicago's recycling ordinance, was successfully pushed by the CAWD—the Resource Center, People for Community Recovery, and Citizens for a Better Environment in the mid 1980s. The economic arguments rose to a furious pitch when the city announced its intention to spend $150 million on a retrofit to modernize the incinerator.[26] The alleged fiscal and social irresponsibility of rebuilding an aging "poison machine" was a constant theme brought up during this campaign. At a meeting of the South Austin Community Coalition (a WASTE member), a mostly African American audience listened to a minister-activist warn:

They want us taxpayers to hand out $150 million dollars for that incinerator that we know is poisoning us. That figure $150 million is interesting to me because that's about the same amount of money that the Chicago Public Schools system is in the hole for right now! So I'm asking you, which one are we going to choose: an incinerator or our children's education?[27]

WASTE immediately hit the streets and got thousands of residents to sign petitions declaring:

> We, the undersigned, believe the Northwest Incinerator is poisoning the air on the West Side. . . . [We] do not want the City to waste $150 million to keep it running . . . [and we] want the City to consider better options like recycling that will not poison the community and will create jobs for community residents.[28]

The third and fourth dimensions of the environmental justice framework are the role of stratification and the capacity of those stakeholders with only a moderate degree of power to shape the outcomes of these conflicts. The WASTE coalition made it clear that the Northwest Incinerator was an example of environmental racism, and this framing, combined with political mobilization, constituted a formidable force.

In the WASTE statement of principles and objectives, the group again called for recycling, specifically a "recycling industrial park in the area that will process a wide range of discarded materials now being burned at the incinerator." During this time, the illegal dumping battles associated with Operation Silver Shovel were raging on Chicago's West Side. WASTE was also heavily involved in those conflicts and made efforts to link fly dumping and the Northwest Incinerator and frame both as forms of environmental injustice.

Environmental racism was hot on the minds of activists in the neighborhoods and among their mainstream environmental organization partners. Lillian Drummond, an African American community leader representing the South Austin Community Coalition, told a reporter her thoughts about the Northwest burner:

> We know they aren't building these things in rich white neighborhoods. . . . They wouldn't stand for it. This is genocide against poor people and all people of color. We will fight it in Chicago, in Springfield, in Washington, DC, and on the streets if necessary.[29]

Underscoring Drummond's accusations, Citizens for a Better Environment reminded the US EPA of its role in producing environmental injustices:

> Too often low-income, minority communities become victims of irresponsible polluting practices. Even when these polluting practices are ultimately identified by your Agency, enforcement actions are less frequent and penalties assessed are much lower.[30]

The resolution that WASTE introduced to the city council (which passed, and the public later voted against the incinerator in a non-binding referendum), read: ". . . the residents in close proximity to the incinerator, who are primarily low income and minority, are becoming increasingly aware of the issue of environmental racism."

So environmental racism was part of the dominant framework activists were presenting to the media, to communities around the incinerator, and to regulatory agencies. The accusation of environmental racism was and remains so politically charged that the city and the US EPA were justifiably worried about the bad publicity and the outcome of this garbage war. In the meantime, WASTE marched on.

In addition to editorials and articles, WASTE used the media in creative ways. They produced an ad in the citywide *Chicago Reader* featuring a photograph of two young girls who were victims of lead poisoning. The caption read: "Their heads are full of dreams. Unfortunately, their brains are full of lead."[31] The coalition made sure that, if city officials produced arguments that the burner was economically and environmentally sound, they would have a hard time combating the politically powerful claims about the facility's impact on human health:

[The incinerator] releases a shocking average of 17 pounds of lead per hour. The community groups . . . are concerned about current and future health problems related to incineration. . . . Health impacts have not been addressed in the city's decision-making process. The Department of Environment maintains that because a rebuild will include better pollution control devices, health concerns are being addressed. However, this view ignores the bioaccumulative nature of toxins produced by incinerators, including heavy metals and dioxin.[32]

A health screening of the Austin neighborhood near the incinerator found that 1,638 children had elevated levels of lead in their blood.[33]

WASTE and its partners were successfully framing the struggle over the Northwest Incinerator as a case of fiscal irresponsibility, environmental racism, and a needless waste of material resources that could be recycled—creating more jobs in the process. The coalition directed its energies at all levels of government, because the city, state, and federal agencies often disagreed over responsibility and accountability, and different regulations and laws often leave communities without a strong claim that their rights are being violated. These inconsistencies and conflicts among multiple levels of government frequently create and exacerbate environmental injustices.[34]

The members of the WASTE coalition played their cards brilliantly. They remembered that, above all, pollution is about politics, and that garbage wars are indeed wars and therefore one must use any and every available tactic. Any scientific, legal, or economic argument activists put forth could be shot down by expert consultants hired by industry and government. When someone is being dumped on and wants to change the situation, the best way to achieve that goal is to mobilize mass opposition and overwhelm the opponents with people rather than to rely solely on well-researched technical data and "facts."

### The Movement-Policy Cycle

In part because of the new expenses incurred as a result of the Supreme Court ruling, but mostly because of the EJ movement's resistance against the burner, Chicago's Northwest Incinerator closed in 1996, after 26 years of operation. One of the oldest waste-to-energy plants in the country, the incinerator had sold steam to the nearby Brach Candy Company, a Chicago landmark of sorts. The Westside Alliance for a Safe and Toxic-free Environment challenged the city's efforts to keep the incinerator open by arguing that, on social, economic, and ecological grounds, recycling was a sounder option. A settlement between the EPA, the Justice Department, and environmentalists resulted in $700,000 being devoted to the cleanup of contaminated land in the community surrounding the incinerator, as well as funds being earmarked for a lead abatement program in the neighborhood. It appeared that the movement was even more victorious when the city of Chicago announced its intentions to close the incinerator *and* develop a comprehensive recycling program. Unfortunately for the activists, the large solid-waste firm Waste Management, Inc. (WMX) was awarded the municipal recycling contract for the Blue Bag program. The Blue Bag program that WMX put into place was in many ways as regressive as the incinerator.[35] This turn of events is yet another example of the movement-policy cycle that has occurred throughout US history with respect to the garbage wars. Environmental activists had a good idea, but they were limited in their ability to control its implementation.

### The Future Is Now: WMX and the Blue Bag System

The previous sections detailed the pre-history of the Blue Bag system and the forces that created it. This section focuses on the second pillar of the environmental justice framework: the role of stakeholders.

The Chicago plan was to adopt what became known as the "Blue Bag" approach to recycling. Many curbside recycling programs are characterized by source separation, which entails putting recyclables into bins to be picked up by recycling (not garbage) trucks. This program is different. Through the Blue Bag program, residents place their recyclables in blue plastic bags, which are then collected along with household garbage in a single garbage truck. The trucks then dump their loads at materials recovery facilities operated by WMX, where the bags are pulled out of the garbage and their contents separated. Recyclable materials not in bags are also pulled out of the garbage for processing.

In addition to meeting the requirements of the city's recycling ordinance (i.e., that 25 percent of the waste stream be recycled by 1996), the city promised that the new recycling system would create between 200 and 400 jobs. Like many industrial cities of the Northeast and the Midwest, Chicago had experienced continuous recessions and bouts with de-industrialization. Between 1967 and 1987 the city lost 326,000, or 60 percent, of its manufacturing jobs.[36] More and more, recycling was shaping up to be the next "win-win" urban policy for Chicago. It would solve the landfill problem, please the environmental community, and provide jobs in some of the city's depressed areas. The Blue Bag system seemed especially advantageous insofar as an infrastructure was in place, with the city already providing waste pickup service using a fleet of trucks and several transfer stations and landfills (owned by WMX). The Blue Bag program would fit right into this structure with no major changes. A cost-benefit analysis of a curbside recycling program versus the mixed-waste Blue Bag system revealed that the latter would cost millions of dollars less. Thus, ignoring ecological and social criteria, the *Solid Waste Management Newsletter* reported that "the primary reason given for adopting the commingled bag/MRRF recycling program is its affordability."[37]

When WMX received the contract for the Blue Bag system, environmental organizations like the Chicago Recycling Coalition cried foul. CRC's executive director, Anne Irving, called the bidding process an example of "bald-faced power playing by a corporation with a monopoly."[38] The Resource Center and other community-based recyclers were not even considered for the contract. Irving and other activists viewed WMX as a shoo-in because of its power in city and state politics. The corporation is headquartered in the Chicago metropolitan area; the brother of Mayor Richard Daley is on the board of directors of a WMX subsidiary, Wheelabrator Technologies; and Wheelabrator was to be the operator of the Northwest Incinerator (which had just been shut down). The fact that the new recycling system was being operated by the same company the movement had just defeated in the battle over the incinerator felt like a slap in the face. Furthermore, WMX has a long history of unsavory behavior. In fact, it has been the target of more lawsuits charging bribery, death threats to politicians, illegal dumping, and environmental racism than any other waste firm.[39] This company, a corporate environmental criminal running a recycling system, was nothing more than a wolf in sheep's clothing as far as environmentalists were concerned. In addition to complaints about a WMX monopoly, environmentalists were upset that the recycling system was a mixed-waste program. Mixed-waste programs had already failed in other cities because recyclable materials become contaminated with garbage waste and are unmarketable.

WMX is the largest waste hauler in the world. With average annual revenues in the neighborhood of $11 billion, WMX has operations in Australia, Canada, Europe, and South Africa. Probably the corporation most vilified by the anti-toxics and environmental justice movements in recent years (owing to its ownership of scores of landfills, incinerators, and hazardous waste facilities), WMX is widely alleged to be an "environmental terrorist" and a perpetrator of flagrant corporate crimes.[40] What is curious is that several local community organizations that had been fighting WMX for years decided to support the Blue Bag program. For example, People for Community Recovery had been fighting WMX since 1982. Specifically, PCR was up in arms about the location of WMX's landfill and chemical waste incinerator in the neighborhood and even held several public protests against the company. For years, PCR's diagnosis of the problem was "too much pollution and not enough good jobs"—a mantra that was taken up by the rest of the environmental justice movement. When WMX announced that it was finally going to address the "jobs versus environment" issue by building a recycling plant that would hire local residents, PCR, the Mexican Community Committee, and several other organizations lent support. WMX made an arrangement with these organizations to recruit, interview, and pre-screen potential employees who later went to work for the company. What only WMX could know at that time was that the jobs at these recycling centers were terribly unsafe and unhealthy. In this way, many environmental justice movement organizations were unwittingly complicit in the imposition of environmental injustices on workers from their own communities. This is but a fraction of the complexity that is missing from much of the research on environmental racism. That is, the systems of institutional racism and classism produce arrangements that place certain people of color in the role of "the oppressed as oppressor," or stakeholders who receive small gains while more powerful actors benefit handsomely from both groups' oppression.[41] This is the story of Operation Silver Shovel and the Robbins incinerator as well, and this dynamic is absent from the traditional "perpetrator-victim" scenario presented in many academic and activist accounts of environmental inequality.[42]

The struggle for valuable post-consumer waste was short, WMX being the nearly predetermined victor. The non-profit recyclers like the Resource Center would have to eke out an existence through more creative means. The City of Chicago provided taxpayer dollars and political will to WMX; neighborhood groups worked with WMX to recruit workers; residents participated in the Blue Bag program by providing their trash and recyclables to the waste haulers; and, while environmentalists were critical of WMX's recycling methods and its political power, they had earlier lent support to the campaign for a citywide recycling program, and they ignored the problems of occupational safety and environmental inequality inherent in the Blue Bag system. They objected mainly to the lack of non-profit involvement and the anticipated low quality of recovered recyclables. The stakeholders generally left out of the debate over the Blue Bag were the workers. This was in large part because the city and WMX had already determined that the jobs would be non-union.[43] And since residents were desperate for any type of work, and environmentalists were paying no attention to job quality or to wages, this exclusion went uncontested.

### Green Business or Global Sweatshop?

### Management's Decisions and Environmental Hazards
The third pillar of the environmental justice framework is institutional inequality and its role in producing environmental hazards. This section

details how WMX created an unbearably hazardous work environment where people of color were concentrated.

The structure of the Blue Bag system and the MRFs in which they were processed was created by managers with a range of options available to them. These decisions had direct impacts on the nature of environmental inequality at the MRFs.

The Blue Bag program went into effect on December 4, 1995, serving single-family homes and low-density buildings in Chicago. Some 750,000 residents were expected to separate their paper and commingled products (plastic, metals, etc.) into blue bags that were to be mixed in with the regular garbage pickup and taken to four colossal MRFs in the city, where they would be processed for end markets. These "dirty MRFs"—MRFs processing both recyclables and garbage—were each the size of several football fields and were staffed by 100 African American and Chicano workers picking, sorting, lifting, and cleaning tons of trash and recyclables. WMX workers faced environmental inequalities in the plants based largely on managerial decision making. Two principal decisions contributed to environmental inequality at this MRF: to accept mixed waste and to maintain an oppressive work culture.

### Decision 1: Accepting Certain Types of Waste

Like the Northwest Incinerator and the Robbins Incinerator, the Blue Bag system was touted as the most sophisticated and advanced waste management technology ever assembled under one roof. WMX's MRFs revealed that these buildings were packed with computer stations, assembly lines, magnetic sorters, air classifiers, balers, cameras, and other forms of machinery and technology. Although designed for efficient recycling, they seemed to neglect two important things: high-quality recycling (mixed-waste systems like the Blue Bag combine trash and recyclables, thus contaminating the latter) and a high-quality work environment. These two issues would haunt this recycling program from day one. The decision to use a capital-intensive production process to make recycling more efficient failed. This decision also created an occupational environment where workers were expected to adapt to machines and regularly increase production.

There are hundreds of MRFs across the United States that receive only source-separated materials and do not accept municipal solid waste (MSW).

WMX departed from this model in an apparent effort to innovate and reap greater value from the entire waste stream. This managerial decision to build a "dirty MRF" had a major impact on the health and safety of workers at the MRF. MSW is material that a Danish inspection service ruled "presents a very high health hazard, and must not be sorted by hand."[44]

In a December 1995 episode of the television series *ER*, one emergency room patient was a man who had fallen from a 15-foot sorting line and impaled himself on a piece of machinery in a recycling center. The WMX recycling workers I interviewed faced hazards no less serious. And while these hazards are both physical and psychological in their impact, they originate in social structures.

WMX grossly miscalculated the environmental and safety issues, which is ironic since Blue Bag recycling was touted as an environmentally responsible initiative. I spoke to more than two dozen workers and managers who worked under the Blue Bag system. The stories they told resemble the experiences of laborers in the sweat shops, the mines, the steel and textile mills, and the slaughterhouses of the nineteenth-century United States and the contemporary Global South.

Recycling workers face a number of health and safety hazards. To the horror of most workers, the Blue Bag system was characterized by the routine manual handling of chemical toxins, hazardous waste, and infectious medical wastes, all of which are found in household garbage (whose contents are not regulated). Bleach, battery acid, paint, paint thinner, inks, dyes, razor blades, and homemade explosives are in the waste stream. Medical waste has recently emerged as a significant problem because, as hospital patients are more frequently sent home under managed care, so is their waste. Garbage and recycling workers are regularly exposed to these substances. One worker told me: "There are tons of medical wastes and construction wastes. Say, for instance, the red bags that have biohazards would drop down the chute. One time a bag went through marked 'asbestos' and I said 'Damn, that looks like asbestos, a cloud of asbestos dust just hanging there!'"[45]

Finger and arm pricks by syringes and hypodermic needles and battery acid sprays are becoming quite common in MRFs around the world.[46] Workers have died as a result of battery acid exposure. Needle pricks are particularly worrisome, as many employees fear exposure to HIV.

The newspapers covered the Blue Bag controversy from day one, but they generally focused on recycling rates and on whether recyclables were being contaminated when mixed with garbage. A few stories about working conditions appeared, but this issue never really concerned environmentalists. When city or WMX officials did address the question of labor, they pointed out that they had "created" 400 jobs in Chicago that were, according to Commissioner of the Department of Environment Henry Henderson, "clean and safe."[47] WMX management insisted that the working conditions were "excellent." A WMX MRF site manager named Mitchell told me:

The enclosures, we have nine of them, where the sorting will be done, are in a climate-controlled area, [which] will be heated and air conditioned. The system will produce six air changes an hour within the enclosure, for the sorters. . . . We've gone pretty far to make that environment safe.[48]

Another manager, Jake, added:

The way the sorting is done, there are very different ways, some of them are "throw-across" into a backboard situation. And other sorts are pulling and dropping into a thing, where there's no lifting, so you don't have the back injuries. And what experts call "depth burden" (i.e. the length one has to reach) is greatly reduced. All of the exchanges of materials are outside of the enclosures, so any dust that's generated will stay out of the enclosure so the environment they're in is good.[49]

However, even the trade journals picked up the negative story about "Chicago's Blues," particularly the abysmally low recycling rate of 6 percent. Other cities had recycling rates exceeding 30 percent, and the Coalition for Appropriate Waste Disposal (CAWD) had earlier claimed that Chicago could attain a rate of 60 percent.[50]

Labor hazards remained problematic too. Eric Keely, a Chicago-based private consultant to the recycling industry, argued that "more than anything, including low recovery rates, what is going to kill this program is the presence of infectious medical waste and various other working hazards."[51] On July 11, 1996, eight months after the Blue Bag program began, the US Occupational Safety and Health Administration slapped WMX with a $10,500 fine for several labor violations. Although the penalty was not heavy, the fact that OSHA (by most accounts an immobile bureaucracy) actually came out and inspected the sites is notable. The violations are listed in table 6.1. These violations correspond strongly with the ethnographic data I gathered, but they fall short of capturing the full reality of the labor process WMX employees confronted every workday, including the oppres-

Table 6.1
WMX's OSHA violations. Source: interview with former WMX manager, summer 1996 (see note 63).

---

Employees subjected to dangerously high sound levels (90.1–90.5 decibels)

No existing sound monitoring system in place

Proper protective equipment not being used

Machines not guarded properly

Inadequate safety training

No recognizable emergency plan or training

Hepatitis B vaccination (required by law for any US workers handling trash) not administered

---

sive work culture maintained at the plants. A year later, OSHA representatives made a follow-up visit to the WMX MRFs and found that the company had engaged in "willful violation" of previous orders to follow labor law and inoculate its employees against Hepatitis B. The penalty this time was $112,500. The charge regarding inoculations was verified by a WMX employee who told me that he and other workers had had "no physical examination, no inoculation":

> That's what made me kind of skeptical . . . because you were working around raw garbage and I was talking with a couple of guys that were *managers* for WMX, and before they were hired, they had to take physicals and they were inoculated. But the people from REM were given no physicals or inoculations.[52]

WMX hired its laborers from a temporary labor service called Remedial Environmental Manpower (REM). WMX therefore deliberately withheld legally mandated vaccinations from the REM "temps," all of whom were men and women of color. This withholding of medical care placed employees at great risk. WMX workers confronted other dangers too, many of which were seemingly unpreventable once the MRF was up and running. One employee told me: "WMX was built on top of a landfill. And for a while before they had the fire suppression systems working, we had to have people walking around with fire extinguishers because there was methane gas seeping through the floor . . . ."[53]

WMX's management made the decision to build this MRF on the methane-producing landfill. This decision contributed directly to a hazardous work environment.

In December of the Blue Bag's first year, a deceased infant was discovered on the recycling line. This was the fourth human body discovered at the city's recycling centers in a year.[54]

The workers I interviewed made it clear that dangerous incidents were routine. In two weeks' time, Ferris (a line sorter in the "primary" department, where the trucks dump the garbage) had witnessed "about six" accidents. He elaborated:

I got cut on my finger with some glass, because the glass went through the glove. And then this other girl, she got stuck in the arm with needles, but they sent her to the company doctor. And they put her back to work the next day when her arm was still hurting. They gave her some medicine and she was still hurting, so I feel that wasn't right. Then this one guy fell down a chute and broke his arm. And then this one guy got burnt with some battery acid.[55]

These psychological and physical hazards intermingled as people desperate for gainful employment and job security continued working in the face of gross health and safety violations. In a city where the unemployment rate in many African American neighborhoods exceeds 50 percent, it is not difficult to understand why, as one worker explained, "you never turn down work when you're looking for it."[56] However, that worker also reasoned, "you also have to think of your safety because that *job* might be there next year, but if you contracted some disease, *you* might not be there next year."[57]

The sociological implications of hazardous jobs have always had effects beyond the workplace.[58] Often a worker exposed to hazards has unknowingly carried dangerous chemicals home on his or her clothing or body. Such transfers of toxins sometimes have direct impacts on the health of family members or friends. Other evidence of dangerous work is also often found in the home, in the form of the social and psychological wounds that risky jobs inflict upon employees and their families. WMX workers were no exception. Workers' families were stuck in a catch where either the lack of work or the presence of socially and physically oppressive work was a routine source of stress. Dee Dee's situation was typical: "People put all their time and effort into this, and they want to spend quality time with their children like they should, and then just to let us go like that [i.e., fire us arbitrarily], you know, that ain't right!"[59] Another quote is typical of families facing the oppressive nature of the work. Jason's mother answered the phone one night when I called to schedule an interview with him. He was not home, but his mother had this to say about WMX: "They were just evil, and they treated him like the devil would treat somebody."[60]

Thus, management's decisions routinely produced an unsafe working environment for WMX employees and impacted their families. The way management "would treat somebody" is a part of what I would call "the work culture."

### Decision 2: Maintaining an Oppressive Work Culture

Most secondary labor markets in which African Americans and Latinos are concentrated are characterized by low wages, a lack of mobility, a lack of health and safety guarantees, and a lack of hope. (Secondary labor markets are characterized by lower wages and lesser opportunities for mobility than are found in primary labor markets.) Thus we should not be surprised to find similar patterns at WMX. Most work in secondary labor markets is also characterized by the fact that workers are not encouraged or allowed to think creatively and independently on the job. Workers employed in hazardous occupations find that this problem is compounded by the job's dangers. "Workers in hazardous occupations are 50–90 percent more likely than workers in safe occupations to describe their jobs as uncreative, monotonous, meaningless, and as providing no worker control over work pace. They are 10–20 percent more likely to report no control over job duties, no control over work hours, and the pervasiveness of rules."[61]

The oppressive social environment at WMX contributes to the problem of dangerous and uncreative work. Richard Edwards's classic book *Contested Terrain* outlines three types of managerial control over labor: simple, technical, and bureaucratic.[62] WMX managers made use of all three. Simple control generally includes direct supervision of labor. WMX managers made the decision to use a disciplinarian management style. For example, workers regularly complained of being harassed by foremen and managers who rarely let them leave the sorting lines to use the bathrooms and arbitrarily instituted mandatory overtime. One whistle-blowing former manager put it as follows:

John and Norm's [the general managers] philosophy was to "keep your foot in their ass." That was their verbal philosophy as communicated to us. That is bound to fail, nothing new about that. . . . Dan Karlson was an REM supervisor and he walked around the plant with a pistol in his holster. His philosophy was "whenever you get a disgruntled worker you have to slap them and shut them up."[63]

As evidence of this philosophy in action, one worker who contacted OSHA to file a complaint in early 1996 was fired within a week of doing so. After several workers spoke to journalists about the deplorable health and safety conditions in the plant, REM issued a memo to its employees "strictly prohibiting" any communication with the news media. Workers were explicitly instructed to respond with "no comment" to any inquiries about working conditions in the MRFs and were warned that "violation of this work rule may result in disciplinary action up to and including immediate termination of employment."[64]

These oppressive conditions had direct impacts on the state of occupational health at the WMX MRF. Collins, a worker at one facility, told of the following experience between the managers and workers who were determined to keep their jobs:

They [management] was always threatening people. . . . They said that if you didn't work Saturdays then you might as well not come back Monday. . . . A couple of guys there had twisted ankles and everything. I looked for medical kits but didn't notice any of that. These guys with hurt ankles were frightened for their jobs because the way that these people were pushing them was like "Hey, I'm gon' tell you. We got more people standing in line waiting on this job." He wasn't lying because I noticed that they started bringing in Mexican Americans late at night who didn't speak English. They would bus them in late at night and then take them out in the morning.[65]

A female worker in the same plant told a similar story:

One lady I know cut her foot. This was in where they pick the trash off the conveyor belts—it's upstairs. She had cut her foot and she was bleeding. And I was thinking you know, if you hadn't had a tetanus shot and you don't know what you stepped on, I thought the company should have took her right away to get her a tetanus shot. They didn't. They gave her a piece of toilet tissue, put it back in her shoes and sent her right back to work. When she got injured, that was part of her 15 minute break. She used her 15 minute break to take care of it.[66]

Workers and management battled over the control and the speed of assembly lines throughout the twentieth century.[67] In Richard Edwards's typology of forms of managerial control, the assembly line is the classic example of technical control. Like many workers on assembly lines, however, some recycling workers had the power to stop the process for emergencies and for certain quality-control purposes, although doing so was strongly discouraged. However, the *speed* of the line was inflexible. One female worker noted:, "There was no way you could control the speed [of the line]. You could control it if you wanted to stop it, but not control how fast or how slow it went."[68]

Like major managerial decisions, the assembly line as technical control influenced occupational safety and health in the WMX MRF. Another worker recounted the following experience: "With the [conveyor] belt constantly running, you're reaching for one thing and, by the time you turn your head back, there's something in your face. . . . You couldn't see what was actually coming and that made it real dangerous for you."[69] For example, one female employee almost "got her neck slit on the line" when landscape clippings and branches poked her as she worked.[70]

The oppressive conditions also impacted workers' social psychological stability with regard to their status as "temps." Temporary status was difficult for many workers to contend with. Being a "temp" is alienating and marginalizing. Temporary status and the informal managerial practices that often accompany it were used as a form of bureaucratic control. That is, the presence or absence of company rules, regulations, and procedures can place many barriers to a worker's compensation, safety, status, power, and job advancement. Bureaucratic control at WMX included a structure of rules and procedures that guaranteed that African Americans and Latinos would remain temporary employees in the lowest-ranking, most dangerous jobs in the plant. The forms of managerial control over labor at WMX are outlined in table 6.2.

As I mentioned above, workers at WMX were hired through a temporary job service called Remedial Environmental Manpower. In recent years, powerful lobbyists for temporary employment firms have fundamentally changed federal labor legislation. For example, workers at the WMX MRFs were technically not employees of WMX or of REM. Rather, as a result of

**Table 6.2**
Forms of managerial control at WMX.

|  | Description | Impact on work conditions |
| --- | --- | --- |
| Simple | Direct supervision | Contributes to stress and endangerment |
| Technical | (Dis)assembly lines | Contributes to physical and psychosocial hazards |
| Bureaucratic | Rules, procedures | Relegates employees of color to riskiest jobs |

recent changes in labor laws, they were "consumers" of REM's services.[71] They therefore had questionable legal rights as workers and an ambiguous legal relationship to WMX. This arrangement encouraged and rewarded abuse and exploitation by management.

All the workers at WMX were "temps," and therefore they could be fired arbitrarily. Two workers recounted the following:

When they did [suddenly] lay us off, they was telling us all that we did a great job . . . and that we'd be first for consideration when they started hiring back again. But I haven't heard anything else from 'em.[72]

They got our hopes up so high. They didn't tell us that we was experimental guinea pigs. They just had us psyched all up like we was gon' be there for a while and they just dropped us like that.[73]

And in view of the highly informal accounting system, an employee was often uncertain as to whether he or she had any official status as an employee of WMX:

They didn't ask me for a W-2 form. There was no paper work that was filled out. You just came in and they just put you straight to work after a brief training session. And a lot of people, I didn't think they should have been put to work that day. They were unprepared in gym shoes without enough clothes on [to do hard, industrial labor].[74]

Being a "temp" also meant that you had little or no power in the workplace and were at the mercy of managers' whims. For example, many times workers worried about when they would be allowed to finish a shift and go home. Angela stated:

I started work at 6 that morning and I got out by 7 that night. And that was during a time when some guys had been working from 6 in the morning until 2 the next morning straight. They had been threatened with immediate dismissal otherwise. The managers said that anybody that didn't want to work until they told them to go home should leave right then. Because they said they might work you 15–20 hours that day. And then it was more of a demand that you stay. It wasn't like eight hours and anybody that wanted to work overtime after eight could stay. It was like "You stay till we tell you to leave."[75]

Surprisingly, many laid-off workers expressed a desire to return. For example, after being laid off, rehired, then laid off again, DJ told me: "I really liked that job and I wouldn't mind going back."[76] Leila, a temporary worker "on call" for WMX, told me she would like to become a permanent WMX worker because any job was better than no job: "It was just a job to get money, you know? Well I'm out of work now. Well, not really out of work because I'm working there, but I would like to do that, yes, for as long as possible. Being a temp is something that you never know what's going to happen."[77]

The decisions by management at the WMX MRF imposed a range of environmental injustices on workers of color. Despite the conditions workers face, WMX has insulated itself somewhat. Because the city was the client and because they recruited workers through a temporary agency and through local community organizations, they have been able to deflect some of the blame for the Blue Bag's shortcomings. WMX's public relations efforts have also helped. In early 1995, before the Blue Bag controversy erupted, WMX issued a "Good Neighbor Policy" indicating commitment to "environmental protection and compliance," "civic and charitable programs," "host community consultation," "communication and disclosure," and "local hiring and purchasing."[78] Relative to these promises, the resources workers sought were basic and direct. Most of them simply wanted better pay, job security, and more attention to occupational safety. Many of them drew on a range of strategies to express their opposition to the system.

### Shaping Environmental Inequalities from Below: Worker Resistance to Occupational Hazards and Recycling Ideology

The final pillar of the environmental justice framework is the capacity of those suffering from environmental injustices to resist them. This is crucial to understanding environmental racism. Communities and workers are not always passive, and in fact they have measurable and powerful effects on government and industrial policies.

WMX workers responded to social subjugation and occupational hazards through various strategies. Resistance included responses to the ideology of recycling in the context of the dirty work it requires. It also included responses to management decisions that contributed to environmental inequalities.

Some workers gave voice to their concerns. One worker, in a letter to the press, pleaded for journalists to exercise "that constitutional freedom I do not [have]." He noted that he and his co-workers experienced "constant colds, flu, diarrhea and coughing"[79] as a result of working at WMX. He continued:

Several people have been struck by discarded hypodermic needles. Air quality is bad. Others, including myself, have been injured by battery acid, muscle strains, lower back pain, pinched nerves, contusion, various types of trauma including emotional or psychological from witnessing dead bodies, parts of animal carcasses, live and dead rats, etc. And let's not forget the supervisors' bogus tactics. . . . [We have been] threatened to be fired by voicing your opinion. . . . Being talked to loud in front of other people. Not being able to take a day off even if you are sick or a family member dies.[80]

This worker was later fired for this action, after which he pressed for an OSHA investigation of unfair labor practices at his former workplace. Another worker, the aforementioned Collins, was very clear about his willingness to speak out and be heard in the media. When I said to him "I will use a false name for you in anything I write up from this interview, unless you would like it otherwise," he responded: "You can write my name anywhere you want to. I want people to know who I am and what I'm saying."[81]

Several workers articulated their circumstances and grievances through their experiences as men and women of color in an unequal society. One female worker referred to her manager as a "prejudiced, chauvinistic, racist."[82] Another female worker declared: ". . . it was mostly all black folks [working in the MRF], about four Mexicans and no white folks. Yes, they had us slaving, we was back in slavery."[83]

Critiquing the racially biased authority structure at one firm, one man said:

I would love to see more people of color in positions of authority over there because all the bigwigs are white. Black folks are the peons over there. And then they shipped illegal immigrants in there at night under cover of darkness. . . . And they probably hired them so they could lower their wages to about half what we [blacks] is making. And if you ever go down to the facility you'll see what goes in and out of there . . . nothing but garbage, blacks, and Mexicans.[84]

Intraracial conflict was a theme in many interviews because the temporary agency (REM) that hired workers for WMX was owned by African Americans. REM and WMX had promised that workers would be eligible to join a union after a 90-day probation period. Few if any workers ever made it through 90 consecutive days, however. One female recycler told me that she had confronted the manager of the agency and accused him of firing and rehiring workers to avoid paying them union wages:

When people are getting their 90 days then you want to lay them off. He said "That ain't got nothing to do with it," but I said "Yes it do, it has a lot to do with it, because you don't want us in the union." And I told [the African American manager]: "You know what, Jack? Instead of you trying to help the next black man, you're a black person up there doing a little something for yourself and you're trying to kick the next black man in the back. You don't want them to get up there, and that ain't right."[85]

This worker's criticism reveals that REM's role in the Blue Bag system parallels that of political leaders in Robbins and on the West Side during the Operation Silver Shovel scandal.

Workers were well aware of the contradictions between recycling's public image and the personal trials they were subjected to. One worker said: "There are so many smells that you come across, they make your stomach queasy. Yet before we went to work, they showed us a safety film where all the stuff was really clean."[86]

A Latina worker who later quit her job at the MRF explained:

. . . they told us that it was going to be a clean work environment. They said that fresh air was going to be pumped through there every 15 minutes, so it wouldn't smell, and stuff like that, but it wasn't. It was a little different than they had described it. One time they had a dead dog . . . go through there. There was all garbage, you know [not just recyclables]. At first we thought they were only talking about plastic bottles and cans going through there. But that was plain garbage, everything, you know? Dirty diapers, cleaning products, and stuff like that.[87]

Many workers exercised their option to leave. The coercive work environment and the extreme occupational hazards were generally cited as the reasons for this type of response. Another Chicana worker told me: "The [heaters] upstairs would make you so hot sometimes we had to turn them off and that's how some people got sick. This one guy he got pneumonia. They told him he had to either work or go home, and that wasn't right. He left."[88]

Workers' responses to hazards and coercion included "everyday forms of resistance."[89] Some common forms this hidden resistance took were muted character assassinations directed at management and silent refusal to touch things on the line that were perceived as "too nasty" or "dangerous." The latter often angered managers because it had a negative impact on the plant's productivity. A worker named Seela explained: ". . . if [a pile of garbage] was too high, I just let it go. Plain and simple. That's what every-body else was doing. [The feeling was] 'Hey, if you can't see nothing, just back away from it and let it pass.'" I asked: "But would that end up mess-ing up the process?" Seela replied: "Yeah 'cause then the manager would come up on the line and be all really bitchy, seeing that so much went down that wasn't supposed to go down. He would be talkin' all crazy."[90]

In one instance, workers' responses included an extreme form of resis-tance. A manager explained:

Did you ever hear about the riot at WMX? You know, it was the week of Christmas and people had been working a lot of overtime. But management didn't keep track of their hours so people were getting checks for like $1.05 and $1.50 for two weeks of work. So the workers rioted. They tore the hell out of the dining room, knock-ing over tables, breaking out windows and all kinds of stuff.[91]

Management responded accordingly:

Ken Carlson was the site supervisor for REM, and when things took a turn for the worse, when everybody started to riot at the plant . . . we had armed guards. I don't know if they were policemen or not, but they looked like street thugs. They were sitting around the dining room making sure that workers weren't going to bust any windows out or anything.[92]

Despite these efforts, the workers remained embedded in a larger social and political process that continued to support and ignore these environmental inequalities. In fact, most of WMX's employees were forced to choose between their safety and a job.

Workers at WMX resisted and shaped the nature of environmental inequalities at the MRFs. Through a variety of strategies, they responded to managerial decision making and environmentalist ideology, and this may have empowered them in significant ways. Even so, workers were never able to organize collectively in a formal sense, particularly since union eli-gibility was routinely denied them. In addition, the environmental injus-tices at WMX remain so entrenched and severe that, despite the range of resistance strategies workers drew on, most report that it remains a highly undesirable and unsafe job.

## Discussion

The stories of the Northwest Incinerator and the Blue Bag are often de-linked in the minds of Chicago environmental activists, who neatly separate the glorious victory over the Northwest burner from the miserable failure of the Blue Bag system. Unfortunately, the two are intimately linked, because the shutdown of the burner ushered in the startup of the Blue Bag. Furthermore, in virtually every proclamation of opposition against the Northwest Incinerator, activists took a stand in favor of recycling. They even had a ready-made infrastructure in place: non-profit community-based recyclers who had been providing recycling services for decades. This is one example where the environmental movement went beyond the typical "Just say no" framework and actually had a tangible, working model of what we could say yes to: recycling. Unfortunately, the movement was overpowered by the largest waste hauler in the world and its close ties with the city. Even so, the existing non-profit recycling centers produced their own problems and were anything but perfect. The point to remember here is that the EJ movement was successful at influencing policy but was not able to achieve its desired goals.

The EJ and anti-toxics movements now seemed to have reached a consensus that city dumps, landfills, and incinerators are bad for the environment and bad for people's health. Thus far, however, there seems to be no such consensus on the recycling industry. Ironically, while the recycling industry enjoys the veneer of environmental responsibility, it is often a source of significant social and environmental inequalities confronting workers and communities of color.

The existence of a hazardous work environment in a materials recovery facility is best understood against the backdrop of a larger profile of secondary labor markets where people of color are concentrated. African Americans, overrepresented in dangerous and "high-risk" jobs, have a national rate of occupational injury and illness 37 percent greater than the rate for white workers.[93] Latinos suffer similarly disproportionate hazards. In California, Latino men were "80 percent more likely to suffer a disabling injury or illness than whites, while black men were 40 percent more likely."[94] Women in California suffered lower injury rates than men, but the proportionate ethnic differences are also present. Latinas "were almost 60 percent more likely than their white co-workers and black women were almost 40 percent more likely than their white co-workers to suffer a disabling injury or illness."[95] Studies also reveal that workers in hazardous occupations have little job security and are rarely rewarded for creativity and innovation.[96]

What caused and shaped the environmental injustices at WMX? Three main factors were at work: (1) Environmentalists, neighborhood groups, the state, and industry collectively praised recycling as a policy that would achieve resource conservation (i.e., it would solve the landfill crisis) and job creation. This ideology, put into action, led to the shutdown of the Northwest Incinerator. (2) WMX's management maintained hazardous working conditions and an oppressive social environment. (3) In response to factors 1 and 2, workers at WMX drew on a range of resistance strategies, from "hidden resistance" to outright rebellion.

Research on environmental racism can benefit from the cases of WMX and the Resource Center in three ways.

First, it is clear that there are variations in the nature and the degree of environmental inequalities. Without question, the environmental inequalities at WMX were more extreme than those at the Resource Center. We should also pay attention to that fact that environmental injustices experienced by residents in close proximity to each of these centers are distinct from those experienced by workers. In other words, there are different types of environmental injustices rather than a monolithic brand of hazard imposed upon communities and workers.

Second, worker resistance was a major factor in the emergence and the nature of environmental inequality. Although worker resistance at WMX was constant, it was largely unorganized and often ineffective. The inefficacy was attributable to several factors, including the lack of union bargaining power and the high turnover rate at the plant (which essentially meant that a new cohort of workers entered the plant every few months to begin the process all over). This is not to dismiss worker resistance at WMX altogether. In fact, because of worker resistance, OSHA inspected and fined the facility (although both times whistle blowers paid for their actions by losing their jobs), and hidden forms of resistance like refusing to sort certain piles of waste had direct impacts on the plant's productivity. These struggles are always in progress, and studies reporting only on success or failure in the siting of LULUs and other hazards miss the important processes that shape these outcomes.

Third, the environmental inequalities at WMX did not result simply from the company's perpetrating injustices against the workers. Rather, they were part of a larger, multi-stakeholder process that involved collaboration, conflict, and cross-cutting allegiances among stakeholders. The government's legitimacy lies in its ability to provide jobs and public security for citizens and workers and in its providing a conducive political economic climate in which capital can flourish. These goals were at odds in this case. Neighborhood and community-based environmental organizations sought good jobs for their residents. On Chicago's Southeast Side, however, these organizations unwittingly connected unemployed residents with hazardous jobs at WMX. And environmentalists wished for a comprehensive recycling system that conserved resources and created jobs. However, their principal criticisms of the Blue Bag program focused on the ecological failures of the system (attributed to low recycling rates), not on the occupational safety risks and the low wages. This oversight is revealing of the continued lack of solidarity between the environmental and labor movements. The environmental justice framework in this book captures the above dynamics in ways that suggest that the origins of and the struggles against environmental hazards are much more complex than was previously thought.

## Conclusion

Chicago has a long history of managing solid waste through both traditional and innovative methods. Traditional methods include waging garbage wars in the neighborhoods, perpetrating environmental racism, and dumping waste along the path of least resistance. More innovative methods include non-profit recycling and composting. Aluminum recycling got its start in Chicago in 1904, the scrap metal industry had its start here, and Chicago was home to the first community-based non-profit recyclers. Chicago is also the city where WMX was born and where its current corporate headquarters are located. This is also the region of the country where the US Supreme Court entered a garbage war and handed down a decision that helped seal the fate of the largest municipal waste incinerator in the Western Hemisphere. The shutdown of the Northwest Incinerator, however, would not have happened if not for the presence of a multi-racial coalition of organizations mobilized in opposition to the burner. The unfortunate aftermath of this victory was the reassertion of control by WMX, the parent company of the incinerator firm. WMX introduced the Blue Bag recycling system, possibly the most high-tech, hazardous, anti-ecological, and fiscally irresponsible waste management program ever devised. Recycling rates were never higher than 6 percent, workers were constantly injured and hospitalized, and city taxpayers shelled out tens of millions of dollars to put this "win-win" policy into motion.[97]

On the eve of the Blue Bag's debut, the non-profit community-based recyclers were in greater jeopardy than ever. Once the Blue Bag program was operational, the city withdrew all fiscal support for the non-profits, except for the mobile buy-back program the Resource Center and WMX developed. The RC's Uptown spinoff folded and sold its assets back to the parent organization, and the RC itself was in dire straits. Some workers warned that alley entrepreneurs and other indigent clientele could "literally starve to death"[98] if the non-profits went under. Jim Burris of the Uptown station remarked wryly: ". . . solid waste recycling had moved from being a type of social movement driven by a set of environmental ideals/assumptions and grounded in a concern for local neighborhoods, to becoming a commercially-driven industry, grounded essentially in competition and profit maximization by well-capitalized corporations and local governments working closely with those corporations. As environmental activists we found this premise to be, at the same time, factual, a sign of a certain type of 'success' of the recycling movement."[99]

This was a dismal period in Chicago's environmental history. Workers of color were being injured, communities of color were still being dumped on, the EJ movement had faltered, and the original community-based recyclers were becoming extinct. Moreover, one of the movement's arch-enemies, WMX, was taking credit for launching a citywide recycling system.

In the next and final chapter, I piece together the many fronts of the Chicago garbage wars I have considered since the first chapter. I revisit the environmental justice framework and raise questions about research, the movement, and policy concerning environmental justice.

# 7

## Toward Environmental Justice

[Mary McDowell] maintained that a garbage disposal system which placed a burden of ill health upon one section of a community, even though it benefited other sections, was unjust and undemocratic and unwise for all concerned. She argued that continued municipal prosperity was impossible while one part of the community suffered unnecessarily.[1]

This book began as a study of environmental racism's causes, its insidious effects on humankind and the biosphere, and the many movements that have emerged to combat it. However, as I observed and spoke with community residents, workers, activists, industry representatives, and government employees of all racial and ethnic backgrounds, it became clear that, to one degree or another, solid waste and pollution are in everyone's back yard. There is no denying that politically marginal, low-income, and people of color populations bear the heaviest burden. But sooner or later, the affluent, the elites, and middle-class white communities will have to confront environmental contamination in their homes, neighborhoods, and workplaces. This is because we in the global North are producing more waste every year and becoming increasingly dependent upon chemical-intensive production for most consumer and commercial products and because pollution knows no boundaries.[2] Following Mary McDowell's warning, I believe that no community will be ecologically sustainable while others suffocate under the burden of toxics and solid waste. The fate of relatively pollution free communities is intimately linked to the fate of contaminated communities. In the meantime, we must confront environmental inequalities head on.

The terms *environmental racism* and *environmental justice* sum up what the problems and solutions are; what the movement in poor neighborhoods and communities of color is fighting against and what they are fighting for. These two polar opposites cannot be overemphasized because, as the late Kwame Túre (formerly Stokely Carmichael of the Black Panther Party) once told an audience, "movements are usually very clear about what they are fighting *against*, but all too frequently they are not very clear about what they are fighting *for*."[3] The transfer of this dilemma to the EJ movement is simple enough, and stated succinctly by another great leader, farm worker organizer, and EJ activist Baldemar Velasquez: "When I walk into a field to organize farm workers, I can tell them to say 'no' to pesticides and herbicides, but then I also have to give them an alternative—something to say 'yes' to."[4]

A recurring theme throughout the garbage wars in Chicago's history was that the solutions to waste problems (i.e., what communities have said "yes" to) were later discovered to create more problems, more injustices. In what I have termed the movement-policy cycle, since the 1880s, communities in Chicago and around the United States have protested polluting and dangerous technologies, directly influencing the next generation of waste management "solutions." Unfortunately, as was the case with reduction plants, waste-to-energy incinerators, sanitary landfills, and recycling technologies, each of these developments created nearly as much (if not more) pollution as the last. Furthermore, in each case, these new solutions were experimented with in communities and workplaces where people of color, immigrants, and low-income persons were concentrated. The good news is that the EJ movement does have a measurable impact on policy. The bad news is that the movement is often faced with limited and inappropriate choices, or is simply excluded from the implementation process.

## The Environmental Justice Framework

A significant body of research concludes that low-income persons and people of color are carrying a heavier toxic load than the rest of us. This is environmental inequality and environmental racism. However, we remain in need of a conceptual framework that would shed light on how this phenomenon unfolds. In this book I have done just that. By building upon previous studies and examining Chicago's garbage wars, I provide an answer to the question: What are the causes and consequences of environmental racism? I propose a framework that emphasizes

• the importance of the history of environmental racism and the processes by which it unfolds

• the role of multiple stakeholders in these conflicts

• the role of social stratification by race and class,

and

• the ability of those least powerful segments of society to shape the contours of environmental justice struggles.

This framework moves us beyond a model of environmental racism where pollution is unilaterally and uniformly imposed upon a population that reacts, toward a vision wherein many stakeholders display their full complexity and would-be victims become active agents in resisting and shaping environmental inequalities before, during, and after they emerge.

Within this framework, we also move beyond a view wherein the outcomes of EJ struggles consist simply of the *presence or absence* of hazards, to a vision in which we can explain variations in patterns of environmental inequalities. Environmental racism develops and changes over time and space. Thus, we cannot overstate the importance of studying history and process. For example, in the stories detailed in this book, different stakeholders accessed varying amounts of resources across the cases. Specifically, environmental inequalities are more or less pronounced across cases because residents, workers, or environmentalists have lesser or greater power relative to government and corporations.

This framework assists us in understanding the process by which environmental injustices unfold. Without a satisfactory explanation of how environmental inequalities develop, our understandings of why and how people suffer from them are lacking. Furthermore, we place policy makers and activists who might seek to remedy these social problems at a disadvantage.

It should be clear from the four dimensions of this framework that environmental inequalities are not always simply imposed unilaterally by one class or race of people on another. Rather, like all forms of inequality, environmental inequalities are relationships that are formed and often change through struggle among many groups—stakeholders. Acts of environmental racism are also acts of social injustice and the abuse of power. But it is also about opposition to these forces—the struggle for environmental justice. This is why we must include worker and community resistance as part of the process whereby environmental inequalities emerge rather than simply as a reaction to them.

What are the driving forces behind environmental racism? In a sentence, it is the quest for political, cultural, psychological, social, and economic dominance and security. Those racial, class, and stakeholder groups with the ability, the power, and the resources to achieve such dominance and security do so at the expense of the less powerful. When different stakeholders struggle for access to valuable resources within the political economy, the benefits and costs of those resources become distributed unevenly. That is, those stakeholders who are unable to mobilize resources (political, economic, etc.) will most likely bear the brunt of environmental inequalities. Conversely, those stakeholders with the greatest access to valuable resources are able to enjoy cleaner and safer working, living, and recreational environments. In communities and workplaces where environmental racism is evident, people of color, low-income populations, and politically marginal groups host more than their fair share of the pollution, the toxins, and the risk. These hazards have an undeniable and often irreversible effect on the health of entire communities.

Thinking back to the garbage wars detailed in chapters 2–6, we can apply this framework to understand the production of environmental racism.

The first dimension of the EJ framework emphasizes the importance of history and the process by which these conflicts unfold. Tracing the history of different methods of waste management in Chicago and other major US cities, we observe the following cycle, indicating the dominant methods used.

- 1880s–1910s: city dumps, reduction plants, reuse
- 1920s–early 1940s: incinerators
- World War II–1950s: sanitary landfills
- 1960s–early 1970s: incinerators
- 1976–1989: sanitary landfills, incineration, recycling
- 1990–present: incinerators, sanitary landfills, recycling

These changes, occurring over more than a century, reflect the movement-policy cycle, wherein environmental and community organizations oppose the dominant waste management technology and spawn the development of new forms. So, for example, when Mary McDowell and other neighborhood reformers protested the discriminatory waste dumping in poor and immigrant wards, the use of reduction technology was proposed and adopted. Years later, a new round of garbage wars produced the next stage in the "evolution" of waste management technology, and so forth. What is unsettling about this history is that it is a cycle. It has repeated itself. This reveals that one or more of the following may be to blame:

• society's lack of creativity

• society's inattention to the past

• efforts by powerful institutions to restrict our ability to discover and develop ecologically sustainable technologies.

The evidence suggests that, while each of these three factors is at work, the third one is the major reason why waste management methods are as rudimentary and anti-ecological as they have ever been. And since the first garbage wars in Chicago, that city's waste continues to be imposed on people of color, immigrants, and the working poor. In that regard, very little has changed. Race and racism have always shaped waste management policies.

The second dimension of the EJ framework underscores the importance of analyzing the role of the many stakeholders in EJ struggles. The Resource Center and People for Community Recovery have perhaps played some of the most intriguing roles as defenders against—and sometimes beneficiaries of—environmental inequality. The Resource Center, like any organization, must take care to ensure its own survival. But this instinct led to the implementation of a solid-waste-management plan that targeted poor neighborhoods and communities of color for the siting of recycling facilities. The Resource Center and many other environmental groups were nearly successful at getting the Illinois Legislature to pass an "Environmental Justice" bill whose goal was to place more recycling firms in communities of color. These policies were well-intentioned, but they would have resulted in the exacerbation of existing environmental injustices via the importation of more waste into these areas. People for Community Recovery is also revered as a veteran EJ organization that has fought some of the world's biggest polluters. When WMX offered to construct a recycling system and provide jobs for unemployed men and women in PCR's neighborhood, this appeared to be a solution to the "jobs versus environment" dilemma. So, as PCR willingly and understandably recruited residents to work in the recycling facilities, they unwittingly sent these folks into one of the most hazardous workplaces in Chicago. These examples underscore that the line between perpetrator and community defender in environmental justice conflicts can become blurred. But the important thing to note is that if we understand this as a complex, multi-stakeholder process, we can also understand *why* environmental justice advocates would sometimes support seemingly environmentally unjust policies.

The third dimension of the EJ framework reminds us that institutional inequality is a major driver of environmental injustices. Without understanding institutional and historic inequality, we can never fully comprehend Operation Silver Shovel and the Robbins Incinerator battles as anything more than "corrupt politicians on the take." In both cases, the political leaders' actions resembled a classic colonial arrangement as much as they resembled old-time Chicago politics. The alderman in the African American community of Lawndale had every incentive to take bribes in return for illegal dumping and the use of unlawful "recycling" operations. He, like most African American aldermen, was neither independently wealthy nor terribly influential in the City Council. His constituents, all African Americans, mostly working-class and poor, were unlikely to raise a fuss over another LULU in the 'hood and were not very politically active. The typical result: White middle-class neighborhoods receive better roads, newer developments, and Lawndale gets their garbage. The Robbins Incinerator war was no different. Robbins, an all-African-American village, could hardly attract a gas station, let alone get any major business developers to set up shop in the area. The only business that agreed to locate in this desperately poor village was a toxics-spewing garbage burner. While many EJ activists portrayed Mayor Brodie as a sellout and a pawn, her only choice at the moment was to accept an incredibly hazardous form of economic development or none at all. The reason why this situation is emblematic of the colonialism that African Americans still struggle against is because Robbins's human, economic, and political capital have always been dependent upon white-dominated businesses and political entities in Chicago, in Springfield, and in Washington. This dependence (not altogether different from the relationship between the Global North and the Global South) is built upon and reinforces racial and class hierarchies.

The fourth and final dimension of the EJ framework emphasizes that "it's not over till it's over." In other words, just because a group of politically marginal people are exposed to environmental hazards does not mean the struggle is finished or that the battle has been lost. Environmental injustices are constantly in process because people are continually resisting them. The struggle against the Northwest Incinerator is a perfect example. This garbage war was connected to the shutdown of Chicago's three other incinerators because their closures required that the Northwest burner take nearly 100 percent of the waste. This struggle was for clean air, fiscal responsibility, neighborhood control, and for the environmentally just development of a citywide recycling program. If we end the story of the Northwest Incinerator at the time of its closing, it would appear that the EJ movement was wildly successful. But if we continue the story to include the development of the Blue Bag recycling system, we understand that the movement's goals were usurped by powerful forces who then imposed more garbage on the city's Latino and African American populations. Resistance on the shop floor at WMX's MRFs was crucial to bringing this case to light and helped activists reframe recycling as a form of environmental racism in communities and workplaces. The struggle against WMX and the Blue Bag is a garbage war that rages on today. The Resource Center and its allies continue to fight to stay afloat and anticipate the day when the Blue Bag contract will expire and the political process opens up once again. The Robbins case is also a good example of the power of continuous resistance. Most observers might have predicted that after the Robbins Incinerator was constructed the battle was over. But EJ activists continued to mobilize until they succeeded in shutting the burner down—three years after it was built. This story should instill hope for environmental justice and a deeper understanding of the processes by which garbage wars unfold and evolve.

Not only do the findings from these cases point to the deeply flawed nature of environmental policy making; they also underscore the fundamental pervasiveness of racial and class inequality in US society. Without attention to race and class divisions within communities of color, we lose sight of the forced choices that low-skilled workers, communities, and social movements have to make every day. A former recycling worker put it best: "It was one of the nastiest jobs I've ever had. No, it was THE nastiest job, right? And the pay wasn't all that hot considering the work we were doing and the danger we were in. But all in all, it was a job."[5]

## Sociology and Environmental Justice

Recently there has been a strong emphasis by some environmental sociologists on the study of political economy and its impact on natural and social systems. This area of research has been led most notably by Allan Schnaiberg and his collaborators (Kenneth Gould, Adam Weinberg, and this author) who have proposed the "treadmill of production" model,[6] wherein, as capital is invested in markets, economic expansion comes at the cost of environmental and social integrity. Profit and shareholder value are prioritized over other concerns, and workers and politically marginal stakeholders tend to bear the brunt of economic, social, and environmental problems. Because of the deep-seated ideology of "growth at all costs," the government (supported by industry, workers, and consumers) continues to provide capital outlays for economic expansion under the logic that fiscal growth will eventually meet society's needs. This model illuminates the contradictory behavior of many stakeholders. For example, the state often disempowers itself by providing massive support and authority to the private sector. Through downsizing and reengineering, the private sector often threatens its own interests by instilling disloyalty among the workers and consumers upon which it depends. Workers tend to support pro-growth policies that boost productivity but often lead to wage cuts or even layoffs. Environmentalists support anti-pollution initiatives without also pushing for a reduction in overall social inequality—the root cause of ecological destruction. When one stakeholder (or more) proposes a policy change that might threaten the treadmill of production, most other stakeholders will generally oppose these measures. Thus the treadmill model provides insight into the fierce resistance that community and environmental activists encountered when they mobilized against the Northwest and Robbins incinerators. But the treadmill model also aids us in understanding why so many stakeholders support recycling, despite its own negative impacts on the natural and working environments.

It is my hope that environmental sociology will begin to shed more light on the links between community-level pollution and workplace environmental issues. The absence of a serious labor component in environmental studies and the lack of an environmental component in labor studies reinforces the popular "jobs versus environment" myth that activists and policy makers routinely contend with. Moreover, theories of social inequality in general will benefit from a serious consideration of the role of environmental inequalities in all institutions. For example, it is often the case that where we find disparities in income and quality of life we also find environmental inequalities.

## Conclusion: The Broader Context

The recent successes and setbacks of the environmental justice movement must be placed against a backdrop of rising political, economic, and social discord around the world. At the root of that discord is the growing disparity between the wealthy and the poor within and between nations. Social inequality has increased dramatically in the past three decades.[7] This increase is due in large part to the acceleration of transnational or global economic activity, which has pitted individuals, social classes, racial and ethnic groups, neighborhoods, cities, regions, and even nation-states against one another in a competitive world system.[8] Urban centers in the United States and around the world are in the midst of a restructuring crisis that has continued through de-industrialization, corporate downsizing, and a commitment to "free trade." My hope is that the environmental justice movement will continue to work with labor, human rights, women's rights, and the global justice movement to directly target the institutions supporting free trade, particularly transnational corporations. Environmental justice in Chicago, the United States, and on Mother Earth will never be achieved without resisting corporate power and the ideology of profit before people and the environment that supports it. A more difficult task, however, will be undoing the colonial legacies that many of us support and reinforce every day.

# Appendix
## The Principles of Environmental Justice

Adopted at the First National People of Color Environmental Leadership Summit, October 24–27, 1991, Washington, D.C.

### Preamble

We, the people of color, gathered together at this multinational People of Color Environmental Leadership Summit, to begin to build a national and international movement of all peoples of color to fight the destruction and taking of our lands and communities, do hereby re-establish our spiritual interdependence to the sacredness of our Mother Earth; to respect and celebrate each of our cultures, languages and beliefs about the natural world and our roles in healing ourselves; to insure environmental justice; to promote economic alternatives which would contribute to the development of environmentally safe livelihoods; and, to secure our political, economic and cultural liberation that has been denied for over 500 years of colonization and oppression, resulting in the poisoning of our communities and land and the genocide of our peoples, do affirm and adopt these Principles of Environmental Justice:

1. Environmental justice affirms the sacredness of Mother Earth, ecological unity and the interdependence of all species, and the right to be free from ecological destruction.

2. Environmental justice demands that public policy be based on mutual respect and justice for all peoples, free from any form of discrimination or bias.

3. Environmental justice mandates the right to ethical, balanced and responsible uses of land and renewable resources in the interest of a sustainable planet for humans and other living things.

4. Environmental justice calls for universal protection from nuclear testing, extraction, production and disposal of toxic/hazardous wastes and poisons and nuclear testing that threaten the fundamental right to clean air, land, water, and food.

5. Environmental justice affirms the fundamental right to political, economic, cultural and environmental self-determination of all peoples.

6. Environmental justice demands the cessation of the production of all toxins, hazardous wastes, and radioactive materials, and that all past and current producers be held strictly accountable to the people for detoxification and the containment at the point of production.

7. Environmental justice demands the right to participate as equal partners at every level of decision making including needs assessment, planning, implementation, enforcement and evaluation.

8. Environmental justice affirms the right of all workers to a safe and healthy work environment, without being forced to choose between an unsafe livelihood and unemployment. It also affirms the right of those who work at home to be free from environmental hazards.

9. Environmental justice protects the right of victims of environmental injustice to receive full compensation and reparations for damages as well as quality health care.

10. Environmental justice considers governmental acts of environmental injustice a violation of international law, the Universal Declaration On Human Rights, and the United Nations Convention on Genocide.

11. Environmental justice must recognize a special legal and natural relationship of Native Peoples to the US government through treaties, agreements, compacts, and covenants affirming sovereignty and self-determination.

12. Environmental justice affirms the need for urban and rural ecological policies to clean up and rebuild our cities and rural areas in balance with nature, honoring the cultural integrity of all our communities, and providing fair access for all to the full range of resources.

13. Environmental justice calls for the strict enforcement of principles of informed consent, and a halt to the testing of experimental reproductive and medical procedures and vaccinations on people of color.

14. Environmental justice opposes the destructive operations of multinational corporations.

15. Environmental justice opposes military occupation, repression and exploitation of lands, peoples and cultures, and other life forms.

16. Environmental justice calls for the education of present and future generations which emphasizes social and environmental issues, based on our experience and an appreciation of our diverse cultural perspectives.

17. Environmental justice requires that we, as individuals, make personal and consumer choices to consume as little of Mother Earth's resources and to produce as little waste as possible; and make the conscious decision to challenge and re-prioritize our lifestyles to insure the health of the natural world for present and future generations.

# Notes

## Chapter 1

1. Schnaiberg 1980, p. 5.

2. Melosi 1980, 1981, 2000.

3. Interview with Mary Ryan, spokesperson for WMX, Oakbrook, Illinois, 1994.

4. Interview with Pat James, fall 1995.

5. Environmental inequality or environmental injustice occurs when a particular social group—not necessarily a racial or an ethnic group—is burdened with environmental hazards.

6. Bullard 1990.

7. Silliman 1997, p. 113.

8. See Melosi 1980.

9. Tuttle 1969. The race riot of 1919 was sparked by the drowning of an African American male at a beach that summer. A stone-throwing melee between blacks and whites prevented Eugene Williams from coming ashore safely and he drowned in Lake Michigan. This is a quintessential example of how recreational spots, or what Alston (1990) terms "where we play," were and remain sites of environmental justice struggles. Gender of course played a major role here as shirtless African American men were perceived to be a terror to white women in bathing suits. Hurley (1995) demonstrates that similar dynamics were occurring at beaches in Gary, Indiana during the 1960s and the 1970s. As Taylor (1989) points out, perhaps when scholars and white environmentalists pay attention to this history of racial terrorism in parks, playgrounds, and beaches, they will understand why some people of color may have reservations about "getting back to nature." Gottlieb (1993) also does a nice job of exploring these racist roots of the early conservation movement.

10. Alston 1990, 1991.

11. Rodney 1982. Divide and conquer takes many forms, one of which is to appoint a local "chief" and/or to elevate one ethnic group over another in status. This strategy creates a dynamic wherein one group has incentives (political power, jobs, and psychological benefits that may accompany various perquisites from the colonizer)

to dominate another, while neither is experiencing true freedom. We see this drama played out all over the world.

12. Bryant 1995, p. 6. Environmental racism also includes the pattern of disparate treatment of marginal groups, regardless of intent.

13. Bryant 1995, p. 6.

14. Bryant 1995, p. 6.

15. Rawls 1971, p. 511.

16. Early studies focusing on the association between social class and pollution include the following: Asch and Seneca 1978; Berry 1977; Freeman 1972; Schnaiberg 1973, 1980, 1994. Research that was more explicit about race and pollution included: Bryant 1995; Bryant and Mohai 1992; Bullard 1990, 1993, 1994; Hofrichter 1993; United Church of Christ 1987; Schnaiberg and Gould 1994; Taylor 1993.

17. Chavis 1993.

18. General Accounting Office 1983.

19. United Church of Christ 1987.

20. Greenpeace 1990.

21. Lavelle and Coyle 1992.

22. Feagin and Sikes 1994.

23. US Environmental Protection Agency 1992.

24. Institute of Medicine 1999.

25. In fact, some community organizations began to target all manner of locally unwanted land uses, such as prisons, liquor stores, and highways as environmentally harmful in a broader sense.

26. Interestingly, much of the research that rejects the environmental racism thesis has paid attention to historical factors in EJ struggles—an element that other academics are only recently tuning into. But this spate of studies is also what some scholars and activists are calling a "backlash" against the movement. This research is also limited in several ways. First, much of the recent work in this area is hampered by a focus on statistical analysis, which attempts to contest the claim that environmental racism is an actual social phenomenon (see Anderton, Anderson, Oakes, and Fraser 1994; Been 1993; Coursey 1994; Mitchell, Thomas, and Cutter 1999). These studies generally seek to dispel the claim that polluting facilities seek out low-income and/or poor communities (sometimes referred to as the "chicken and egg debate"). There are myriad problems with this research. First, as Bullard (1994a) points out, these studies fail to consider the range of hazardous facilities confronting communities of color. Instead, each of these studies has focused on a narrow category of waste facilities, with highly questionable claims that the selected sites have been sampled "randomly" (Coursey 1994). Second, there is an infinite regression that occurs in these "chicken and egg" debates over exactly which statistical measures to employ, which unit of analysis is more appropriate (zip code versus census tract) (see Daniels 2000) and other minutiae. Almost all of these dis-

cussions miss what I view as the major point of EJ research and EJ movement struggles: no community should be disproportionately exposed to pollution. (See the appendix.) Some of these studies are so misguided that they cheerfully proclaim that environmental justice is a moot cause because pollution is distributed by class, not race! The problem with such a claim is that the environmental justice movement (and much of the research) has, from the beginning, stressed that race and class are intertwined and that both people of color and low-income populations are disproportionately impacted (Pastor, Sadd, and Hipp 2001). Thus, such researcher "findings" almost explicitly conclude that it is fine to dump toxins on white/low-income populations. Third, with statistical analysis, one always runs into the problem of overlooking the sociopolitical context in which these activities occur. So, for example, even those statistical studies that conclude environmental racism is alive and well can only show correlations and provide little, if any, understanding as to why and how these things happen. Fourth and finally, while we should always consider the role of funding sources behind any research, the study by Anderton et al. (1994) deserves particular mention. This research concluded that waste sites did not disproportionately impact communities of color in the US. While some scholars may want to spend an inordinate amount of time and energy re-analyzing the authors' data, others (including and especially movement activists) underscored that the major source of funding for this research came from Waste Management, Inc. (WMX). WMX is the world's largest waste hauler and is, without a doubt, the corporation most vilified by the environmental justice movement. The fact that it is nearly universally labeled an "environmental criminal" by EJ activists stems from its ownership of numerous landfills, incinerators, and waste transfer stations across the globe *and* from its often scurrilous efforts to undermine grassroots movements and influence (even threaten) politicians and government agencies. Thus, any study of environmental racism funded by this corporation is highly suspect.

27. Since most environmental justice conflicts have occurred over facility siting in neighborhoods, it is clear that housing and real estate markets play a strong role in these dynamics. Housing is an issue in EJ struggles for two principal reasons. First, housing markets reflect long-standing patterns of institutional racism, thus locking people of color out of certain neighborhoods and keeping them concentrated in other, less desirable communities. Secondly, housing quality itself is a primary contributor to environmental health problems in communities of color, with widespread lead-based paint and asthma-causing agents rampant. Housing markets and real estate practices in the US reflect the desires and will of the more politically powerful, the more affluent. This often means that white communities are able to control who moves in and who can leave. Research demonstrates that from restrictive covenants, to redlining, and outright mob violence, white Americans desire communities free of people of color and have worked skillfully and often brutally to achieve this goal (Bullard, Grigsby, and Lee 1993). White communities may sometimes allow a certain number of people of color access to these markets, but will react strongly when the "tipping point" is reached (Massey and Denton 1993). Cities with significant populations of color often engaged in massive experiments to literally "house" people in concentrated, restricted spaces—urban ghettoes and

housing projects (Hirsch 1990). Other municipalities (e.g., Boulder, Colorado) developed specifically around plans to keep a "city beautiful." This meant driving out and/or repelling both certain types of industry and their associated less desirable working class and ethnic elements (Delgado and Stefancic 1999). Every year there are reports that African American housing applicants are denied mortgage loans in record numbers while white applicants with identical qualifications are accepted. African Americans at every socioeconomic status level are highly segregated in the US. Chicago, Illinois, for example, was more racially segregated than apartheid-era South Africa during the 1980s. What this means for people of color is that when neighborhoods become inundated with pollution they are less likely to be able to move "up and out" into cleaner communities. Whites, on the other hand, are more likely to be able to "buy their way into" more desirable areas. Recent research also has begun to make links among race, environmental quality, and transportation systems (Bullard and Johnson 1997; Bullard, Johnson, and Torres 2000). Robert Bullard and his colleagues at Clark Atlanta University have traced the history of America's two-tiered, racially biased transportation infrastructure, from early conflicts over "separate but equal" accommodations, through the "urban renewal" that followed development of the interstate highway system that disrupted, displaced, bisected, and bypassed many inner city neighborhoods, to today's "auto addiction" and sprawl that exacerbates the problems of pollution and ecological damage. A former Director of the United Church of Christ Commission on Racial Justice, Charles Lee, has described sprawl as "a scenario where we are literally driving each other apart." Resistance to "transportation racism" in the US dates at least as far back as the 1896 *Plessy vs. Ferguson* Supreme Court decision that racial segregation in rail cars was constitutional as long as the facilities were "equal." The 1948 March on Washington Movement was initiated by the great labor leader A. Philip Randolph and the Brotherhood of Sleeping Car Porters. The civil rights movement saw its first major successes in the form of city bus boycotts. And the student movement linked with civil rights activists on the Freedom Rides, with students testing the Supreme Court's ruling against discrimination in interstate travel by riding through the South in racially integrated buses. As the activist-scholar Eric Mann has argued, the two-tiered transportation system in the US is both classist and racist. Mann's Labor/Community Strategy Center in Los Angeles has successfully challenged these inequities on several occasions. Today, church leaders, politicians, community activists and environmentalists alike have come together to combat urban sprawl and the myriad environmental, social, and economic problems associated with it. So transportation is an EJ issue because it creates urban and suburban sprawl, auto pollution, and inefficient and inequitable distribution of resources by class and race.

28. Bullard and Wright 1993; Chavez 1993; Johnson and Oliver 1989; Robinson 1991.

29. Perfecto and Velasquez 1992.

30. Castleman 1987; Roberts 1993.

31. Robinson 1991.

32. LaDou 1985.

33. Berman 1978; Kazis and Grossman 1982; Nelkin and Brown 1984; Roberts 1993, 2001.

34. Navarro 1982.

35. For excellent analyses and critiques of traditional US-based conservation movements, see Gottlieb 1993, 2001; Hays 1969; Jacoby 2001; Taylor 1989.

36. Alston 1990.

37. I am indebted to Adam Weinberg for pointing out this distinction between process and outcomes and the fact that so little EJ research focuses on the former. See Weinberg 1998.

38. Been 1993; Bullard 1990, 1994b; Bryant 1995; Cole and Foster 2001; Foster 2000; Lavelle and Coyle 1992.

39. Hurley 1995, Hersch 1995, Pulido et al. 1996, Szasz and Meuser 1998. Roberts and Toffolon-Weiss (2001) have written a ground-breaking historical and ethnographic study of a range of EJ conflicts in Louisiana.

40. Coursey 1994; Mitchell, Thomas, and Cutter 1999.

41. See Weinberg 1997. The unique value of ethnographic investigation over all other methodologies is that the researcher can actually observe people in everyday situations, in the context in which social behavior naturally occurs. Researchers can also use this method to verify that what people claim they do (in interviews or surveys) is actually what they do.

42. For studies that reveal how grassroots groups shape corporate and state policies, see Hurley 1995, Pulido 1996b, and Walsh, Warland, and Smith 1997. Walsh et al. reveal that many grassroots "technology movements" successfully defeat incinerators before they are ever built. Pulido demonstrates that Chicanos in one Southwestern town proactively created a sustainable enterprise that provided economic and ecological benefits to the community, thereby defining their own identity and life circumstances. Hurley documents the "give and take" and the ebbs and flows of progress in the struggle by the Hatcher administration, residents, and neighbors of Gary, Indiana to ensure that US Steel (USX) complied with environmental regulations while remaining economically solvent. An example of how the environmental inequality process is shaped was the success (and later failures) this coalition achieved in making USX change their production practices. Again, my intention here is to propose that scholars synthesize these findings into a more coherent theoretical understanding of environmental inequality.

43. For more on resistance as an important theoretical issue in understanding how the face of environmental quality changes over time, see Pellow 2000.

44. See Gould, Schnaiberg, and Weinberg 1996; Schnaiberg 1980; Schnaiberg and Gould 1994.

45. See Weinberg, Pellow, and Schnaiberg 2000—the first major study of the US recycling industry.

46. Nyden, Figert, Shibley, and Burrows 1997; Park and Pellow 1996; Stoecker 1996; Stoecker and Bonacich 1992. Advocacy research should not be confused with

"participatory research," but the main distinction is that in the first model, the academic accepts responsibility and accountability for the entirety of the work; advocacy research is viewed as a vehicle through which the activist-scholar can advocate for a cause, not necessarily the result of a partnership and collaboration between the scholar and community members (as is the case in participatory research).

47. Peer-reviewed research is that which has been subjected to the scrutiny of other academic peers before it is published. Activists from People for Community Recovery, the Chicago Recycling Coalition, Citizens for a Better Environment, the South Cook County Environmental Action Coalition, the Center for Neighborhood Technology, and the Midwest Center for Labor Research have read and critiqued portions of this book prior to publication.

48. Much of the data I gathered from documents, interviews, and observations with environmentalists or managers and workers at recycling plants were reciprocated with voluntary labor (as participant observation), informal consulting, and the presentation of research findings. Voluntary labor at some of the field sites greatly enhanced data quality. In my capacity as an environmental justice activist in the city of Chicago, I also gained a great deal of information and entree to settings that would have otherwise been inaccessible. I served on the Board of Directors of the Chicago Recycling Coalition, an organization committed to promoting community-based, non-profit recycling. The CRC is adamantly opposed to the recycling program run by WMX, the for-profit company highlighted in chapter 6. I served on the board of directors of Uptown Recycling, which later merged with the non-profit organization featured in chapter 5, the Resource Center. I also worked as a volunteer and staff member for People for Community Recovery, an organization that has been fighting environmental racism on Chicago's South Side since 1982. I openly used those positions to gather information and make policy recommendations to community and movement organizations, the recycling public, and the waste industry.

49. Bullard 1993.

## Chapter 2

1. Heuchling 1913.

2. Along with Mary McDowell, Hull House founder Jane Addams led the fight against unsound waste disposal practices in Chicago, calling garbage "the greatest menace in a ward such as ours" (Gottlieb 1993, p. 61). Successfully bidding to become the garbage inspector in the 19th Ward, Addams formed a patrol that monitored the garbage wagons as they traveled through the neighborhoods to the city dump. The Hull House was virtually *the* center of community-based political activity during the Progressive Era of municipal reform in Chicago. It was recognized nationally and internationally as such. Jane Addams and Mary McDowell were much sought after for speaking engagements around the US and Europe. Journalists and political radicals like Upton Sinclair spent a good deal of time at Hull House. Addams and her associates also worked hard to provide better lives for at-risk children in immigrant neighborhoods.

3. It is important to remember that, although the term "environmental justice" and the movement fighting for this cause came into being in the 1980s, immigrants, indigenous peoples, the poor, and people of color have been dealing with these issues for a much longer time. I also note that Addams was a tireless crusader for racial justice, writing and speaking publicly against discrimination and violence directed at people of color.

4. Chicago's garbage problems were many. First, there was simply too much waste being generated by the city's residents, due both to an increase in per capita production *and* to large increases in population. Second, the Chicago Reduction Company (Chicago's principal waste management facility at the time) broke down and was no longer receiving materials. So the city began to fill up clay pits and wetlands, which some observers decried as "crude and primitive." Finally, there were constant protests from communities who either were the unfortunate hosts of waste sites, or felt they were not receiving adequate city services in the form of waste collections, or both.

5. Mary McDowell. 1913. *City Club Bulletin*. December 20 (emphasis added).

6. These "smoking guns" of environmental racism and state-corporate repression continue to surface. The Cerrell Report was a 1984 publication commissioned by the California Waste Management Board during the height of the post-RCRA "NIMBY" battles wherein it seemed like no community would accept a waste facility. Cerrell and Associates conducted a study and concluded that the easiest places to site waste facilities were lower income neighborhoods populated with less politically active and less educated persons. Later the Epley report surfaced. This was a study commissioned by the state of North Carolina that profiled those communities least likely to resist the placement of a low level nuclear waste site. The community profiles paralleled those in the Cerrell Report. And more recently, a memo written by Lawrence Summers, then the Vice President of the World Bank (and later the Secretary of the Treasury under President Clinton) was leaked. Summers writes: ". . . shouldn't the World Bank be encouraging *more* [his emphasis] migration of the dirty industries to LDCs [Less Developed Countries]?. . . A given amount of health impairing pollution should be done in the country with the lowest cost, which will be the country with the lowest wages. I think the economic logic behind dumping a load of toxic waste in the lowest wage country is impeccable and we should face up to that." (Gibbs 1992, p. 2) In many activists' opinion, this memo is the smoking gun of global environmental racism. The discovery of these reports and memos enraged EJ activists and only confirmed their suspicions that environmental racism is not the result of impersonal and invisible "market forces" (see Been 1993) at work; rather, it is deliberate and by design.

7. For example, in medieval German principalities street cleaning work was often assigned to Jews. In caste-era India, the lowest caste (untouchables) were generally assigned the task of refuse removal. Immigrant neighborhoods throughout nineteenth-century Europe and the United States were not only the sites of disproportionate waste dumping, they were also the lowest priorities for city services like waste collection (see Melosi 1980; Gottlieb 1993).

8. Mumford 1961.

9. Melosi 1981, p. 41.

10. Carless 1992, p. 11.

11. Gottlieb 1993, p. 54.

12. Gottlieb 1993, p. 54. Also see Melosi 1981, p. 43. Other examples abound. In the January 1883 issue of *The Sanitary News*, one observer wrote: "A strong argument for the continuance of the Immigrant Inspection Service is found in the work which has been accomplished since its inauguration in June last. . . . Small pox is introduced into this country by immigrants who have such an inexcusable dread of vaccination that they will resort to almost any measures to avoid it." (p. 53) In March of that year, the same publication carried an equally inflammatory article on the topic. A report by an author concerning contagion and the spread of illness from waste facilities and factories illustrates the racist assumptions held by many authorities in the planning and medical communities at the time: "A form of blood poisoning among factory people . . . which has come to be known as the 'wool sorter's disease.' The germs are introduced in bales . . . which come from certain localities in the East where people are notorious for their utter disregard of all sanitary precautions and regulations." (p. 111)

13. In 1907 the International Association for the Prevention of Smoke incorporated. It defined its concern as "pollution control." (The concept of pollution prevention did not emerge until the 1980s.) While these groups generally defined the pollution problem in civil engineering terms, reformers at Chicago's Hull House promoted a perspective informed by environmental and social justice.

14. While the 1880s saw pollution and solid waste hit the public agenda like never before, the fouling of air, land, and water in Chicago began at least as far back as 1869 and 1875 when the first steel plants sprang up (Colten 1984, 1994).

15. *Chicago Tribune*, July 9, 1881.

16. Ibid.

17. The *Chicago Tribune* took many anti-environmental positions throughout the next 115 years with regard to landfills, incinerators, and the question of environmental justice. (See chapters 4–6.) At other times, such as during the 1880s, its editorial page served as a pulpit for pro-environmental sentiments.

18. In the 1890s community protests against smoke were occurring as neighborhood activists recognized that companies were violating the 1881 Smoke Control Ordinance with impunity. The Health Department was, again, forced to respond: "Considering the enormity of the nuisance of smoke, the Chicago Department of Health was pleased with its progress on regulating this hazard. . . . As a result of prosecutions for the violation of the smoke ordinance there has been a very general adoption [by industry] of smoke-consuming devices. . . . Since the organization of the Smoke Bureau under the present administration, for the year 1895, the Chief Smoke Inspector and his six Inspectors have discovered and investigated 11,232 violations of the smoke ordinance in all portions of the city, prosecuting 259 suits. During the year 1896 there have been discovered and investigated 9,876 places and

567 suits have been prosecuted. These prosecutions have resulted in an abatement of fully 90 per cent of the causes of the complaints." (Chicago Department of Health, Biennial Report, 1895–1896, pp. 305, 306, 308).

19. *Chicago Tribune*, January 17 and January 28, 1881. This last article referred to the sewage and other wastes in this neighborhood as "One Festering Mass of Abomination." The *Tribune*'s editors regularly referred to solid waste and the neglect of these nuisances as "evil."

20. *Chicago Tribune*, January 28, 1881.

21. Mohai 1990.

22. Ibid.; Taylor 1989.

23. Melosi 1980, p. 21.

24. Ibid., p. 123. "Protests from the unfortunates who lived near the putrefying mounds often went unheard or were ignored. As the concentration of people in the inner cities became acute in the 1880s and 1890s, and as more dumps were created to meet the needs of the rapidly multiplying population, widespread outcries were heard, and these outcries could not easily be ignored" (Melosi 1981, p. 41). In the late nineteenth century, pollution flowed from Chicago's Calumet River into Lake Michigan, threatening the city's drinking water intake off 68th street. Public outcry led to a ban on sewer construction south of 95th street until 1907 (Henderson 1986).

25. Melosi 1981, p. 34.

26. Colten 1984, 1994.

27. Citizens' Association of Chicago Bulletin No. 28, 1912, p. 3.

28. *City Club Bulletin*, December 20, 1913, p. 331.

29. Ibid., p. 336.

30. Greeley 1914.

31. Colten 1984, 1994.

32. People for Community Recovery, an EJ organization featured in chapter 4, is based in the Altgeld Gardens public housing development in Chicago. This entire neighborhood was built on an old waste dump and was later found to contain a range of pollutants, including PCBs, in the soil. As Colten (1984, 1994) demonstrates, much of Chicago's Southeast Side was in fact constructed atop old dumps, slag pits, and other in-fill used to create new land in an ever-expanding city during the nineteenth and the early twentieth centuries. Additionally, this area—in fact the South Side as a quadrant of the city—has always been home to Chicago's greatest numbers of African Americans.

33. Colten 1984, 1994. "NIMBY" was often used derogatorily to deride neighborhood activists as irrational persons placing roadblocks in front of the inevitable (and therefore positive) path to change and progress. When these criticisms began to emerge, EJ and anti-toxics activists made it clear that they were concerned about "everyone's back yard" and wanted to reduce and prevent waste and pollution, rather than simply spread it around (First National People of Color Leadership Summit 1991; Taylor 1989).

34. Schnaiberg 1980, 1994.

35. This sociological framework also ushered in the adoption of innovative research methods for the study of industrial disease among poor and ethnic communities. For example, following the advice of several social scientists, Hamilton became famous for her use of shop floor observations, personal interviews with workers, and medical records. Despite the strength of her studies, Hamilton's use of such non-traditional qualitative methods drew scorn from some medical elites entrenched in quantitative, traditionally hands-off techniques. However, as Christopher Sellers (1997) argues, when Hamilton's methods were supplanted in later years by larger quantitative studies, the influence of workers and the public receded almost entirely from health policy debates. More to the point, the leading authorities in the field made a bargain with some of the most powerful and polluting industries, allowing researchers access to workers' bodies in return for maintaining a veil of secrecy around many of the studies. The impact of this *pax toxicologica* on the well-being of workers and on the state of scientific knowledge of hazards was often negative, as the profit motive was never challenged and as studies were kept under lock and key. One of Sellers's major contentions is that much of the knowledge we have today about environmental health problems is rooted in the early studies of the workplace. This is an important point that underscores the links between the health of the workplace environment and the health of the ecosystem.

36. Gottlieb 1993, p. 63.

37. Kelley 1895, p. 36.

38. Kelley and Stevens 1895, pp. 58–59.

39. In the 1990s and in 2000, home-based piece work again reared its head in the garment, travel, and electronics industries in particular (Pellow and Park 2000).

40. On the evening of May 4, 1886, a workers' rally was held in Chicago to protest state and corporate violence against strikers at the McCormick Reaper Works the previous day. As the rally drew to a close, 176 policemen moved in, demanding the immediate dispersal of the crowd. A bomb exploded and shots were fired by officers (and perhaps protesters), killing and injuring several. A witch hunt for well-known anarchists and socialists led to the kangaroo-court-style conviction of eight men, four of whom were executed.

41. Taylor 1989. In my view, given the evidence of high levels of environmental concern among African Americans, this question is certainly debatable.

42. DuBois [1898] 1973, pp. 144, 287.

43. Spear 1967, p. 29.

44. Hughes 1925, p. 55.

45. Ibid., p. 52.

46. Duncan and Duncan 1957. These drastic differences in life chances between African and European Americans—during good times and bad—bring to mind an old saying: "When white folks sneeze, black folks have a cold." A familiar variant: "When white America is in a recession, black America is in a depression."

47. Bullard and Wright 1993.

48. Hughes 1925, p. 53.

49. Herbst 1932, p. 109.

50. Illinois Interracial Commission, 1948 p. 61.

51. Tuttle 1969. The higher rents blacks paid were commonly referred to as the "Black Tax" or the "Poor Tax."

52. Hughes 1925, p. 3.

53. Duncan and Duncan 1957.

54. Chicago's 1894 Annual Report of the Department of Health reported the following: "The death rate among the colored element of the population of Chicago is, relatively much in excess of the mortality of the race in the country at large—which is about 50% higher than that of the white population. The official census fixed the colored population of the city in 1894 at 24, 889, among which number there were 664 deaths being an annual death rate of 26.67 per thousand. The white death rate—colored excluded—was 15.05 per thousand, and the excess of the colored mortality is thus seen to be more than 77 per cent." The report also noted that, among the general population of Chicago, there had been an "enormous increase in cancer—812%, in 44 years." Perhaps much of this increase was due to the introduction of pollution intensive industrial technologies during that time.

55. Jacobson 1992, p. 48.

56. Department of Development and Planning 1976.

57. Citizens' Association of Chicago Bulletin no. 25, June 1910, p. 6. Throughout the twentieth century there were several scandals in Chicago's waste industry, related to graft, political corruption, and organized criminal activity (see "Jury Probes Sanitary-Mob Link," *Chicago Tribune*, November 20, 1962).

58. Perry 1978, p. 15.

59. Hoy and Robinson 1979, p. 11.

60. Perry 1978, p. 19.

61. Gould, Schnaiberg, and Weinberg 1996, p. 140.

62. Eastwood 1992, p. 28. See also Gould, Schnaiberg and Weinberg 1996, p. 140.

63. Ginsburg 1983.

64. Szasz 1994.

65. Hurley 1995.

66. Perry 1978, p. 16.

67. Light and Bonacich 1988. The scavenging or waste hauling business was a classic example of how "self-exploitation" produced upward mobility for some immigrant groups.

68. Weber 1978.

69. Jacobson 1992, p. 61.

70. Perry 1978, p. 22.

71. Melosi 1981, p. 149.

72. Fannon 1955, p. 99.

73. Jacobson 1992, p. 55.

74. There is a long history of labor displacement resulting from the introduction of automation in the waste industry. Early in the twentieth century, when street sweeping machines were introduced, city leaders embraced this idea with great enthusiasm because it would reduce the amount of labor needed. And a "reduction in the labor force would cut costs, as well as eliminate many worker-employer conflicts (this was an especially attractive argument for anti-union management)" (Melosi 1981, p. 142). In 1955, a water-resistant paper bag was introduced in Hartford, Connecticut for garbage pickup. "The use of the bags appears to have reduced the collection work load. The crew in the test district has been cut from 29 to 20 men, with no loss of efficiency" (*The American City* 1955b). The introduction of the compactor machine in garbage trucks had a similar effect. That same year, the city of Superior, Wisconsin reported that, after replacing its six trucks with "Load Packer" trucks, it was able to use one-third fewer workers at 200% greater productivity than before (Berg 1955).

## Chapter 3

1. Cichonski and Hill 1993, p. 3. The Martin Company was the predecessor of Martin Marietta and Lockheed Martin, both of which have been enormous sources of toxic waste.

2. Hoy and Robinson 1979, pp. 20–21.

3. Ibid., p. 19.

4. Ibid., p. 5.

5. This includes the ideology of cleanliness (i.e., which groups are dirty and which are clean), assumptions about which groups have the moral fortitude to exhibit environmental concerns, and using the recycled materials to launch military assaults against nations populated by people of color.

6. Ginsburg 1983.

7. Kimball 1992, p. 32.

8. Ibid., p. 2.

9. This neo-classical argument, exemplified by Williamson 1985, is rejected by Gould, Schnaiberg, and Weinberg (1996), by Packard (1963), by Rifkin (1995), and by Schnaiberg (1992a,b).

10. The "first" and "second" pollutions were air and water; see Jacobson 1992. Air pollution was still a major issue in Chicago during the 1960s. In fact, in 1960 residents marched on Mayor Richard J. Daley's office to protest the fallout from steel mills on the South Side (Brown 1987, p. 67).

11. Jacobson 1992, p. 84.

12. Carless 1992, p. 12.

13. Ibid., p. 22.

14. Jacobson 1992, p. 119.

15. Perry 1978, p. 30. The decline in the waste industry's ethnic family business orientation is said to occur because of the legal requirement—via civil rights legislation—that all persons be given an equal opportunity for employment. This necessarily meant that mono-ethnic businesses might come under greater scrutiny, particularly those receiving government contracts for public services, such as waste haulers.

16. Jacobson 1992, p. 69.

17. I should note that industry was not the only enemy of labor, particularly workers of color. In fact, it could be said that labor was often its own worst enemy when it came to racial integration and cooperation. Historically, there have been major divisions within and between unions on the question of allowing people of color into their membership. The Congress of Industrial Organizations (CIO) and other socialist-influenced unions were so adamant about including African Americans that they often used violence and intimidation to coerce black workers to sign union cards (Tuttle 1969). Many unions, like the American Federation of Labor (AFL), were so staunchly racist that they often negotiated "sweetheart deals" with industry, wherein white workers would not receive the gains unions got elsewhere, but, in return, they kept the union all-white (or at least kept the shop under the control of a white union). Companies would actually seek out and allow the AFL or the Teamsters to have a plant upon realizing they were the target of an organizing drive by the more radical CIO or the United Farm Workers. The latter two unions were in favor of recruiting people of color to their membership rolls and were frequently amazed at the willingness of white male workers to take a pay cut to ensure racial homogeneity and/or white control over their unions. These dynamics present serious challenges to academic and lay theories of racism premised solely on economics (i.e. protecting wages and profit-making) (see Honey 1993; Roediger 1999).

18. Thompson 1989.

19. Jacobson 1992, p. 83. Buntrock assumed that workers were tired because they failed to take care of themselves (e.g., they didn't get enough sleep) rather than as a result of overwork or job-related stress. Accident prevention, therefore, was the responsibility of the employee not the employer.

20. Ginsburg 1983.

21. See Braun 1991.

22. Perry 1978, p. 158.

23. Melosi 1981, p. 47.

24. Carless 1992. The same rhetoric is being used today in the US and Britain, where a shift toward incinerators is occurring during the "energy crisis" of 2001. Parallels can be seen in the Canadian and US governments' drive to mine natural

resources on Native American lands in order to protect "national security." The end result is the same: dependence on unsustainable technologies and an increase in the degree of environmental racism being practiced (see Gedicks 1993).

25. Carless 1992, p. 12. Incinerators had been used for "resource recovery" long before the 1960s and the 1970s. For example, Chicago's Goose Island Incinerator (1929–1934) was a 600 tons per day capacity burner where workers recovered various metals for sale. Chicago's Medill Incinerator (1956–1972) also featured a metal recovery system.

26. Resource "recovery" from incinerators often took two forms. First, separating out non-combustible materials that might be recyclable. Second, and more attractive for governments and industries, was the conversion of the thermal energy that incinerators produce, into electricity used to power nearby businesses and homes. This idea has been put into practice since the late 19th century in Britain and the US. Unfortunately, it is anything but "clean and sanitary," as many planners, engineers, and environmentalists have claimed.

27. Bullard 1990; Szasz 1994.

28. Bryant and Mohai 1992; Bullard 1990, 1993, 1994; United Church of Christ 1987; Szasz 1994; Walsh, Warland, and Smith 1993.

29. Gottlieb 1993.

30. Interview by the author's assistant, Mary Beth Slusar, 1996.

31. CAWD also supported the Stockyards Incinerator project and an upgrade of the Northwest Incinerator because, they reasoned, not all waste can be recycled and incinerators have some advantages over landfills (CAWD 1986c).

32. Interview with Robert Ginsburg, January 2001.

33. Gottlieb 1993, pp. 189–90.

34. The anti-toxics movement is said to have begun with Lois Gibbs's battle against the Hooker Chemical Corporation at Love Canal, New York, in 1978. This movement continues today, but during the early 1980s and the 1990s it blended with the environmental justice movement significantly. Although both movements were strongly focused on the intersections between social justice and environmental quality, the EJ movement stressed *racial justice* and leadership in communities of color much more openly.

35. Szasz 1994.

36. Gottlieb 1993, p. 185.

37. Cichonski and Hill 1993, p. 4.

38. Gould, Schnaiberg, and Weinberg 1994.

39. It is also important to note that significant arms of the labor movement were making efforts to fight environmental pollution, particularly in the steel, coal, and the oil and chemical sectors. There were several coalition-building ventures and joint conferences between labor and environmental activists during the 1970s and the 1980s around questions of economic and environmental justice. However, as the decline of living standards set it in—brought on by the deindustrialization of US

cities—the class divisions between workers and environmentalists became more pronounced, rendering effective alliances all but impossible. At the turn of the new millennium, however, we have seen impressive efforts to realign labor and environmental organizations with the emergence of the Alliance for Sustainable Jobs and the Environment, which made a major appearance at the November-December 1999 mobilization against the World Trade Organization.

40. Schwab 1994.

41. Support for recycling as an antidote to runaway jobs and dirty technology appears throughout many publications from grassroots anti-toxics and EJ organizations. For example, the Citizens Clearinghouse for Hazardous Waste (Lois Gibbs's organization) and People for Community Recovery (a Chicago EJ organization) both touted the benefits of recycling in their publications (see Jackson 1993; Lester 1996). Also see chapter 4 for a discussion of environmentalists' claims that recycling would create more jobs than incineration.

42. Moberg 1994, p. 11.

43. Szasz 1994.

44. Baker 1995.

45. See Gedicks 1993; Taylor 1995.

46. Gould, Weinberg, and Schnaiberg 2000.

47. See Moyers 1990 for a discussion of the transnational trade in hazardous wastes and its impacts on the Global South.

48. Cichonski and Hill 1992, p. 3.

49. Beck and Associates 1987.

50. US Environmental Protection Agency 1989.

51. World Resources Institute 1993, p. 59.

52. Gordon 1995.

53. Goldman 1994.

54. Gove and Masotti 1982.

55. Schnaiberg and Gould 1994.

56. *Solid Waste Technologies* 1996, p. 9.

57. Hochshild 1989.

58. *Consumer Reports* 1994, p. 91. Ironically, with the removal of phosphates from detergents (to protect waterways like the Great Lakes from algae blooms), household cleaners are actually more hazardous to human skin because abrasive surfactants were substituted for the more ecologically harmful substances (personal communication from J. Timmons Roberts of Tulane University, September 12, 2000).

59. Colorado People's Environmental and Economic Network (COPEEN) 2001.

60. *New York Times* 1996.

61. The use of the term "garbage men" is deliberate because until very recently waste hauling was strictly a male occupation. Also, household hazardous waste is

a relatively recent addition to the arsenal of unsavory items found in the American garbage can.

62. Miller 1995, p. 62.

63. Malloy 1995, p. 48.

64. Western Disposal Services 2000. The OSHA policy this letter refers to was the set of ergonomic rules made during the last days of Bill Clinton's administration. George W. Bush immediately overturned the rules upon taking office.

65. Malloy 1995, p. 54.

66. The argument that automation saves or displaces labor was often paired with the public relations pitch that new technologies can ease the burden of physical strains on workers. For example, when packer trucks were introduced into waste hauling, workers had to do less heavy lifting (Berg 1955). Both arguments are true. But the second argument should also include the observation that, while new technologies may do away with *old* health and safety hazards, they are also generally accompanied by *new* ones. So, for example, when automated lifters appeared on the scene, managers downsized the work force, requiring the few remaining employees to work harder, longer hours. Packers are notorious for crushing the hands and arms of waste collectors, and, more recently, for spewing out lethal chemicals from hazardous materials being compacted.

67. McAdams and McAdams 1995.

68. Larane 1995, p. 76.

69. Schnaiberg 1980.

70. See Gould, Schnaiberg, and Weinberg 1996; Schnaiberg and Gould 1994; Weinberg, Pellow, and Schnaiberg 2000. My own framework seeks to place a more central focus on historical forces shaping environmental conflicts and on the role of race and racism in these struggles.

71. Griffith 1993; Parker 1994; Schnaiberg and Gould 1994; Smith and Feagin 1987.

72. Tierney 1996.

73. Kazis and Grossman 1978.

74. Schnaiberg 1992a,b.

75. Gottlieb 2001, p. 281.

76. Bullard 1990, 1993; Melosi 1981; Schnaiberg 1973, 1980; Szasz and Meuser 1997.

## Chapter 4

1. William Edward Burghardt DuBois, address to City Club of Chicago, 1912.

2. Specifically, there are 31 landfills and 22 factories that are officially described as "major point sources" because each releases 100 tons or more of at least one type of pollutant annually. (See Brown 1987.) One of the incinerators is the only PCB

burner in North America that is located in an urban area (Henderson 1986). I should note that the South Side has not always been heavily populated with African Americans. However, it has always been populated by working-class ethnic groups (European immigrants and/or people of color). Thus, the marginal populations have generally always played host to the majority of pollutants generated there.

3. US Department of Health and Human Services 1992.

4. Nelson 1988.

5. Ibid.

6. Goering 1988.

7. Aterno 1993, p. 4.

8. Henderson 1986. Angering many environmentalists, in April of 1984, the Illinois Environmental Protection Agency—often regarded as a friend of business rather than a steward of environmental interests—released a report that "concludes that there is no imminent danger to human health in the area due to environmental pollution" (Illinois EPA News 1984). In a later study, the IEPA essentially confirmed these "findings," with the caveat that some "short-term health problems and complaints . . . are due to the sum of the effects of some of the chemicals addressed above plus the effects of many other natural and man-made chemicals not addressed in the study. . . ." (Illinois Environmental Protection Agency 1987)

9. Author's field notes, 1993.

10. Henderson 1986.

11. Personal communication with author. As I noted in chapter 1, I worked with and for many grassroots organizations, including PCR, where I was a volunteer, then staff member, Public Policy Director, and Research director, from 1992–1996.

12. Cohen 1992.

13. Author's field notes, July 1993.

14. Ibid.

15. Ibid.

16. Author's interview with Robert Ginsburg, January 2001. See also Henderson 1991; Joravsky 1991.

17. Lazaroff 2000.

18. Szasz 1994.

19. Melosi 1981.

20. The Urban Environment Conference was titled Taking Back Our Health: An Institute on Surviving the Toxics Threat to Minority Communities. The UEC was an alliance of labor, people of color, and environmental organizations founded in 1971. It was the only national organization whose first priority was the environmental and occupational health of people of color and working people in the United States (Urban Environment Conference 1985).

21. "Big Ten," or "Group of Ten": the ten major national conservation and environmental organizations in the US. At that time, these were the Sierra Club, the

Sierra Club Legal Defense Fund, the Audubon Society, the Izaak Walton League, the Natural Resources Defense Council, the National Parks and Conservation Association, the Wilderness Society, Friends of the Earth, the Environmental Defense Fund, and the National Wildlife Federation.

22. Alston 1991.

23. Szasz 1994.

24. United Church of Christ 1987.

25. Bryant and Mohai 1992.

26. Reprinted in *Voces Unidas* (South West Organizing Project, Albuquerque, 1995). The critique of racism compounded the newly emerging class critique of "Big Ten" or "beltway" environmental organizations, particularly regarding "executive compensation." For example, in 1998–99 the salaries of the top executives at eleven of these organizations exceeded $200,000: Ducks Unlimited ($346, 882), the National Wildlife Federation ($247,081), the World Wildlife Fund ($241,638), National Audubon Society ($239,670), the Natural Resources Defense Council ($238,964), the Wilderness Society ($204,591), the Environmental Defense Fund ($262,798), the Nature Conservancy ($210,151), Conservation International ($203,049), the Conservation Fund ($211,048), and Defenders of Wildlife ($201,337) (Knudson and Flodin 2001).

27. Hispanos are persons of Mexican descent who live on Land Grant areas set up during the nineteenth century.

28. Certain firms charged with and/or convicted of corporate and environmental justice crimes (Waste Management, for example) had representatives on the boards of directors of the National Audubon Society and the National Wildlife Federation. I do not use the term "corporate criminal" casually. WMX has been charged with and convicted of many environmental and labor crimes, making that firm a "repeat offender." I should note that the divisions between mainly white environmental organizations and people of color-led EJ groups were not always so stark. For example, in the major battle against the Shintech corporation's efforts to site a PVC factory in Saint James Parish, Louisiana, Greenpeace and the Sierra Club were major collaborators with EJ groups and collectively won. And more generally, white-led organizations such as the Highlander Center's STP school, Clean Water Action, the National Toxics Campaign, the Citizens Clearinghouse for Hazardous Wastes, the Environmental Support Center, and the Institute for Energy and Environmental Research have all been cited for their outstanding support of EJ campaigns (see Alston and Bastian 1993). Furthermore, we must not make the false assumption that all environmental organizations led by whites are in perfect harmony with each other. For example, during the 1990s, local chapters of the Sierra Club were involved in lawsuits against the national Sierra Club organization. Also, working-class white anti-toxics organizations have had many conflicts with national and international environmental groups. In one such incident, Group Against Smoke and Pollution (GASP), a Pittsburgh-based organization complained that Greenpeace strolled into town like white knights and took over a battle against a LULU that GASP had initiated.

29. Author's field notes, July 1993.

30. PCR's former development director, Orrin Williams, was often heard making this astute observation.

31. It is often difficult, and sometimes impossible, to prove that someone has *intentionally* discriminated against someone else. And with private corporations, this task becomes even more challenging because they are, by their very nature, insulated against most public scrutiny. However, as early as 1964, civil rights lawyers were successful at circumventing this difficult standard, by including Title VI in the Civil Rights Act. Title VI allows courts to move beyond individual *intent* to discriminate and, instead, consider larger patterns, trends in unequal treatment, or what the law terms a "disparate impact." That is, regardless of whether or not corporations deliberately site polluting facilities in communities of color, if there is a pattern of such behavior, then we can demonstrate a "disparate impact" on these communities that requires a legal remedy.

32. *Frontline: Justice for Sale?* (hosted by Bill Moyers), Public Broadcasting Service, aired November 1999.

33. Bullard 2000; Roberts and Toffolon-Weiss 2001.

34. In 1998 the African American mayor of Detroit, Dennis Archer, launched a major criticism of environmental justice campaigns because they "would kill new investment in industrial sites in . . . depressed Michigan cities" (Johnson 1998). Archer, Michigan governor John Engler, the US Chamber of Commerce, the National Conference of Mayors, and the National Black Chamber of Commerce were unified on this point and publicly worked to undermine the implementation of the executive order on Environmental Justice. This attack not only included the criticism that the EJ movement was stifling economic development in the African American community, but also levied the charge that claims of environmental racism were unfounded. This conflict resembled age-old divisions within the black community between those individuals, class categories, political leaders, and institutions who benefit from the continued subjugation of African American people, and those who do not. This was in effect, a classic conflict between the appointed chieftains and the masses played out in countless colonies of European powers in the Global South. Perhaps most importantly, those African American leaders attacking the movement for its "naysaying," missed the point that EJ activists have been making for years: we need economic development as much as anyone; the difference is, since we've been inundated with toxics for years, we are now demanding a voice in *what kind of development* we will allow.

35. Chinweizu 1975; Rodney 1982.

36. The ordinance against illegal or "fly dumping" or "midnight dumping" goes at least as far back as 1914: "Refuse on vacant property. Passed 1914. Prohibits dumping on private property or vacant grounds without a permit." (Department of Health, City of Chicago. Report for 1911–1918, p. 302)

37. In 1910 the Superintendent for the Department of Health was dismissed after an investigation concluded that several incidents involving graft and extortion at a waste dump were occurring on his watch (see Citizens Association of Chicago

1910). During the height of the garbage wars (around 1900) in the immigrant enclave of the 29th Ward (Mary McDowell's territory), Alderman Tom Carey got very rich from creating large pits in the neighborhood (to make bricks for his own construction company) and then getting paid by the city to fill them in (see Hull House 1895, chapter VII).

38. Lavelle and Coyle 1992.

39. Christopher later admitted to paying bribes in the late 1980s of approximately $5,000 per month to the late Alderman William Henry of the 24th Ward in return for his agreement to aid Christopher in using and operating the site without interference from the city of Chicago (Vinik and Harley 1997).

40. During the 1990s, the National Parent Teachers Association noticed the pattern of waste sites being located near schools and passed a resolution stating their opposition, specifically, to the location of *concrete recycling and manufacturing* operations near schools.

41. Vinik and Harley 1997, p. 20.

42. Ibid., p. 26.

43. Ibid., p. 14.

44. Ibid., p. 22.

45. Ibid., p. 16.

46. Ibid., p. 24.

47. Cohen 1992.

48. Vinik and Harley 1997, p. 18.

49. Sunya Walls, "Rev. Jackson Plans Dump Site Clean Up," *Chicago Weekend*, February 20, 1996.

50. *Chicago Defender*, December 17, 1997.

51. Vinik and Harley 1997, p. 27.

52. Ibid., p. 31.

53. Ibid., p. 34.

54. *Austin Weekly*. July 16, 1993.

55. Nolan 1993.

56. Michaeli 1993.

57. *Austin Voice*. October 18, 1994.

58. *Austin Voice*. May 26, 1993.

59. *Austin Voice*. July 20, 1993.

60. Michaeli 1994.

61. McNeil 1998.

62. Ibid.

63. Gitlin 1992.

64. One editorial read: "Illinois is on its way to becoming the garbage burning capital of the nation. King of the Burn. Incinerator Heaven. Smokin'" (*Chicago Sun-Times*, December 4, 1995). By one count, the number of existing and proposed incinerators around the state shortly after the Retail Rate Law was passed into law was 29.

65. Haymore 1988.

66. Ibid.

67. Goering 1989.

68. Fegelman 1987.

69. Incinerator supporters claimed that this infusion of capital would double the city's revenue but environmental activist Jeff Tangel calculated that "the proceeds wouldn't balance the village budget" (personal communication, February 2001).

70. *Chicago Tribune*, February 5, 1986.

71. Citizens for a Better Environment/People for Community Recovery memo, April 19, 1994.

72. Schwab 1994b.

73. Schwab 1994a.

74. According to one activist (Jeff Tangel, personal communication), this permit was "so lax that it was a good example of environmental racism" and was a revealing indicator of how few controls the government felt were necessary for a burner in a poor, all-African-American town.

75. See *Chicago Tribune* 1992. One *Tribune* editorial read: "This is a project that has good planning as well as good intentions and it should finally be allowed to proceed. . . . The Robbins incinerator can reduce future demand for more landfill space. That makes it a potential part of the environmental solution, not necessarily a new element of the problem" (*Chicago Tribune* 1991).

76. Goering 1995.

77. Goering 1990.

78. Goering 1991.

79. A similar situation has occurred in some Native American environmental justice struggles. For example, on one reservation, tribal leaders sought to attract a hog farm and environmentalists opposed this idea. Native leaders responded that environmentalists opposing this measure were in effect also opposing Native sovereignty, and therefore were acting in opposition to environmental justice (see Krakoff 2000).

80. Jeter 1998.

81. Ibid.

82. Schwab 1994a, p. 41.

83. *American City and County* 1996.

84. Schwab 1994a, p. 9.

85. Ibid., p. 30.

86. Ibid., p. 40.

87. Stevenson 1991.

88. Interestingly, much of the force behind the anti-Retail Rate Law mobilization came from white suburban communities outside of Chicago who felt that one day their own areas might be targeted for incinerator sitings (*Crains Chicago Business,* January 22, 1998).

89. Jeter 1998.

90. Elrick 1998.

91. Citizens for a Better Environment/People for Community Recovery 1994.

92. Jeter 1998.

## Chapter 5

1. See Bryant 1995; Bullard 1990.

2. Bryant 1995, pp. 21–22; Bullard 1990; Collin and Harris 1993, pp. 105–106; Gould, Schnaiberg and Weinberg 1996; Pellow, Weinberg and Schnaiberg 1995; Schnaiberg 1992a,b; Weinberg, Pellow, and Schnaiberg 2000.

3. Buhrmann 1999; Derksen and Gartrell 1993.

4. Derksen and Gartrell 1993; DeYoung 1986.

5. Greenpeace 1995.

6. Lester 1996, pp. 9–13.

7. Author's interview with Marjorie Isaacson, Secretary, Chicago Recycling Coalition, 1997. The Chicago Recycling Coalition essentially replaced the CAWD in 1989.

8. Jaffe 1988, p. 75.

9. Greene 1993, published by the Center for Neighborhood Technology. See also Eyring, Greene, and Lomax 1994, p. 21.

10. Natural Resources Defense Council 1997.

11. Jaffe 1988, p. 74.

12. Chicago Department of Environment 1995. See Horowitz 1994 for an excellent discussion of dirty MRFs.

13. CAWD 1986.

14. CAWD 1985.

15. Author's interview with Joanna Hoelscher, Policy Director, Citizens for a Better Environment, winter 1996. Hoelscher is one of the most knowledgeable and politically astute environmentalists I have encountered.

16. Pickus 1998. The Creative Reuse Warehouse is a facility where the public—especially school teachers and children—is welcome to fill bags with a variety of

odds and ends for $3 each. Or, patrons can bring their own bag of materials and exchange it for a bag of items from the warehouse, in what Dunn calls a "creative exchange."

17. Gottlieb 1993, p. 185.

18. Resource Center 1985.

19. d'Anjou 1976.

20. Brewer 1984.

21. McIntyre 1994.

22. Jacobson (1993) provides historical insight into land pollution as the "third pollution."

23. Resource Center 1983, p. 3.

24. Brewer 1984.

25. *RC Newsletter*, 1983 and 1984.

26. Resource Center 1986.

27. Interview by author, fall 1995.

28. Interview by author, fall 1995.

29. Resource Center 1984a.

30. Resource Center 1984b.

31. Squires, Bennett, McCourt, and Nyden 1987.

32. Bluestone and Harrison 1982.

33. Wilson 1996, p. 19.

34. Brownfields are vacant, abandoned, or underutilized commercial and industrial properties where the fear of unknown environmental liability is a serious obstacle to their successful redevelopment or improvement. Although the majority of brownfields proliferate in inner cities, most brownfield cleanups have occurred in suburban and rural areas. This reveals yet another example of environmental inequalities with regard to both impacts and cleanup practices.

35. Ken Dunn began the RC when he was still a student at the University of Chicago. Many of his partners were also affiliated with the university at that time.

36. Rush proposed a mandatory recycling ordinance in October 1987 (Finley 1987).

37. Resource Center 1984b.

38. In 1985, the city of Chicago was facing a dilemma. In addition to a strong community-based environmental movement against any proposed landfills, the Department of Planning predicted that the "capacity of current operating sanitary landfills in Chicago will be exhausted in six to seven years" (Chicago Department of Planning 1985, p. 1).

39. Brewer 1984.

40. CAWD 1984; Chicago Department of Planning 1985, p. 1.

41. Giloth and Moe 1999.

42. CAWD 1984.

43. CAWD 1987. Furthermore, CAWD proposed that "collections and sorting of household hazardous waste [be] mandatory" (ibid), something that the Blue Bag system ignored altogether.

44. Michaeli 1993b.

45. In the late 1980s, CAWD was "immobilized" and divided over questions concerning future directions, particularly considering that the recycling ordinance—CAWD's major reason for existence—looked like it was a done deal. There was also internal criticism by groups like PCR and others that neither landfills nor incinerators were acceptable (although CAWD had endorsed these practices under limited conditions). In 1988, several activists urged that CAWD was no longer viable and argued that what was needed was a "fearless subversive, guerrilla tactics group" that would oppose both landfills and incinerators (Chicago Innovations Forum 1988).

46. Interview by author, fall 1996. The Resource Center should be credited with taking chances on workers that most employers in Chicago would shun, particularly African American males, who constitute perhaps the least "desirable" segment of the labor force. See Wilson 1996 for a discussion of employers' racist hiring practices with regard to African American men.

47. Author's field notes, summer 1997.

48. Interview by author, fall 1996.

49. Fordism did not stop with the assembly line. When scholars use this term, they generally mean the broader system and ideology of worker control by management. Even more fascinating, Henry Ford himself felt that in order to control workers on the job, he had to also control them *off the job*. So, with the help of sociologists and other experts, he created a "social department" through which he could monitor and enforce particular social mores among his employees (Pena 1997).

50. Interview by author, fall 1996.

51. Interview by author, winter 1997. Burris was always clear that recycling's social movement origins were fading fast, as for-profit firms began taking over the industry in the 1980s and the 1990s.

52. This reality contradicts some scholars' theories on "hazard pay" (Baker 1985) wherein it is argued that dangerous work is compensated with higher wages. Other scholars have proven this thesis to be flawed (see Robinson 1991).

53. Resource Center 1983, p. 2.

54. Author's field notes, summer 1997.

55. Author's field notes, summer 1997.

56. Author's field notes, summer 1997.

57. In 1994, thousands of US waste industry employers failed to keep a log of injuries and illness, provide proper protective gear and equipment to workers, post signs and notices detailing safety procedures and worker's rights, and communicate

all possible work-related hazards to each employee—all of which are required by federal law and enforced by the Occupational Safety and Health Administration (Vogel 1995, p. 80). Siegel and Kwass (1995, p. 35) note that recycling jobs "tend to be of relatively low quality" and that "with little attention given to job quality or job ladder issues, there is little likelihood that these new jobs will provide an effective avenue for rising out of poverty."

58. Author's field notes, spring 1996.

59. Ibid.

60. Ibid.

61. Ibid.

62. Ibid.

63. Ibid.

64. Van Eerd 1996. Also see Perry 1978, p. 8: "The National Safety Council has recently reported that refusemen have nine times the on-job injury rate of all other industries combined. Their statistics reported that no other occupation had a higher risk of injury. . . .Joseph Cimino, a public health physician, has determined that the New York City refusemen he studied have higher rates of heart trouble and other general health problems than comparable working populations. . . ."

65. Author's field notes, spring 1996.

66. Interview by author, fall 1995.

67. Sennett and Cobb 1972.

68. Hughes 1971.

69. Interview by author, winter 1996.

70. Interview by author, fall 1995.

71. Perry 1978, p. 8.

72. Interview by author, fall 1995.

73. Ibid.

74. Interview by author, spring 1996.

75. Ibid. This worker's comments are a textbook case of the tradition of paternalism and subjugation that has long characterized management-worker relationships, which are magnified for workers of color under the authority of white supervisors and bosses (Pena 1997).

76. Interview by author, winter 1997.

77. Chappell 1993, p. xv. Tom's of Maine is a "green" company specializing in bath products.

78. Edwards 1979.

79. Interview by author, spring 1996.

80. Ibid.

81. Ibid.

82. Ibid.

83. In her book *Dishing it Out*, the anthropologist Greta Paules (1993) examines how waitresses in a New Jersey roadside diner make considerable efforts to control the labor process and resist the ethos of servitude that customers attempt to impose upon them. By engaging in impression management (Goffman 1959) and direct confrontation, recycling workers and waitresses exert power and maintain dignity in otherwise undignified occupations.

84. Joravsky 1993.

## Chapter 6

1. Chicago Department of Planning 1985, p. 9.

2. Chicago Department of Public Works 1973, p. 151. Also see Stabenow 1973. Stabenow claimed the Northwest Incinerator "meets the highest standards."

3. *Chicago Tribune* 1972. The *Tribune* was also one of the leading proponents of the Robbins incinerator project. (See chapter 4.)

4. *Chicago Today* 1972.

5. McMullen 1972.

6. The Calumet Incinerator was creating a local nuisance of its own, which residents repeatedly complained about. In 1975, Illinois Environmental Protection Agency agents interviewed residents living in close proximity to the burner, one of whom stated: "I can smell odors all summer from the incinerator. It smells like old garbage. I know the source by the wind direction. It bothers me very much. I notice it about once per week. In the summer it gets in the house. It also makes you want to go inside. It is a nauseating odor which makes you sick to your stomach." "She will testify," the agent noted (US Environmental Protection Agency 1975b).

7. Enstad 1963.

8. Ibid. I arrived at this calculation by beginning with the observation that the Calumet Incinerator processed about 22% of Chicago's waste (one-fourth of the 88% total waste stream that went to the incinerators), the Calumet landfill accepted 12% of the waste, and during peak seasons these figures would rise. Moreover, the recycling facility would have accepted an estimated 36,000 tons per year. And each of these facilities was located in this one neighborhood.

9. Smith 1970.

10. Emmons 1986.

11. *Calumet Index* 1973.

12. US Environmental Protection Agency 1975.

13. For an excellent discussion of RCRA's impact on the anti-toxics and EJ movements, see Szasz 1994.

14. Chicago Department of Planning 1985. This plan was supported and influenced by the RC and the CAWD, both connected to the anti-toxics and EJ movements.

"Recycling," the report claimed (p. 10), "is compatible with resource recovery incineration, since the diversion of metals, glass and paper from the waste stream increases heat value and reduces residue (ash) volume."

15. Henderson 1995.

16. Brewer 1983.

17. Chicago Department of Planning 1985, foreword.

18. Barry 1987.

19. Briggs 1994. Lead has been found to produce neurological disorders, hearing loss, learning disabilities, and behavioral problems in children and reproductive disorders in women. Cadmium is a probable human carcinogen. According to the EPA, it may cause lung cancer, and is linked to kidney disorders. Other pollutants incinerators emit include acid gases such as sulfur dioxide, nitrogen oxides, and hydrochloric acid, organic chemicals such as dioxin, and heavy metals such as mercury, chromium, and arsenic, all of which are extremely harmful to the ecosystem and human health.

20. Montague 1994. Incinerators have a lifetime of 20–25 years, after which they must either be scrapped or rebuilt. By 1994, the Northwest Incinerator was 23 years old.

21. Citizens for a Better Environment 1994b.

22. Friedman 1994.

23. There is a history of divisions and conflicts between workers and environmentalists (Gottlieb 1993). Perhaps the root of the problem is the lack of a shared understanding that the environment and the workplace are linked. In Chicago, for example, Citizens for a Better Environment regularly granted funds to community organizations and non-profit groups fighting pollution around the region. One funding proposal that was rejected, however, was submitted by Dr. Quentin Young and the Occupational Health Project of the Medical Committee for Human Rights. Young and his group sought funding to create a forum through which industrial workers, environmentalists, and the medical community could unite in an educational and action-oriented program around problems of industrial health in Chicago (Young 1971). For whatever reasons, CBE rejected this proposal, which was years ahead of its time.

24. Eyring, Greene, and Lomax 1994, pp. 21, 14.

25. Fary 1994. The goal of 25% recycling by 1996 was actually a revised (and overambitious) target. In 1986, Mayor Harold Washington promised to achieve this level of recycling by 2000 (CAWD 1986a).

26. By 1994, the Northwest Incinerator was the only burner operating in the state and had been plagued by chronic mechanical failure, pollution problems, and an inability to meet more stringent federal environmental standards (Spielman 1994). Environmentalists urged Mayor Daley to introduce a "pay as you throw" or "volume-based" garbage disposal system. Such a system has been shown to provide an immediate economic incentive for households to reduce their trash disposal

volume and to look toward recycling. However, several aldermen, the mayor, and the commissioner of the Department of Environment all rejected this proposal as it would have been viewed as a back-door increase in property taxes (ibid.).

27. Author's field notes, July 1994.

28. WASTE 1994.

29. Henderson 1995, p. 17.

30. CBE 1994b. For the definitive study documenting the government's racial disparities in enforcement against polluters, see Lavelle and Coyle 1992 .

31. *Chicago Reader* 1995.

32. Chicago Recycling Coalition 1994.

33. Citizens for a Better Environment 1999.

34. Operation Silver Shovel is a classic example of inconsistent and uncoordinated government regulations producing and exacerbating environmental injustices. Polluters were operating without any permits and few if any governmental entities took responsibility for it.

35. The movement-policy cycle we have seen since chapter 2 demonstrates that the EJ and environmental movements are faced with limited choices, between a rock and a hard place. Landfills and incinerators are both hazardous, yet activists and policy makers have periodically favored one over the other, depending on the circumstances. The research reveals that these choices are not based on sound data: "There is some evidence that landfill emissions to the air are comparable to incinerator emissions. . . . The March-April 1994 issue of *Solid Waste Technologies* . . . compared a new landfill with a new incinerator and found that the landfill 'appears to pose greater health and environmental risks.' [The author] found that the cancer risk from dioxin emitted from an incinerator was .07 chances per million, while the risk from a landfill that burns off its methane gas was .25 chances per million." (Henderson 1995, p. 13)

36. Wilson 1996.

37. *Solid Waste Management Newsletter* 1990. This turn of events is fascinating for several reasons. First, it is actually not surprising, given Chicago's historical focus on efficiency in its waste management systems, while other major cities have had a much stronger emphasis on ensuring that such systems protected public health. (See Melosi 1981, p. 30.) But damning evidence that the Blue Bag program had little or nothing to do with ecological concerns comes from the city's 1985 Waste Management Plan, which stated: "Large-scale recycling is economically feasible only if recoverable materials are separated from the waste stream at the source. Although other methods of separating recyclable materials do exist, it is too costly and inefficient to separate them, once they are mixed into the combined municipal waste stream." Furthermore, in 1990, the City Council also passed an ordinance forbidding the inclusion of infectious wastes into the municipal waste stream. The Blue Bag system would later violate both the Waste Management Plan's recommendation and the city ordinance—it was a mixed-waste system in which hospital wastes would find their way into the garbage via home-based health care practices. Both of these issues were articulated and pushed onto the city's agenda early on by

the Coalition for Appropriate Waste Disposal, an environmental organization with a seat on Mayor Harold Washington's Solid Waste Management Task Force.

38. Interview by author, fall 1995.

39. *Rachel's Environment and Health Weekly* 1997.

40. WMX's ChemWaste subsidiary was the owner of a hazardous waste landfill whose expansion was challenged by El Peublo para Agua y Aire Limpio and the California Rural Legal Assistance Foundation in what became a landmark environmental justice case. In June of 1994, WMX attempted to convene a symposium under the title Environmental Justice: The Search for Balance. The conference was to be held in the Chicago area but was cancelled as EJ groups became irate at what they viewed as WMX's efforts to co-opt the movement and "cool out" many EJ leaders with soothing words and false promises. (WMX 1994). WMX also worked diligently to get corporate secrecy laws passed in several states, restricting citizen access to previously public information about health, environment, and safety practices in a range of corporations. In 1987, People for Community Recovery teamed up with Greenpeace and blocked 57 trucks from importing hazardous waste to ChemWaste's incinerator on the Southeast Side.

41. Stockdill 1996.

42. This is what has been referred to as the "perpetrator-victim scenario" common to many accounts of environmental justice struggles (Pellow 2000). Briefly, this involves the portrayal of EJ conflicts as overly simplistic, where the villains and the victims are clearly defined. The cases in this book underscore that, while there clearly are powerful institutions benefiting from environmental injustices, there are many stakeholders who sometimes play roles that blur the line between the victim or target and the perpetrator (e.g., the RC and PCR). Furthermore, intra-racial or intra-ethnic divisions within communities of color are dynamics that have yet to be fully explored in the EJ literature. Operation Silver Shovel and the Robbins and Northwest Incinerators make it clear that these divisions are real and have major consequences for the health of workers, residents, and the ecosystem.

43. There are conflicting reports about the union issue at the MRFs because, allegedly, some workers were allowed (or forced) to join a "union" that was clearly company run, while many others were fired before even being considered for union eligibility.

44. Ritter 1996. The RC's decision *not* to accept MSW had a positive impact on that work environment.

45. Interview by author, fall 1996.

46. Horowitz 1994; Powell 1992; Ritter 1996; van Eerd 1996.

47. *Chicago Tonight* 1996.

48. Interview by author, fall 1996.

49. Ibid.

50. CAWD 1988 (minutes of general meetings, January 25 and February 24). Prior to the Blue Bag program, Chicago recycled somewhere between 2% and 3% of its

waste. In 1994, Seattle claimed to recycle 45% of its residential waste and nearly as much commercial waste. That same year, Newark, New Jersey reported recycling 30% of all waste (Moberg 1994, p. 10).

51. Interview by author, summer 1996.

52. Interview by author, fall 1996. Remedial Environmental Manpower is a temporary firm that hires out day labor for all manner of environmental companies in the Chicago area. REM was officially touted as a minority or female-owned contractor, but this claim was constantly challenged by workers who felt this was a "white man's company." REM was, on its best day, perhaps one of the shadiest operations in town.

53. Interview by author, fall 1996. Upon hearing this story, one of my colleagues responded: "Talk about lighting a fire under somebody's ass!" Like the Medill and Calumet Incinerators, one generation of waste management technology is often coupled with or taken over by the next on the same plot of land. The predictable result is that this new technology is just as polluting as the last and is located in the same community of color—thus extending environmental injustices into the future.

54. Sullivan 1996. Another infant's body was discovered at a WMX MRF on December 7, 1995; on December 12, 1996, the body of a west suburban man was found in a garbage can at a Blue Bag MRF; and on December 30, 1995 the body of a woman who was the victim of a serial killer's 12 murder rampage, was discovered at a WMX MRF.

55. Interview by author, fall 1996.

56. Ibid. The 50% unemployment figure is from Wilson 1996.

57. Interview by author, fall 1996.

58. Nelkin and Brown 1984.

59. Interview by author, summer 1996.

60. Ibid.

61. Robinson 1991, p. 84.

62. Edwards 1979.

63. Interview by author, summer 1996.

64. Memo to REM Employees 1996.

65. Interview by author, fall 1996.

66. Ibid.

67. Braverman 1974; Burawoy 1978; Edwards 1979; Thompson 1989.

68. Interview by author, summer 1996.

69. Interview by author, fall 1996.

70. Ibid.

71. Gonos 1997.

72. Interview by author, fall 1996.

73. Ibid.

74. Ibid.

75. Ibid.

76. Ibid.

77. Ibid.

78. WMX 1995.

79. REM Employees 1996.

80. Interview by author, fall 1996.

81. Ibid.

82. Ibid.

83. Ibid.

84. Ibid.

85. Ibid.

86. Ibid.

87. Ibid.

88. Scott 1990.

89. Interview by author, summer 1996.

90. Interview by author, fall 1996.

91. Ibid.

92. Bullard and Wright 1993; Johnson and Oliver 1989.

93. Robinson 1991, p. 97.

94. Ibid.

95. Ibid.

96. After an outside consultant released a report on the Blue Bag system, the city and WMX claimed to have addressed many of the concerns over worker health and safety. (See Weinberg, Pellow, and Schnaiberg 2000.) However, no reforms, short of removing the mixed-waste component of the system itself, would address the fact that infectious and hazardous wastes were an inherent part of the program. That fact alone means that any modifications to the Blue Bag would be of limited value.

97. Interview by author, winter 1996.

98. Ibid.

99. Author's interview with Jim Burris, spring 1996.

## Chapter 7

1. Hull House 1895, p. 148.

2. Thornton 2000.

3. Túre 1994.

4. People for Community Recovery 1992.

5. Author's field notes, fall 1996.

6. See Gould, Schnaiberg and Weinberg 1996; Schnaiberg 1980; Schnaiberg and Gould 1994.

7. Braun 1991.

8. Nash 1987; Sassen 1988; Smith and Feagin 1987.

# References

Alston, Dana. 1990. *We Speak for Ourselves*. Panos Institute.

Alston, Dana. 1991. Moving Beyond the Barriers. Speech delivered at First National People of Color Environmental Leadership Summit, Washington.

Alston, Dana, and Ann Bastian. 1993. "An Open Letter to Funding Colleagues: New Developments in the Environmental Justice Movement."

*American City and County*. 1996. "Issues and Trends." September, p. B20.

Anderton, Doug, A. B. Anderson, J. M. Oakes, and M. Fraser. 1994. "Environmental Equity: The Demographics of Dumping." *Demography* 31: 229–248.

Aneshensel, Carol. 1992. "Social Stress: Theory and Research." *Annual Review of Sociology* 18: 15–38.

Apotheker, Steve. 1993. "Curbside Recycling Collection Trends in the 40 Largest US Cities." *Resource Recycling*, December: 27–33.

Aquino, John. 1996. "Consolidations in the Solid Waste Industry." *Waste Age*, May: 127–136.

Asch, P., and J. L. Seneca. 1978. "Some Evidence on the Distribution of Air Quality." *Land Economics* 54: 278–297.

Aterno, Kathleen. 1993. Statement before the Subcommittee on Transportation and Hazardous Material Committee on Energy and Commerce. Washington, November 18.

Auletta, Kenneth. 1982. *The Underclass*. Random House.

*Austin Voice*. 1993a. "Lawndale Residents Trashing Garbage Dump Scheme." May 26.

*Austin Voice*. 1993b. "North Lawndale Dumps the Dumpers." July 20.

*Austin Voice*. 1994. "Ald. Miller & Flood Bros. Trying to Sneak Dump into Lawndale." October 18.

*Austin Weekly*. 1993. "Permit Denied for West Side Transfer Operation." July 16.

Baker, Beth. 1995. Curbing Recycling Revisionists. *Environmental Action*. (Washington), summer.

Baker, Dean. 1985. "The Study of Stress at Work." *Annual Review of Public Health* 6: 367–381.

Barry, Patrick. 1987. A Five Year Recycling Plan for Chicago. Statement by Patrick Barry, Coalition for Appropriate Waste Disposal, Chicago, July 1.

Beary, Jack. 1995. "Recycling Plans in the Bag." *Daily Southtown* 18, November 10: 1.

Beck, R. W., and Associates. 1987. The Nation's Public Works: Report on Solid Waste. National Council on Public Works Improvement.

Beck, Ulrich. 1992. *Risk Society*. Sage.

Been, Vicki. 1993. "Locally Undesirable Land Uses in Minority Neighborhoods." *Yale Law Review* 103: 1383.

Berg, E. W. 1955. "200% Better Refuse Sanitation." *American City*, February.

Berman, Daniel. 1978. *Death on the Job*. Monthly Review Press.

Berry, B. J. L., ed. 1977. *The Social Burdens of Environmental Pollution: A Comparative Metropolitan Data Source*. Ballinger.

Bluestone, Barry, and Irving Bluestone. 1992. *Negotiating the Future*. Basic Books.

Bluestone, Barry, and Bennett Harrison. 1982. *The Deindustrialization of America*. Basic Books.

Braun, Denny. 1991. *The Rich Get Richer: The Rise of Income Inequality in the United States and the World*. Nelson-Hall.

Braverman, Harry. 1974. *Labor and Monopoly Capital*. Monthly Review Press.

Brewer, Gretchen. 1983. "Burning Waste—And Money." *Chicago Tribune*, June 7.

Brewer, Gretchen. 1984. "State of the Resource Center." Newsletter of Resource Center, Inc. (Chicago) 1, no. 4.

Briggs, Michael. 1994. "High Court: Incinerator Ash Must Be Separated." *Chicago Sun-Times*, May 3.

Brown, Michael. 1987. *The Toxic Cloud*. Harper & Row.

Brown, Phil. 1992. "Popular Epidemiology and Toxic Waste Contamination." *Journal of Health and Social Behavior* 33: 267–281.

Brown, Phil, and Edwin Mikkelsen. 1990. *No Safe Place: Toxic Waste, Leukemia and Community Action*. University of California Press.

Brown, Phil, and Faith Ferguson. 1995. "'Making a Big Stink': Women's Work, Women's Relationships, and Toxic Waste Activism." *Gender and Society* 9: 145–172.

Bryant, Bunyan, ed. 1995. *Environmental Justice: Issues, Policies, and Solutions*. Island.

Bryant, Bunyan, and Paul Mohai. 1992. *Race and the Incidence of Environmental Hazards: A Time for Discourse*. Westview.

Buhrmann, Jan. 1999. "The Impact of Social Context on Environmental Attitudes, Behaviors, and the Attitude-Behavior Relationship." Paper presented at annual meeting of American Sociological Association, San Francisco.

Bukro, Casey. 1989. "The True Greenhouse Effect." *Chicago Tribune*, December 31.

Bukro, Casey. 1991. "From Coercion to Cooperation." *Chicago Tribune*, Ecology-Special Report, November 17.

Bullard, Robert. 2000. *Dumping in Dixie: Race, Class and Environmental Quality*. Third Edition. Westview.

Bullard, Robert, ed. 1993. *Confronting Environmental Racism: Voices from the Grassroots*. South End.

Bullard, Robert. 1994a."The Legacy of American Apartheid and Environmental Racism." *St. John's Journal of Legal Commentary* 9: 445–474.

Bullard, Robert, ed. 1994b. *Unequal Protection*. Sierra Club Books.

Bullard, Robert, Eugene Grigsby, and Charles Lee, eds. 1994. *Residential Apartheid: The American Legacy*. CAAS.

Bullard, Robert, and Glenn Johnson, eds. 1997. *Just Transportation: Dismantling Race and Class Barriers to Mobility*. New Society.

Bullard, Robert, Glenn Johnson, and Angel Torres, eds. 2000. *Sprawl City: Race, Politics, and Planning in Atlanta*. Island.

Bullard, Robert, and Beverly Wright. 1993. "The Effects of Occupational Injury, Illness and Disease on the Health Status of Black Americans." In *Toxic Struggles: The Theory and Practice of Environmental Justice*, ed. R. Hofrichter. New Society.

Bunker, Stephen. 1985. *Underdeveloping the Amazon: Extraction, Unequal Exchange and the Failure of the Modern State*. University of Illinois Press.

Burawoy, Michael. 1979. *Manufacturing Consent: Changes in the Labor Process Under Monopoly Capitalism*. University of Chicago Press.

Buttel, Frederick, Charles Geisler, and Irving Wiswall. 1984. *Labor and the Environment: An Analysis of and Annotated Bibliography on Workplace Environmental Quality in the United States*. Greenwood.

Cable, Sherry. 1992. "Women's Social Movement Involvement." *Sociological Quarterly* 33: 35–50.

Cable, Sherry, and Charles Cable. 1995. *Environmental Problems, Grassroots Solutions: The Politics of Grassroots Environmental Conflict*. St. Martin's Press.

*Calumet Index*. 1973. "File Your Complaints On Incinerator Pollution." July 23.

Canan, Penelope. 1996. "Bringing Nature Back In." *Sociological Inquiry* 66: 29–37.

Capek, Stella. 1993. "The 'Environmental Justice' Frame: A Conceptual Discussion and an Application." *Social Problems* 40: 5–24.

Carless, Jennifer. 1992. *Taking Out the Trash*. Island.

Castleman, Barry. 1987. "Workplace Health Standards and Multinational Corporations in Developing Countries. In *Multinational Corporations, Environment, and the Third World*, ed. C. Pearson. Duke University Press.

Center for Neighborhood Technology (Chicago). 1993. Four Strategies for Sustainable Communities.

Cerny, C., and S. Seriff, eds. 1996. "Recycled, Re-seen." *El Palacio*, summer-fall: 24–35.

Chappell, Tom. 1993. *The Soul of a Business*. Bantam.

Chavez, Cesar. 1993. "Farm Workers at Risk." In *Toxic Struggles: The Theory and Practice of Environmental Justice*, ed. R. Hofrichter. New Society.

Chavis, Ben. 1993. "Environmental Racism." In *Confronting Environmental Racism: Voices from the Grassroots*, ed. R. Bullard. South End.

*Chicago Defender*. 1997. "City Swats Down Illegal Fly Dumpers." December 17.

Chicago Department of Environment. 1995. Chicago's Blue Bag Recycling Program.

Chicago Department of Health. 1894. Annual Report of the Department of Health.

Chicago Department of Health, Biennial Report, 1895–1896.

Chicago Department of Health. Report for 1911–1918.

Chicago Department of Planning. 1985. Waste Management Options for Chicago.

Chicago Department of Public Works. 1973. "First Incineration Facilities." In *Chicago: A History*. Rand McNally.

Chicago Innovations Forum. 1988. Neighborhood Economic Interests in Chicago's Mandatory Waste Separation Ordinance. March 17 and 18.

Chicago Recycling Coalition. 1994. Letter to Loomis Mayfield, Coordinator of Policy Research Action Group, Loyola University, July 1.

Chicago Recycling Coalition. 1997. Problems with the Blue Bag Program (memorandum).

*Chicago Reader*. 1995. March 10.

*Chicago Sun-Times*. 1995. "Taxpayers Burned by Incinerator Deal." December 4.

*Chicago Today*. 1971. Editorial. "Chicago Can Salvaging Keeps our City Cleaner." October 17.

*Chicago Tonight*. 1996. PBS Television (WTTW).

*Chicago Tribune*. 1881. "Public Health: Wretched Condition of a West Side Tenement Block." January 17.

*Chicago Tribune*. 1881. "City Sanitation: Another Investigation by the Tribune Commission." January 28.

*Chicago Tribune*. 1881. "Chicago Stenches: Reid and Sherman's Packing-House and Its Horrible Smells." July 9.

*Chicago Tribune*. 1962. "Jury Probes Sanitary-Mob Link." November 20.

*Chicago Tribune*. 1972. Editorial. May 7.

*Chicago Tribune*. 1986. (no title). February 5.

*Chicago Tribune*. 1991. "Clearing the Air over an Incinerator." August 23.

*Chicago Tribune*. 1992. "Avoiding the Burner." August 7.

Chinweizu. 1975. *The West and the Rest of Us: White Predators, Black Slavers, and the African Elite.*. Random House.

Cichonski, Thomas, and Karen Hill, eds. 1993. *The Recycling Sourcebook*. Gale Research.

Citizens' Association of Chicago. 1910. Bulletin No. 25, June.

Citizens' Association of Chicago. 1912. Bulletin No. 28, June.

Citizens for a Better Environment/People for Community Recovery. 1994a. Memo, April 19.

Citizens for a Better Environment. 1994b. Letter to David Mucha, Attorney, Region V, USEPA.

Citizens for a Better Environment. 1999. "Chicago Incinerator Settlement Will Improve Environment for Westside." April 29. www.cbemw.org/fact/nwincerpress. htm.

Clavel, Pierre, and Nancy Kleniewski. 1990. "Space for Progressive Local Policy: Examples from the United States and the United Kingdom." In *Beyond the City Limits: Urban Policy and Economic Restructuring in Comparative Perspective*, ed. J. Logan and T. Swanstrom. Temple University Press.

Clawson, Dan. 1980. *Bureaucracy and the Labor Process: The Transformation of US Industry, 1860–1920*. Monthly Review Press.

CAWD (Coalition for Appropriate Waste Disposal). 1984. Letter to David Mosena, Deputy Commissioner, Department of Planning, City of Chicago. This letter contains a comprehensive revision of the City's waste disposal ordinance.

CAWD. 1985. Letter to Mayor Harold Washington. August 2.

CAWD. 1986a. Letter to Richard J. Carlson, Director, Illinois Environmental Protection Agency. February 20.

CAWD. 1986b. Letter to Aldermen. April 22.

CAWD. 1986c. Comments on the City of Chicago Preliminary Budget Estimate Report. Chicago, Illinois. August 28.

CAWD. 1987. Minutes, General Meeting. October 19.

Cohen, Linc. 1992. "Waste Dumps Toxic Traps for Minorities." *Chicago Reporter*. April.

Cole, Luke, and Sheila Foster. 2001. *From the Ground Up: Environmental Racism and the Rise of the Environmental Justice Movement*. New York University Press.

Collin, Robert, and William Harris, Sr. 1993. "Race and Waste in Two Virginia Communities." In *Confronting Environmental Racism: Voices from the Grassroots*, ed. R. Bullard. South End.

Colorado People's Environmental and Economic Network (COPEEN) 2001. "Newell Recycling Off the Hook." *COPEEN News* 7, no. 1: 5.

Colten, Craig. 1984. Industrial Wastes in the Calumet Area, 1869–1970: An Historical Geography. Hazardous Waste Research and Information Center, Illinois Deparment of Energy and Natural Resources, Champaign.

Colten, Craig. 1994. "Chicago's Waste Lands: Refuse, Disposal and Urban Growth, 1840–1990." *Journal of Historical Geography*, 20: 124–142.

*Consumer Reports*. 1994. "A Guilt-Free Guide to Garbage." February.

Coombs, S. 1991. "MRFs Multiplied in '91 Despite Economic Recession." *Recycling Times* 31: 8.

Coursey, Don. 1994. "Environmental Racism in the City of Chicago." Paper presented at Irving B. Harris School of Public Policy, University of Chicago. October.

*Crain's Chicago Business*. 1998. Burn, Baby, Burn: Illinois' Wicked Signal to Wall Street." January 22.

Daly, Herman. 1973. *Toward a Steady State Economy*. Freeman.

Daniels, Glynis. 2000. "Ecological Fallacy or Environmental Fact?: An Investigation of Aggregation Bias in the Study of Environmental Justice." Paper presented at annual meeting of American Sociological Association. Washington.

d'Anjou, Charlotte. 1976. "Energy: A Great Resource." *ONE*, May: 4–5.

Davidson, Marilyn, and Cary Cooper. 1981. "A Model of Occupational Stress." *Journal of Occupational Medicine* 23: 564–574.

Davis, Morris. 1977. "Occupational Hazards and Black Workers." *Urban Health*, August: 16–18.

Delgado, Richard, and Jean Stefancic. 1999. Home-Grown Racism: Colorado's Historic Embrace, and Denial, of Equal Opportunity in Higher Education. Latino/a Research and Polic Center, University of Colorado, Denver.

Denzin, Norman. 1970. *The Research Act*. Aldine.

Department of Development and Planning (Chicago). 1976. Historic City: The Settlement of Chicago.

Derksen, Linda, and John Gartrell. 1993. "The Social Context of Recycling." *American Sociological Review* 58: 434–442.

DeYoung, R. 1986. "Encouraging Environmentally Appropriate Behavior." *Journal of Environmental Systems* 15: 281–292.

DuBois, W. E. B. 1912. Address to the City Club of Chicago.

Duncan, Otis Dudley, and Beverly Duncan. 1957. *The Negro Population of Chicago: A Study of Residential Succession*. University of Chicago Press.

Eastwood, Carolyn. 1992. "Sidewalk Sales: Remembering the Heyday of Jewish Street Peddlers in Chicago. *Jewish United Fund News*, May, 22–33.

Edelstein, Michael. 1988. *Contaminated Communities: The Social and Psychological Impacts of Residential Toxic Exposures*. Westview.

Edwards, Richard. 1979. *Contested Terrain: The Transformation of the Workplace in the Twentieth Century*. Basic Books.

Ellingson, Stephen. 1996. "Understanding the Dialectic of Discourse and Collective Action: Public Debate and Rioting in Antebellum Cincinnati." In *Social Movements: Readings on Their Emergence, Mobilization, and Dynamics*, ed. D. McAdam and D. Snow. Roxbury.

Elrick, M. L. 1998. "Burner Facing New Heat." *Daily Southtown*. July 4.

Emmons, David. 1986. "Community Organizing and Urban Policy: Saul Alinsky and Chicago's Citizens Action Program." Unpublished Dissertation, University of Chicago, Department of Sociology.

Enstad, Robert. 1963. "City Switches to Incineration for Waste Disposal." *Chicago Tribune*. May 9.

Environmental Defense Fund. 1993. National Recycling Media Campaign. Fundraising letter to membership.

Erikson, Kai. 1994. *A New Species of Trouble*. Norton.

Evans, Peter, Dietrich Rueschemeyer, and Theda Skocpol, eds. 1985. *Bringing the State Back In*. Cambridge University Press.

Evans, Sara, and Harry Boyte. 1986. *Free Spaces*. Harper and Row.

Eyring, Bill, Kevin Greene, and Franklin Lomax. 1994. *An Alternative to the Northwest Incinerator: Reducing Waste, Stimulating Economic Development and Creating Jobs Instead of Pollution*. Center for Neighborhood Technology, Chicago.

Fannon, William. 1955. "Sanitary Fills to Go in Baltimore." *American City*, January: 99.

Fary, Mark. 1994. "Resolution." September. Chicago City Council.

Feagin, Joe, and Melvin P. Sikes. 1994. *Living with Racism: The Black Middle-Class Experience*. Beacon.

Fegelman, Andrew. 1987. (no title) *Chicago Tribune*. February 3.

Fenwick, Rudy, and Mark Tausig. 1994. "The Macroeconomic Context of Job Stress." *Journal of Health and Social Behavior* 35: 266–282.

Fieldnotes. This generally refers to interviews and observations made by the author between 1992–1998 in Chicago.

Finley, Larry. 1987. "Legislator Rips Chicago on Waste 'Crisis.'" *Chicago Sun-Times*, October 20.

First National People of Color Leadership Summit. 1991. Principles of Environmental Justice.

Fletcher, Ben. 1988. "The Epidemiology of Occupational Stress." In *Causes, Coping and Consequences of Stress at Work*, ed. C. Cooper and R. Pane. Wiley.

Foster, Sheila. 2000. "Community Based Environmental Protection and Justice: A Critical Assessment." Paper presented at "Environmental Justice and Natural Resources" Conference. Tattered Cover Bookstore, Denver.

Freeman, A. M., III. 1972. "The Distribution of Environmental Quality." In *Environmental Quality Analysis: Theory and Method in the Social Sciences*, ed. A. Kneese and B. Bower. Johns Hopkins University Press.

Freudenberg, Nicholas. 1984. *Not in Our Backyards*. Monthly Review Press.

Freudenburg, William, Scott Frickel, and Robert Gramling. 1995. "Beyond the Society-Nature Divide." *Sociological Forum* 10: 361–392.

Friedman, Fred. 1994. WASTE letter to Deputy Regional Administrator, Michelle Jordon, USEPA. December 17.

Gamson, William. 1975. *The Strategy of Social Protest*. Dorsey.

Gamson, William. 1992. "The Social Psychology of Collective Action." In *Frontiers in Social Movement Theory*, ed. A. Morris and C. Mueller. Yale University Press.

Gamson, William, Bruce Fireman, and Steven Rytina. 1982. *Encounters With Unjust Authority*. Dorsey.

Gaventa, John. 1980. *Power and Powerlessness*. University of Illinois Press.

Gedicks, Al. 1993. *The New Resource Wars: Native and Environmental Struggles Against Multinational Corporations*. South End.

Geertz, Clifford. 1973. *The Interpretation of Cultures*. Basic Books.

Gereffi, Gary, and Miguel Korzeniewicz, eds. 1994. *Commodity Chains and Global Capitalism*. Greenwood.

Gibbs, Lois. 1992. "How Dare They!!!" *Everyone's Backyard*, June: 2

Giloth, Robert, and Kari Moe. 1999."Jobs, Equity, and the Mayoral Administration of Harold Washington in Chicago." *Policy Studies Journal* 27, no. 1: 129–146.

Ginsburg, Robert. 1983. "The Dirt Comes Out From Under the Carpet." *CBE Environmental Review*, March-April: 3–5.

Gitlin, Lisa. 1992. "Overlooked." *Recycling Today*. September: 37–40.

Goering, Laurie. 1988. "South Suburbs' Cancer Rate Studied." *Chicago Tribune*. July 22.

Goering, Laurie. 1989. "Robbins is Scrambling to Pay Workers, Debts." *Chicago Tribune*. May 17.

Goering, Laurie. 1990. "Incinerator Risks Seen by Hospital." *Chicago Tribune*. December 27.

Goering, Laurie. 1991. "Incinerator Foes Score Big at Polls." *Chicago Tribune*, April 8.

Goering, Laurie. 1995. "Foes of Robbins Incinerator United in Opposition, and Fears." *Chicago Tribune*, April 24.

Goffman, Erving. 1959. *The Presentation of Self in Everyday Life*. Doubleday Anchor.

Goffman, Erving. 1974. Frame Analysis. Harvard University Press.

Goldman, Benjamin. 1994. *Toxic Wastes and Race Revisited*. Center for Policy Alternatives, Washington.

Gonos, George. 1997. "The Contest over 'Employer' Status in the Postwar United States: The Case of Temporary Help Firms." *Law and Society Review* 31: 81–110.

Gordon, David. 1995. *Fat and Mean: The Corporate Squeeze of Working Americans and the Myth of Managerial "Downsizing."* Martin Kessler Books.

Gottlieb, Robert. 1993. *Forcing the Spring: The Transformation of the American Environmental Movement*. Island.

Gottlieb, Robert. 2001. *Environmentalism Unbound: Exploring New Pathways for Change*. MIT Press.

Gould, Kenneth. 1991. "The Sweet Smell of Money: Economic Dependence, and Local Environmental Political Mobilization." *Society and Natural Resources* 4: 133–150.

Gould, Kenneth. 1992. "Putting the (W)RAPs on Public Participation." *Sociological Practice Review* 3: 133–139.

Gould, Kenneth. 1993. "Pollution, and Perception: Social Visibility, and Local Environmental Mobilization." *Qualitative Sociology* 16: 157–178.

Gould, Kenneth. 1994. "Legitimacy, and Growth in the Balance." *Industrial and Environmental Crisis Quarterly* 8: 237–256.

Gould, Kenneth, Adam Weinberg, and Allan Schnaiberg. 1993. "Legitimating Impotence: Pyrrhic Victories of the Modern Environmental Movement." *Qualitative Sociology* 16: 207-246.

Gould, Kenneth, Adam Weinberg, and Allan Schnaiberg. 1995. "Natural Resource Use in a Transnational Treadmill." *Humboldt Journal of Social Relations* 21: 61–93.

Gould, Kenneth, Allan Schnaiberg, and Adam Weinberg. 1996. *Local Environmental Struggles: Citizen Activism in the Treadmill of Production.* Cambridge University Press.

Gove, Samuel, and Louis Masotti. 1982. *After Daley: Chicago Politics in Transition.* University of Illinois Press.

Granovetter, Mark. 1974. *Getting a Job: A Study of Contacts and Careers.* Harvard University Press.

Greeley, Samuel A. 1914. "Experiences with Refuse Collection, and Disposal with Reference to Odors." Paper presented before the Sanitary Engineering Section of the American Public Health Association. Jacksonville, Florida. December 2.

Greene, Kevin. 1993. *Incineration versus Recycling.* Center for Neighborhood Technology.

Greenpeace. 1995. "African-American Population in Pulp Mill Towns, Southeast US." In *It's About TIME.*

Greer, Edward. 1979. *Big Steel: Black Politics and Corporate Power in Gary, Indiana.* Monthly Review Press.

Griffith, David. 1993. *Jones's Minimal: Low Wage Labor in the US.* State University of New York Press.

Harrison, Bennett. 1994. *Lean and Mean: The Changing Landscape of Corporate Power in the Age of Flexibility.* Basic Books.

Haymore, Tyrone. 1988. *The Story of Robbins, Illinois.* Robbins Historical Society. Publication No. 2.

Hays, Samuel. 1969. *Conservation and the Gospel of Efficiency: The Progressive Conservation Movement, 1890–1920.* Atheneum.

Henderson, Harold. 1986. "Don't Dump on Us." *Chicago Reader.* May 23.

Henderson, Harold. 1991. "Will it Fly? Six Questions that Need to be Asked About the Lake Calumet Airport." *Chicago Reader,* January 4.

Henderson, Harold. 1995. "Talking Trash." *Chicago Reader*, April 14.

Herbst, Alma. 1932. *The Negro in the Slaughtering and Meat Packing Industry in Chicago.* University of Chicago.

Hersch, R. 1995. "Race, and Industrial Hazards: An Historical Geography of the Pittsburgh Region, 1900–1990." Discussion Paper 95-18, Resources for the Future, Washington.

Heuchling, Fred. 1913. *City Club Bulletin.* December 20. Chicago.

Higgins, Lorie, and Loren Lutzenhiser. 1995. "Ceremonial equity." *Social Problems* 42: 468–492.

Hirsch, Arnold. 1990. *Making the Second Ghetto: Race and Housing in Chicago, 1940–1960.* Cambridge University Press.

Hirschman, Albert. 1970. *Exit, Voice, and Loyalty.* Cambridge University Press.

Hochshild, Arlie. 1989. *The Second Shift.* Avon.

Hoeling, A. A. 1966. *Homefront, US A.* Thomas Crowell.

Hoetmer, Gerard. 1988. "Police, Fire, and Refuse Collection, 1988." *Municipal Yearbook 1988.* International City Management Association.

Hoffman, Andrew. *From Heresy to Dogma: An Institutional History of Corporate Environmentalism.* New Lexington Press.

Hofrichter, Richard, ed. 1993. *Toxic Struggles: The Theory and Practice of Environmental Justice.* New Society.

Holusha, John. 1994. "Rich Markets for Business of Recycling." *New York Times*, October 8.

Honey, Michael K. 1993. *Black Labor and Southern Civil Rights: Organizing Memphis Workers* University of Illinois Press.

Horowitz, Tony. 1994."Inside a 'Dirty MuRF': The Offal Part of the Recycling Boom." *Wall Street Journal*, December 1.

House, James, and M. F. Jackman. 1979. "Occupational Stress, and Health." In *Toward a New Definition of Health*, ed. P. Ahmed and G. Coelho. Plenum.

Hoy, Suellen M., and Michael C. Robinson. 1979. *Recovering the Past: A Handbook of Community Recycling Programs, 1890–1945.* Public Works Historical Society.

Hughes, Elizabeth. 1925. Living Conditions for Small Wage Earners in Chicago. Department of Public Welfare, City of Chicago.

Hughes, Everett. 1956. *Men and Their Work.* Free Press.

Hughes, Everett. 1971. *The Sociological Eye.* Aldine-Atherton.

Hull House. 1895. *Hull-House Maps and Papers.* T. Y. Crowell.

Hurley, Andrew. 1995. *Environmental Inequalities: Class, Race and Industrial Pollution in Gary, Indiana, 1945–1980.* University of North Carolina Press.

Illinois Environmental Protection Agency. 1975. Inter-Office Correspondence Regarding the Calumet Incinerator. February 20.

Illinois Environmental Protection Agency. 1987. An Environmental Manifesto for Southeast A Comprehensive Program for Restoring, and Enhancing the Quality of Life in Chicago's Forgotten Neighborhood. August.

Illinois EPA News. 1984. "IEPA Releases Initial Findings on Southeast Chicago Study." April 25

Illinois Interracial Commission. 1948. Special Report on Employment Opportunities in Illinois.

Institute of Medicine. 1999. *Toward Environmental Justice: Research, Education, and Health Policy Needs*. National Academy Press.

Jacobson, Timothy. 1993. *Waste Management: An American Corporate Success Story*. Gateway Business Books.

Jacoby, Karl. 2001. *Crimes Against Nature: Squatters, Poachers, Thieves, and the Hidden History of American Conservation*. University of California Press.

Jaeger, Carlo. 1994. *Taming the Dragon: Transforming Economic Institutions in the Face of Global Change*. Gordon and Breach.

Jaffe, Martin. 1988. *The Recycling of Municipal Solid Waste: Issues for Illinois Communities*. Office of Technology Transfer, University of Illinois Center for Solid Waste Management, and Research.

Jakubiak, Joyce. 1993."Implementing a community recycling program." In *The Recycling Sourcebook*, ed. T. Cichonski, and K. Hill. Gale Research.

Jeter, Jon. 1998. "Poor Town That Sought Incinerator Finds More Problems, Few Benefits." *Washington Post*, April 11.

Johnson, Bill. 1998. "Save Detroit's Development, and Minorities from Eco-Justice." *Detroit News*, June 12.

Johnson, John H. Jr., and Melvin Oliver. 1989. "Blacks, and the Toxics Crisis." *Western Journal of Black Studies* 13: 72–78.

Jones, R., and Riley Dunlap 1992. "The Social Basis of Environmental Concern." *Rural Sociology* 59: 28–47.

Joravsky, Ben. 1991. "Trouble in Paradise: Airport Agony." *Chicago Reader*. July 26.

Joravsky, Ben. 1993. "Talking Trash: City Hall's Spat with Uptown Recycling." *Chicago Reader*, April 14.

Karasek, Robert, and Tores Theorell. 1990. *Healthy Work: Stress, Productivity, and the Reconstruction of Working Life*. Basic Books.

Kazis, Richard, and Richard Grossman. 1982. *Fear at Work*. Pilgrim.

Kelley, Florence. 1895. "The Sweating-System." In*Hull House Maps and Papers*. Crowell.

Kelley, Florence, and Alzina Stevens. 1895. "Wage-Earning Children." In *Hull House Maps and Papers*. Crowell.

Kelley, Robin. 1993. "'We Are Not What We Seem': Rethinking Black Working-Class Opposition in the Jim Crow South." *Journal of American History*: June 75–112.

Kimball, Debi. 1992. *Recycling In America: A Reference Handbook*. ABC-CLIO.

Kitschelt, Herbert. 1986. "Political Opportunity Structures, and Political Protest: Anti-Nuclear Movements in Four Democracies." *British Journal of Political Science* 16: 57–85.

Klandermans, Bert. 1984. "Mobilization, and Participation: Social-Psychological Expansions of Resource Mobilization Theory." *American Sociological Review* 49: 583–600.

Knudson, Tom, and Scott Flodin. 2001. "Environment, Inc." *Sacramento Bee*, April 22–24.

Krakoff, Sarah. 2000. "A Framework for Considering Whether Exercises of Tribal Sovereignty are Environmental Justice Questions." Paper presented at "Environmental Justice, and Natural Resources" Conference, Denver.

Kroll-Smith, Steve. 1994. "Multiple Chemical Sensitivity, and Negotiated Codes." Paper presented at annual meeting of American Sociological Association, Los Angeles.

LaDou, Joseph. 1985. "Health Issues in the Microelectronics Industry." *Occupational Medicine* 1: 1–12.

Lamphere, Louise, Patricia Zavella, Felipe Gonzales, and Peter Evans. 1993. *Sunbelt Working Mothers: Reconciling Family and Factory*. Cornell University Press.

Larane, A. 1995. "Lille Takes Lead in High-Tech French Recycling." *Waste Age*, November: 75–76.

Lavelle, Marianne, and Marcia Coyle. 1992. "Unequal Protection: The Racial Divide in Environmental Law." *National Law Journal* 15: S1–S12.

Lazaroff, Cat. 2000. (no title). *Environmental News Service*, February 11.

Leidner, Robin. 1993. *Fast Food, Fast Talk: Service Work and the Routinization of Everyday Life*. University of California Press.

Lester, Stephen. 1996. "Recycling: A Modern Day Success Story." In *Everyone's Backyard*. Citizens Clearinghouse for Hazardous Waste.

Light, Ivan, and Edna Bonacich. 1988. *Immigrant Entrepreneurs: Koreans in Los Angeles, 1965–1982*. University of California Press.

Lindstrom, Bonnie, Ann Traore, and Marcia Untermeyer. 1995. "Evanston." In *The Chicago Community Fact Book*.

Lingeman, R. R. 1976. *Don't You Know There's a War On? The American Home Front, 1941–1945*. Putnam.

Lo, Clarence. 1984. "Mobilizing the Tax Revolt: The Emergent Alliance between Homeowners, and Local Elites." *Research in Social Movements: Conflicts and Change* 6: 293–328.

Logan, John, and Harvey Molotch. 1987. *Urban Fortunes: The Political Economy of Place*. University of California Press.

Logan, John, and Todd Swanstrom, eds. 1990. *Beyond the City Limits: Urban Policy and Economic Restructuring in Comparative Perspective*. Temple University Press.

Lukes, Steven. 1974. *Power: A Radical View*. Macmillan.

McAdam, Doug. 1983."Tactical Innovation, and the Pace of Insurgency." *American Sociological Review* 48: 735–754.

McAdam, Doug. 1996."The Framing Function of Movement Tactics: Strategic Dramaturgy in the American Civil Rights Movement." In *Comparative Perspectives on Social Movements*, ed. D. McAdam et al. Cambridge University Press.

McAdam, Doug, and David Snow, eds. 1997. *Social Movements: Readings on their Emergence, Mobilization, and Dynamics*. Roxbury.

McAdam, Doug, John McCarthy, and Mayer Zald, eds. 1996. *Comparative Perspectives on Social Movements*. Cambridge University Press.

McAdams, Cheryl, and Walter McAdams. 1995. "Computer Technology in the Waste Industry." *Waste Age*, September: 125–130.

McCarthy, John, and Mayer Zald. 1973. *The Trend of Social Movements in America*. General Learning Press.

McCarthy, John D., and Mayer Zald. 1977. "Resource Mobilization, and Social Movements: A Partial Theory." *American Journal of Sociology* 82: 1212–1241.

McCarthy, John, and Michael Wolfson. 1992. "Consensus Movements, Conflict Movements, and the Cooptation of Civic, and State Infrastructures." In *Frontiers in Social Movement Theory*, ed. A. Morris and C. McClurg Mueller. Yale University Press.

McIntyre, Gina. 1994. "Rockwell Neighbors on Bumpy Road to Recycling." *The Inside*. December 14.

McMullen, Jay. 1972. "City to Recycle Residue, Sell Metal, Glass." *Daily News*, June 1.

McNeil, Brett. 1998. "City Tries to Trash Illegal Dumping in Austin." *Austin Weekly News*, June 4.

Malloy, Michael. 1995. "Truck Technology: Bodies Shaping up for the 21st Century." *Waste Age*, December: 48–56.

Massey, Douglas, and Nancy Denton. 1993. *American Apartheid and the Making of the Underclass*. Harvard University Press.

Masterson-Allen, S., and Phil Brown. 1990. "Public Reaction to Toxic Waste Contamination." *International Journal of Health Services* 20: 485–500.

Marx, Karl. 1977. *Capital*, volume 1. Random House.

Melosi, Martin, ed. 1980. *Pollution and Reform in American Cities, 1879–1930*. University of Texas Press.

Melosi, Martin. 1981. *Garbage in the Cities: Refuse, Reform, and the Environment, 1880–1980*. Texas A&M University Press.

Melosi, Martin. 2000. *The Sanitary City: Urban Infrastructure in American from Colonial Times to the Present*. Johns Hopkins University Press.

Michaeli, Ethan. 1993a. "West Siders Protest Onslaught of Garbage" *Chicago Defender*, May 8.

Michaeli, Ethan. 1993b. "Recycling Could Come to Low-Income Areas." *Chicago Defender*, July 27.

Michaeli, Ethan. 1994. "Group Vows to Stop 2nd Mountain." *Chicago Defender*, July 16.

Miller, Chaz. 1993. "Washington State: Recycling Creates Jobs, and Value." *Recycling Times*, November 16, p. 7.

Miller, Chaz. 1995. "The Shape of Things to Come." *Waste Age*, September: 60–71.

Mitchell, Jerry, Deborah Thomas, and Susan Cutter. 1999. "Dumping in Dixie Revisited: The Evolution of Environmental Injustices in South Carolina." *Social Science Quarterly* 80: 229–243.

Moberg, David. 1994. "West Side Story: Controversy Surrounds the Proposed Rebuilding of Chicago's Northwest Incinerator." *The Neighborhood Works*. December-January, pp. 9–12.

Montague, Peter. 1994. "Ash Controversy Smolders." *Environmental Action*, fall: 36.

Moyers, Bill. 1990. *Global Dumping Ground: The International Traffic in Hazardous Waste*. Seven Locks Press.

*Multinational Monitor*. 1997. "The Workplace Toll." July-August.

Mumford, Lewis. 1961. *The City in History: Its Origins, Its Transformations, and Its Prospects*. Harcourt, Brace & World.

Natural Resources Defense Council. 1997. Too Good to Throw Away: Recycling's Proven Record.

Navarro, Vincente. 1982. "The Labor Process, and Health: A Historical Materialist Interpretation." *International Journal of Health Services* 12: 5–29.

Nelkin, Dorothy, and Michael Brown. 1984. *Workers at Risk*. University of Chicago Press.

Nelson, Deborah. 1988. "Our Toxic Trap: The Far South Side." Special report, *Chicago Sun-Times*.

*New York Times*. 1995. "The Trashman Cometh." May 30.

*New York Times*. 1996. "Fumes Kill Sanitation Worker." November 13.

Nolan, Karen. 1993. "Protesters Help to Dump Garbage Site." *Chicago Defender*, July 7.

Nyden, Phil, Anne Figert, Mark Shibley, and Darryl Burrows. 1997. *Building Community: Social Science in Action*. Pine Forge.

O'Connor, James. 1973. *The Fiscal Crisis of the State*. St. Martin's Press.

O'Neill, Hugh, and Megan Sheehan. 1993. Exploring Economic Development Opportunities in Recycling. Urban Research Center, New York University.

Packard, Vance. 1963. *The Waste Makers*. Pocket Books.

Park, Lisa Sun-Hee. 1997. "Navigating the Anti-Immigrant Wave." In *Community Activism and Feminist Politics*, ed. N. Naples. Routledge.

Park, Lisa Sun-Hee, and David N. Pellow. 1996. "Washing Dirty Laundry: Organic-Activist Research in Two Social Movement Organizations." *Sociological Imagination* 33: 138–153.

Parker, Robert. 1994. *Flesh Peddlers and Warm Bodies: The Temporary Help Industry and Their Workers.* Rutgers University Press.

Pastor, Manuel, Jr., Jim Sadd, and John Hipp. 2001. "Which Came First? Toxic Facilities, Minority Move-in, and Environmental Justice." *Journal of Urban Affairs* 23: 1–21.

Paules, Greta. 1993. *Dishing It Out: Power and Resistance among Waitresses in a New Jersey Restaurant.* Temple University Press.

Pellow, David N. 2000. Environmental Inequality Formation: Toward a Theory of Environmental Injustice. *American Behavioral Scientist* 43: 581–601.

Pellow, David N., and Lisa Sun-Hee Park. 2000. "The Hazards of Work: Environmental Racism at the Point of Production." Paper presented at annual meeting of American Sociological Association, Washington.

Pena, Devon. 1997. The Terror of the Machine: Technology, Work, Gender, and Ecology on the US -Mexico Border. Center for Mexican American Studies, Austin.

People for Community Recovery. 1992. Conference on Environmental Justice in the Midwest. October.

Perfecto, Ivette, and Baldemar Velasquez. 1992. "Farm Workers: Among the Least Protected." *EPA Journal* 18, March-April: 13–14.

Perrolle, Judith. 1993. "The Emerging Dialogue on Environmental Justice." *Social Problems* 40: 1–4.

Perrow, Charles. 1984. *Normal Accidents.* Basic Books.

Perry, Stewart. 1978. *San Francisco Scavengers: Dirty Work and the Pride of Ownership.* University of California Press.

Pickus, Abigail. 1998. "Garbage in, Reusables Out." *Streetwise*, June 23.

Porter, Michael. 1990. "The Competitive Advantage of Nations." *Harvard Business Review*, March-April: 73–93.

Powell, Jerry. 1992. "Safety of Workers in Recycling, and Mixed Waste Processing Plants." *Resource Recycling*, September.

Pulido, Laura. 1996. "A Critical Review of the Methodology of Environmental Racism Research." *Antipode* 28: 142–159.

Pulido, Laura, S. Sidawi, and R. O. Vos. 1996. "An Archaeology of Environmental Racism in Los Angeles." *Urban Geography* 17: 419–439.

Quadagno, Jill. 1992. "Social Movements, and State Transformation: Labor Unions, and Racial Conflict in the War on Poverty." *American Sociological Review* 57: 616–634.

Rabasca, Lisa. 1993. "Recycling Plays Key Role in Philadelphia's Expanding Economy." *Recycling Times*, November 16, p. 5.

*Rachel's Environment and Health Weekly.* 1997. "Waste Management Accused of Gangster Death Threats against New Orleans Officials." July 24.

Ranney, David, and William Cecil. 1993. Transnational Investment, and Job Loss in Chicago. Center for Urban Economic Development, University of Illinois, Chicago.

Rawls, John. 1971. *A Theory of Justice.* Harvard University Press.

Reich, Robert. 1992. *The Work of Nations.* Random House.

REM. 1996. "Memo to REM Employees."

REM Employees. 1996. "Open letter to the Press."

Renner, Michael. 1992."Creating Sustainable Jobs in Industrial Countries." In *State of the World*, ed. L. Brown et al. Norton.

Resource Center (Chicago). 1983. Newsletter, vol. 1, no. 3.

Resource Center (Chicago). 1984a. Contribution solicitation letter, December 1.

Resource Center (Chicago). 1984b. Newsletter, vol. 1., no. 5.

Resource Center (Chicago). 1985. Newsletter, vol. 2, no. 2. Chicago.

Resource Center (Chicago). 1986. Newsletter, vol. 2, no. 3.

Rifkin, Jeremy. 1995. *The End of Work: The Decline of the Global Labor Force and the Dawn of the Post-Market Era.* Putnam.

Ritter, Jack. 1996. "Recycling Plant Blues." *Chicago Sun-Times*, March 10.

Roberts, Timmons. 1993. "Psychosocial Effects of Workplace Hazardous Exposures." *Social Problems* 40: 74–89.

Roberts, Timmons. 1996. "Negotiating Both Sides of the Plant Gate." Paper presented at annual meeting of American Sociological Association, New York.

Roberts, Timmons, and Melissa Toffolon-Weiss. 2001. *Chronicles from the Environmental Justice Front Line.* Cambridge University Press.

Robinson, James. 1991. *Toil and Toxics: Workplace Struggles and Political Strategies for Occupational Health.* University of California.

Rodney, Walter. 1982. *How Europe Underdeveloped Africa.* Howard University Press.

Roediger, David. 1999. *The Wages of Whiteness: Race and the Making of the American Working Class.* Verso.

Rollins, Judith. 1985. *Between Women: Domestics and Their Employers.* Temple University Press.

Salimando, J. 1986. "A Tale of Two Californians." *Waste Age* 17: 39–46.

Sassen, Saskia. 1988. *The Mobility of Labor and Capital.* Cambridge University Press.

Schnaiberg, Allan. 1973. "Politics, Participation, and Pollution: The 'Environmental Movement,'" In *Cities in Change: Studies on the Urban Condition*, ed. J. Walton and D. Carns. Allyn & Bacon.

Schnaiberg, Allan. 1975. "Social Syntheses of the Societal-Environmental Dialectic." *Social Science Quarterly* 56: 5–20.

Schnaiberg 1980. *The Environment: From Surplus to Scarcity*. Oxford University Press.

Schnaiberg, Allan. 1992a. "Recycling Versus Remanufacturing." Working paper, Institute for Policy Research, Northwestern University.

Schnaiberg, Allan. 1992b. "The Recycling Shell Game." Working paper, Institute for Policy Research, Northwestern University.

Schnaiberg, Allan. 1993. "Paradoxes, and Contradictions: A Framework for 'How I Learned to Reject Recycling.'" Paper presented at annual meeting of American Sociological Association, Miami Beach.

Schnaiberg, Allan. 1994. "The Political Economy of Environmental Problems." *Advances in Human Ecology* 3: 23–64.

Schnaiberg, Allan, and Kenneth Gould. 1994. *Environment and Society: The Enduring Conflict*. St. Martin's Press.

Schnaiberg, Allan. 1997. "Sustainable Development, and the Treadmill of Production." In *The Politics of Sustainable Development*, ed. S. Baker et al. Routledge.

Schneider, Keith. 1991. "As Recycling Becomes a Growth Industry, its Paradoxes also Multiply." *New York Times*, January 20.

Schor, Juliet. 1991. *The Overworked American: The Unexpected Decline of Leisure*. Basic Books.

Schwab, James. 1994a. *Deeper Shades of Green: The Rise of Blue-Collar and Minority Environmentalism in America*. Sierra Club Books.

Schwab, James. 1994b. Presentation at Forum on Environmental Racism, Irving B. Harris Graduate School of Public Policy, University of Chicago.

Schwarz, John, and Thomas Volgy. 1992. *The Forgotten Americans*. Norton.

Schwartz, Michael, and Shuva Paul. 1992. "Resource Mobilization Versus the Mobilization of People: Why Consensus Movements Cannot Be Instruments of Social Change." In *Frontiers in Social Movement Theory*, ed. A. Morris and C. Mueller. Yale University Press.

Scott, James. 1990. *Domination and the Arts of Resistance*. Yale University Press.

Seager, Joni. 1993. *Earth Follies: Coming to Feminist Terms with the Global Environmental Crisis*. Routledge.

Sellers, Christopher. 1997. *Hazards of the Job: From Industrial Disease to Environmental Health Science*. University of North Carolina Press.

Sennett, Richard, and Jonathan Cobb. 1972. *The Hidden Injuries of Class*. Knopf.

Sheehan, Helen, and Richard Wedeen, eds. 1992. *Toxic Circles: Environmental Hazards from the Workplace into the Community*. Rutgers University Press.

Sheehan, Kathleen. 1993. "Recycling, Composting, and Jobs." *Recycling Times*. March 9, p. 3

Siegel, Beth, and Peter Kwass. 1995. Jobs and the Urban Poor: Publicly Initiated Sectoral Strategies. Mt. Auburn Associates, Somerville, Mass.

Silliman, Jean. 1997. "Making the Connections: Women's Health, and Environmental Justice." *Race, Gender and Class* 5: 104–129.

Simon, Ellen. 1998. "Illinois Sues Clinton, N.J. -Based Firm over Chicago Garbage-Burning Plant." *Knight-Ridder/Tribune Business News*, April 30.

Smith, Michael. 1970. No title. *Chicago Tribune*, January 4.

Smith, Michael, and Joe Feagin, eds. 1987. *The Capitalist City*. Basil Blackwell.

Smith, Suzanna, and Michael Jepson. 1993. "Big Fish, Little Fish: Politics, and Power in the Regulation of Florida's Marine Resources." *Social Problems* 40: 39–49.

Solid Waste Management Newsletter (Office of Technology Transfer, University of Illinois Center for Solid Waste Management, and Research). 1990. "Chicago Announces 1991 Recycling Plan." Vol. 4, no. 12.

*Solid Waste Technologies*. 1996. "Municipal Solid Waste Generation Rate Flattens: US Recycles 24 Percent." May-June, p. 9.

*Solid Waste Technologies*. 1996. "Yale Releases Waste Policy Papers." January-February, p. 45.

SouthWest Organizing Project (Albuquerque). 1995. Voces Unidas..

Spear, Allan. 1967. *Black The Making of a Negro Ghetto, 1890–1920*. University of Chicago Press.

Spielman, Fran. 1994. "Incinerator Foes Propose Trash Fee as Alternative." *Chicago Sun-Times*, June 30.

Squires, Gregory, Larry Bennett, Kathleen McCourt, and Philip Nyden. 1987. *Race, Class, and the Response to Urban Decline*. Temple University Press.

Stall, Susan, and Randy Stoecker. 1994. "Community Organizing or Organizing Community?" Paper presented at annual meeting of American Sociological Association, Los Angeles.

Stabenow, G. 1973. "Results of the Stack Emissions Tests at the New Chicago Northwest Incinerator." *Journal of Engineering for Power*, July: 137–141.

Stockdill, Brett. 1996. Multiple Oppressions, and Their Influence on Collective Action: The Case of the AIDS Movement. Ph.D. thesis, Northwestern University.

Stoecker, Randy. 1995. "Community, Movement, Organization: The Problem of Identity Convergence in Collective Action." *Sociological Quarterly* 36: 1–30.

Stoecker, Randy. 1996. "Sociology, and Social Action: An Introduction." *Sociological Imagination* 33: 3–17.

Stoecker, Randy, and Edna Bonacich. 1992. "Why Participatory Research." *American Sociologist* 23: 5–14

Strauss, Anselm. 1987. *Qualitative Analysis for Social Scientists*. Cambridge University Press.

Stretton, Hugh. 1976. *Capitalism, Socialism and the Environment.* Cambridge University Press.

Sullivan, Molly. 1996. "Baby Found Dead in Trash." *Daily Southtown.* December 27.

Swanson, Stevenson. 1991. "Recycling Grows into a Way of Life." *Chicago Tribune,* June 16.

Swanson, Stevenson. 1991. "Federal EPA Upholds State Incinerator OK." *Chicago Tribune,* August 7.

Swanson, Stevenson. 1991. "The No. 1 Second City." *Chicago Tribune,* November 17.

Szasz, Andrew. 1994. *EcoPopulism: Toxic Waste and the Movement for Environmental Justice.* University of Minnesota Press.

Szasz, Andrew, and Michael Meuser. 1997. "Environmental Inequalities: Literature Review, and Proposals for New Directions in Research, and Theory." *Current Sociology* 45: 99–120.

Szasz, Andrew, and Michael Meuser. 1998. "Unintended, Inexorable: The Production of Environmental Inequalities in Santa Clara County, California." *American Behavioral Scientist* 43: 602–632.

Tarrow, Sidney. 1983. *Struggling to Reform: Social Movements and Policy Change During Cycles of Protest.* Cornell University Press.

Taub, Richard. 1988. *Community Capitalism.* Harvard Business School Press.

Taylor, Bron. 1995. *Ecological Resistance Movements: The Global Emergence of Radical and Popular Environmentalism.* State University of New York Press.

Taylor, Dorceta. 1989. "Blacks, and the Environment: Toward an Explanation of the Concern, and Action Gap between Blacks, and Whites." *Environment and Behavior* 21: 175–205.

Taylor, Dorceta. 1993. "Minority Environmentalism in Britain." *Qualitative Sociology* 16: 263-295.

Taylor, Dorceta. 1997. "American Environmentalism: The Role of Race, Class, and Gender in Shaping Activism, 1820–1995." *Race, Gender and Class* 5: 16–62.

*The American City.* 1955. "Experts Analyze Air-Pollution Problems." April, p. 106.

*The American City.* 1955. "Paper Bag Liners for Refuse Containers." February, p. 199.

*Sanitary News* (Chicago). 1883a. Vol. 1, no. 5.

*Sanitary News* (Chicago). 1883b. Vol. 1, no. 10.

Thompson, John. 1990. *Ideology and Modern Culture.* Stanford University Press.

Thompson, Paul. 1989. *The Nature of Work: An Introduction to Debates on the Labour Process.* Macmillan.

Thornton, Joe. 2000. *Pandora's Poison.* MIT Press.

Tierney, John. 1996. "Recycling Is Garbage." *New York Magazine.* June 30.

Túre, Kwame. 1994. Black History Month Address. Northwestern University.

Tuttle, William. 1969. "Labor Conflict, and Racial Violence: The Black Worker in Chicago, 1894–1919." *Labor History* 10: 408–432.

United Church of Christ. 1987. *Toxic Wastes and Race in the United States*. United Church of Christ Commission for Racial Justice.

US Department of Health, and Human Services. 1992. Proposal for Southeast Chicago Petitioned Public Health Assessment. USDHHS Public Health Service, Agency for Toxic Substances, and Disease Registry, Division of Health Assessment, and Consultation, Atlanta.

US Environmental Protection Agency. 1975a. Correspondence from James O. McDonald, Director, Enforcement Division to Richard Briceland, Director of the IEPA, February 14.

US Environmental Protection Agency. 1975b. Inter-Office Correspondence from S. Rosenthal Regarding Chronology of Milestone Dates Re: City Incinerators. Chicago.

US Environmental Protection Agency. 1989. *The Solid Waste Dilemma: An Agenda for Action*.

US Environmental Protection Agency. 1992. Environmental Equity: Reducing Risk For All Communities.

US Environmental Protection Agency. 1992. "Special Issue: Environmental Protection: Has it Been Fair?" *EPA Journal*, March-April: entire issue.

US General Accounting Office. 1983. *Siting of Hazardous Waste Landfills and Their Correlation with Racial and Economic Status of Surrounding Communities*. Government Printing Office.

Valenti, Robert. 1988. "Urban Recycling Comes of Age." *The Neighborhood Works* 11, May-June: 1–9.

van Eerd, Maartje. 1996. *The Occupational Health Aspects of Waste Collection and Recycling*. Working document 4, part I, Urban Waste Expertise Programme, Netherlands.

Vinik, Nina, and Keith Harley. 1997. Environmental Injustice: Community Perspectives on Silver Shovel. Chicago Legal Clinic.

Viscusi, Kip, and Wesley Magat. 1987. *Learning about Risk: Consumer and Worker Response to Hazard Information*. Harvard University Press.

Vogel, Kimberly 1995. "What to Do When the OSHA Inspector Cometh." *Waste Age*, December: 75–81.

Walley, Noah, and Bradley Whitehead. 1994. "It's Not Easy Being Green." *Harvard Business Review*, May-June: 46–52.

Walls, Sunya. 1996. "Rev. Jackson Plans Dump Site Clean Up." *Chicago Weekend*, February 20.

Walsh, Edward, Rex Warland, and D. Clayton Smith. 1993. "Backyards, NIMBYs, and Incinerator Sitings." *Social Problems* 40: 25–38.

WASTE. 1994. Petition, "More Jobs, Less Pollution! Let the Community Choose!" Chicago.

Weber, Max. 1978. *Economy and Society*, ed. G. Roth and C. Wittich. University of California Press.

Weinberg, Adam S. 1994. "Citizenship, and Natural Resources." Working paper 94-26, Center for Urban Affairs and Policy Research, Northwestern University.

Weinberg, Adam. 1998. "The Environmental Justice Debate: A Commentary on Methodological Issues, and Practical Concerns." *Sociological Forum* 13: 25–32.

Weinberg, Adam S., and Kenneth A. Gould. 1993. "Public Participation in Environmental Regulatory Conflicts." *Law and Policy* 15: 139–167.

Weinberg, Adam, David N. Pellow, and Allan Schnaiberg. 1996. "Sustainable Development as a Sociologically Defensible Concept." *Advances in Human Ecology* 5: 261–302.

Weinberg, Adam, David N. Pellow, and Allan Schnaiberg. 2000. *Urban Recycling and the Search for Sustainable Community Development*. Princeton University Press.

Western Disposal Services (Boulder). 2000. A Quarterly Update for Our Customers. Summer.

Williams, Gary. 1996. "Forces of Change in the Solid Waste Industry: A Survey." *Waste Age* May: 163–168.

Williamson, Oliver. 1985. *The Economic Institutions of Capitalism*. Free Press.

Wilson, William Julius. 1978. *The Declining Significance of Race*. University of Chicago Press.

Wilson, William J. 1987. *The Truly Disadvantaged*. University of Chicago Press.

Wilson, William J. 1996. *When Work Disappears*. Random House.

WMX. 1994. "Environmental Justice: The Search for Balance." Symposium. Oakbrook, Illinois (cancelled).

WMX. 1995. "Good Neighbor Policy." Oakbrook, Illinois.

Woods, Randy. 1993. "NYC Economic Development Study Sparks Recycling Expansion Plans." *Recycling Times*. September 21, p. 3.

Woods, Randy. 1993. "NYC Job-Creation Plan Includes Outline for Recycling Growth." *Recycling Times*, October 19. p. 1.

World Resources Institute. 1993. *The 1993 Information Please Environmental Almanac*. Houghton Mifflin.

Young, Quentin. 1971. Funding Proposal Submitted to Citizens for a Better Environment, by the Occupational Health Project of the Medical Committee for Human Rights. Chicago.

Young, David. 1991. "Green Is Also the Color of Money." *Chicago Tribune*, November 17.

# Index

Ace Disposal, 46
ACORN, 88
Addams, Jane, 22, 48
Advocacy research, 17, 18
African Americans, 2–5, 9–12, 17, 18,
    21, 29, 30, 33–35, 45, 50, 56, 57,
    73–90, 94, 97, 98, 109–116, 122,
    128, 133, 137, 144, 148–151,
    154–157, 166, 167
Alinsky, Saul, 4, 133
Alley entrepreneurs, 109–122
Altgeld Gardens housing project,
    67–70
American Planning Association, 93
American Public Health Association,
    29, 94
Asian Americans, 3, 12, 17, 56, 80
Asian Pacific Environmental Network,
    76
Asian Pacific Islander Americans, 9
Assembly lines, 117, 144, 150, 151
Association of Community
    Organizations for Reform Now, 88
Austin (Chicago community), 81,
    85–89, 109, 137–139

Bethel New Life Community
    Development Organization, 113
Black Belt (Chicago), 30, 34, 133. *See
    also* South Side
Block clubs, 109
Blue Bag, 106, 130, 132, 140–148,
    153–160, 167
Boston, Massachusetts, 27

Brewer, Gretchen, 113, 134
Brodie, Irene, 95, 97, 166
Brownfields, 111
*Brown vs. Board of Education*, 79
Bryant, Bunyan, 8, 75
Buntrock, Dean, 46
Burris, Jim, 93, 118, 160
Burris, Roland, 93
Bush, George H. W., 56, 63, 73
Buy-back recycling centers, 52,
    108–111, 119

C & S Recycling, 87, 96, 105, 114
California Rural Legal Assistance
    Foundation, 77
Cancer Alley, 57
Carson, Rachel, 43
Center for Neighborhood Technology,
    137
Cerrell Report, 74
Chandler, Michael, 87, 88
Chavez, Cesar, 11
Chavis, Ben, 68
Chemical plants, 2, 78
Chester, Pennsylvania, 78, 79
Chester Residents Concerned for
    Quality Living, 78
Chicago and Suburban Ash and
    Scavenger Association, 45
Chicago and Suburban Refuse
    Disposal Association, 45
Chicago City Health Department, 25
*Chicago Defender*, 86
Chicago Legal Clinic, 82

*Chicago Reader*, 139
Chicago Recycling Coalition, 118, 141
Chicago Reduction Company, 28
Chicago Smoke Control Ordinance,
    24, 25
*Chicago Tribune*, 25, 26, 93, 132–134
Chicanos, 56, 74, 77, 144, 155
Child labor, 31, 32 37
Christopher, John, 81–85
Citizens Association of Chicago, 28,
    35
Citizens Clearinghouse for Hazardous
    Waste, 53, 104
Citizens for a Better Environment, 70,
    92, 113, 133, 135–138
Citizens In Action, 87, 88
Citizens United to Reclaim the
    Environment, 70
City Club of Chicago, 21, 22, 28
City Council, Chicago, 81
Civic organizations, 109
Clean Air Act, 94
Clinton, Bill 67, 71, 78
Coalition for Appropriate Waste
    Disposal, 49, 50, 70, 106, 109,
    113–115, 137, 146
Cole, Luke, 77
Coleman, Adolph, 93, 96
Collins, Cardiss, 89
Colonization, 80, 99
Committee to Protect the Prairie, 70
Concerned Citizens of South Central
    Los Angeles, 74
Concerned Parents of Summer,
    Webster, and Frazier Schools, 82, 87
Congressional Black Caucus, 79
Connett, Paul 92
Construction and demolition debris,
    81, 82, 84, 89
Conveyor belts, 60, 117, 129, 151

Daley, Richard M., 88, 112, 130, 142
Dempster Dumpster, 39
Dennis, Josephine, 118
Disparate impact, 78
Diversion credit, 114
Duluth, Minnesota, 27

Dunn, Ken, 106, 107, 109, 116, 117,
    121, 128

Earth Day, 51, 57, 75
Earth Summit, 67
Edwards, Richard, 125, 149, 150
El Pueblo para Aire y Agua Limpio, 77
Environmental Defense Fund, 135
Environmental inequality, 3, 8, 15, 16,
    23, 24, 28–31, 68, 72, 97, 101, 102,
    112, 115, 118, 128–131, 143, 144,
    153, 156–158, 162, 163
Environmental injustice, 13
Environmental justice, 3–15, 19–22,
    29, 30, 54, 71–74, 79, 80, 97, 99,
    101, 102, 125, 131, 134, 138, 140,
    143, 153, 159, 161, 164–169
Environmental organizations, 73, 75,
    76
*Environmental Protection Agency
    Journal*, 10
Environmental Protection Agency, US,
    9, 52, 55–58, 72, 78, 84, 95, 108,
    133, 136–140
Environmental racism, 2–10, 14, 16,
    21, 22, 30, 53, 74, 84, 88, 89,
    93–95, 98, 99, 101, 135, 138, 139,
    142, 143, 153, 158–164, 167
European Americans, 21, 29, 56, 71,
    78, 90, 123
Executive Order 12898, 67, 71, 77, 78

Fair Labor Standards Act, 46
Federal Bureau of Investigation, 84–86
First National People of Color
    Environmental Leadership Summit,
    76
Flood Brothers, 87, 96, 105, 114
Foster Wheeler Inc., 91–97
Friedman, Fred, 136, 137

General Accounting Office, US, 73
Gibbs, Lois, 53
Ginsburg, Robert, 49
Global North, 1, 161, 167
Global South, 5, 55, 72, 80, 145
Good Neighbor Policy, 64, 153

Gottlieb, Robert, 49–51, 64
Gould, Kenneth, 61
Grand Crossing (Chicago neighbor-
    hood), 111
Greene, Kevin, 134
Greenpeace, 9, 71, 79, 92
Gulf Coast Tenants Association, 75

Hamilton, Alice, 30, 31
Haymarket Square riots, 4, 32
Hazards
  environmental, 101, 102, 127, 143,
    157
  household, 58, 120, 145
  landfill, 5, 9
  occupational, 24, 63, 120, 121, 125,
    127, 129, 143–149, 153, 159
  psychological, 102, 125, 127, 129,
    145, 148, 151
Hegewisch Organized to Protect the
    Environment, 70, 71
Henderson, Henry, 87, 146
Henry, William, 86
Hitler, Adolf, 41
Hochschild, Arlie, 58
Homeless, 107, 109
Huizenga, Harm, 35
Hull House, 21, 22, 30, 31, 32
Human Action Community
    Organization, 92
Hurley, Andrew, 13

Illinois Environmental Council, 92
Illinois Environmental Protection
    Agency, 83, 84, 86, 93, 95, 97, 133
Immigrants, 3, 12, 15, 22, 31–38, 45,
    77, 109, 110, 116, 121, 128, 163,
    165
Incineration, 28, 36, 37, 42, 44, 47,
    54, 70, 90, 92, 95, 113, 131, 134
Incinerators, 2, 3, 5, 28, 39, 48, 54, 74,
    106, 113, 132–135, 142, 157, 164
  Calumet, 42, 132–134
  chemical, 10
  medical waste, 10, 78, 90
  Medill, 132–134
  municipal, 10

Northwest, 90, 113, 132–144,
    156–159, 167, 168
  Robbins Resource Recovery Facility,
    9, 18, 93–97, 113, 143, 144, 155,
    166–168
  Southwest, 132–134, 144
  waste-to-energy, 48–50, 91, 95, 132,
    133, 140, 158, 162
  resource-recovery, 47, 48
  siting of, 9, 90
Indigenous Environmental Network,
    76, 77
Industrial Areas Foundation, 4
Institute of Medicine, 10
Institutional inequality, 30
Institutional racism, 86, 143
Interracial conflict, 7, 17, 154
Irondalers Against the Chemical
    Threat, 70
Irving, Anne, 141

Jackson, Jesse, 79, 84
Jacobson, Timothy, 38
Johnson, Cheryl, 69
Johnson, Hazel, 5, 67–69, 71, 73, 76

Keely, Eric, 146
Kelley, Florence, 30–32
Khian Sea, 54
Knights of Labor, 32
Krisjon company, 81–87, 114
Kuehn, Bob, 79

Labor movement, 32, 53, 64, 159
Labor process, 46, 61, 121, 125–128,
    146
Lake Calumet Wetlands, 42, 70
Lake Michigan, 30
Landfills, 3, 5, 10, 37, 42–49, 57, 68,
    70, 73, 74, 78, 90, 102, 105, 106,
    112–114, 132–135, 141, 142, 147,
    157, 158, 162, 164
Latinos, 2, 3, 9–12, 17, 35, 49, 56, 71,
    75, 77, 80–84, 109, 114, 149, 151,
    157, 167
Lawndale (Chicago community),
    81–89, 96

Leaching, 49
Lead smelters, 10
Locally unwanted land uses, 2, 30, 48, 50, 53–55, 65, 74, 78, 90, 135, 158, 166
Louisiana, 75, 78, 79
LULUs. *See* Locally Unwanted Land Uses
Lutheran Volunteer Corps, 116

Marx, Karl, 11
Maryland Manor, 68
Materials-recovery facilities, 3, 103–106, 116, 120, 128–131, 144–147, 150–156, 166, 167
Mayfield, Zulene, 78
McClain, Mildred, 71
McDowell, Mary, 1, 21, 22, 28, 161–165
Meat Inspection Act, 32
Mexican Americans, 4, 33, 34, 45, 154
Mexican Community Committee, 142
Michigan Conference on Race and the Incidence of Environmental Hazards, 74
Midwest Great Lakes Environmental Justice Network, 76
Miller, Jesse, 87, 88
Mobro 4000 barge, 55
Mohai, Paul, 75
Mothers of East Los Angeles, 74
Movement-policy cycle, 29, 74, 136, 140, 162, 164
Municipal housekeeping, 27
Municipal Order League of Chicago, 27

Nance, Willis, 28
National Association for the Advancement of Colored People, 79
National Audubon Society, 75
National Council of Public Works Improvement, 55
National Council of Refuse Disposal Trade Association, 45
National Environmental Policy Act, 108

*National Law Journal*, 9
National Toxics Campaign, 53
National Wildlife Federation, 76
Native Americans, 9, 72, 80
Natural Resources Defense Council, 105
Nature Conservancy, 75
Needles, hypodermic, 145, 148, 154
New poverty areas, 111
New York City, 23, 27, 28, 36, 39
*New York Herald*, 28
North American Free Trade Agreement, 77, 169
North Carolina, 5, 60, 73
Northeast Environmental Justice Network, 76
North Side (Chicago), 30

Oakbrook, Illinois, 5
Occupational Safety and Health Administration, US, 60, 146, 147, 150, 154, 158
Operation PUSH, 79, 84
Operation Silver Shovel, 18, 80, 84–89, 95, 96, 105, 138, 143, 155, 166

Packing houses, 25, 30, 34
Palmer, Alice, 115
People for Community Recovery, 5, 67–73, 76, 89, 92, 94, 113, 137, 142, 165, 166
People of color, 2, 22, 26, 30–36, 53, 56, 69–74, 80, 81, 90, 102, 103, 115, 157, 162, 164, 165
People of Color and Disenfranchised Communities Environmental Health Network, 71
Perpetrator-victim scenario, 30, 143
Philadelphia, Pennsylvania, 33
*Plessy vs. Ferguson*, 33
Pollution, 2, 24, 25, 27, 37, 47, 68, 101–103, 108, 131, 139, 162
  air, 24, 37, 47, 49
  land, 37, 44
  noise, 120
  water, 24

Progressive era, 24, 48
Pure Food and Drug Act, 32

Reading Energy Company, 91
Reagan, Ronald, 56, 63, 73
Recycling, 2, 5, 16, 43, 48–57, 64, 89,
    101–104, 107, 125, 128, 131, 136,
    138, 140, 141, 155–167
  community-based, 16, 53, 101, 102,
    107, 108, 116, 126, 141, 157, 160
  for-profit, 52, 103, 130
  of mixed waste, 144
  non-profit, 18, 56, 60, 101–103, 106,
    112, 130, 131, 143, 157–160
  source-separated, 128, 141
Reduction, 3, 23, 28, 39, 164
Remanufacturing, 103, 104
Remedial Environmental Manpower,
    147, 150–156
Resistance, 11, 25, 28, 29, 37, 46, 80,
    81, 99, 125, 127, 129, 133, 134,
    140, 153–158, 165, 169
Resource Center, 56, 101, 105–119,
    123–130, 134–137, 143, 158, 160,
    165
Resource Conservation and Recovery
    Act, 50, 53, 54, 57, 65, 68, 134, 135
Resource recovery, 47, 48
Resource Recovery Act, 52, 108, 131
Retail Rate Law, 90, 91, 94, 96, 98
Riots, 2, 4, 6, 156
Robbins, Illinois, 5, 89–98
Rush, Bobby, 109, 112

Sanctuary movement, 110
San Francisco, California, 35, 38
Sanitarians, 24, 29
Sanitation workers, 123
Scavengers, 23, 26, 35–39, 44, 45,
    109, 110, 122
Scavengers' Protective Association, 37,
    38
Schnaiberg, Allan, 16, 61, 168
Schwab, Jim, 53, 93
Scott, Gloria, 93
Scrap collection, 23, 42
Secondary labor markets, 149

Sewage treatment plants, 2,10
Shintech, 79
Sierra Club, 76, 92, 94, 113
*Silent Spring*, 43
Simple control, 125
Sinclair, Upton, 32
Smith, Damu, 71
Solid Waste Disposal Act, 44, 52, 108,
    131. *See also* Resource Recovery Act
Solid waste facilities, 2
Solid waste industry, 5
*Solid Waste Management Newsletter*,
    141
South Austin Community Coalition,
    137
South Cook County Environmental
    Action Coalition, 92, 96
Southeast Side (Chicago), 68, 70, 135,
    157, 159
Southern Organizing Committee For
    Environmental and Economic
    Justice, 76
South Lawndale Community Block
    Club, 83, 85
South Shore Recycling Station, 109
South Side (Chicago), 30, 49, 50, 67,
    68, 70, 73, 90, 92, 107, 110, 111,
    123, 133
Southwest Network for Environmental
    and Economic Justice, 75–77
Southwest Side (Chicago), 49
Southwest Supplementary Fuel
    Processing Facility, 49
St. Francis Hospital and Health Center,
    69, 94
Stakeholders, 7, 13, 18, 21, 24, 25, 30,
    34, 47, 52, 54, 57, 61–65, 104, 112,
    128, 134, 138, 140, 143, 158, 159,
    163–165, 169
Steel plants, 10, 25, 33, 110, 125, 145
Strikes, 4, 34, 39
Sunset Company, 36, 38, 46
SunShares, 35, 36, 60
Supreme Court, US, 33, 78, 135, 140,
    159
Sweatshops, 30, 32, 72, 145
Szasz, Andrew, 13

Tangel, Jeff, 96
Taylor, Dorceta, 33
Third pollution, 44, 108
Transfer stations, 2
Treadmill of production, 61, 64, 168
Treatment, storage, and disposal facili-
    ties, 50
Tulane Environmental Law Clinic, 79
Ture, Kwame, 162

Unions, 56, 124, 143, 155
United Church of Christ Commission
    for Racial Justice, 9, 68, 90
United Farm Workers, 11
United Nations Conference on
    Environment and Development, 67
United Neighborhood Organization,
    70, 71
University of Chicago, 106, 111
Uptown Recycling Station, 109, 110,
    118, 120, 124, 130, 160
Urban Environment Conference, 73

Velasquez, Baldemar, 162
Volunteers in Service to America, 116,
    119

Waring, George, 36
Warren Country, North Carolina, 73
Washington Harold, 56, 70, 109,
    112–114, 130, 135
Waste, 37, 47, 58, 59, 15, 127
  commingled, 119, 141
  dumping of, 11, 28, 53, 111
  fly, 81, 87, 88, 138
  hauling of, 26, 38, 45, 103
  hazardous, 50, 58, 59, 73, 84, 121,
    136, 142, 145
  illegal, 69, 80–87, 138, 142
  mixed, 141–144
  municipal solid, 116, 144, 145
  recovery of, 48, 50
  recycling of, 41, 43, 48–52
  reuse of, 36, 43, 48, 49, 56, 103, 128,
    164
  solid, 6, 25, 28, 30, 36, 41, 44, 46,
    50, 55, 101–103, 108, 128, 161

Waste Management, Inc. (WMX), 5,
    35, 77, 130, 135, 140–160, 166,
    167
Waste Reclamation Service, 41
Weinberg, Adam, 61
Western Disposal Services, 60
Westside Alliance for a Safe and Toxic
    Free Environment, 136–140, 148,
    149
West Side (Chicago), 81, 87–89, 113,
    114, 136, 138, 155
Wheelabrator Technologies, 142
Win-win policy, 60, 64, 102, 104, 112,
    141, 160
WMX. *See* Waste Management, Inc.
Work
  dangerous, 31, 119, 157
  high-risk, 125, 157
  lethal, 50, 58
  low-status, 98, 106, 122, 123, 151
  low-wage, 81, 98, 106, 125, 149,
    155, 156, 159
  temporary, 147, 151–153
World War I, 41
World War II, 39, 41, 43, 59

Zoning, 87, 109